The Impossibility of Palestine

THE IMPOSSIBILITY OF PALESTINE

HISTORY, GEOGRAPHY, AND THE ROAD AHEAD

MEHRAN KAMRAVA

Yale
UNIVERSITY PRESS

New Haven and London

blished with assistance from the foundation established in memory of
Calvin Chapin of the Class of 1788, Yale College

Yale University Press books may be purchased in quantity for
educational, business, or promotional use. For information, please e-mail
sales.press@yale.edu (U.S. office) or sales@yaleup.co.uk (U.K. office).

Set in Gotham and Adobe Garamond type by IDS Infotech, Ltd.
Printed in the United States of America.

Library of Congress Control Number: 2015947224
ISBN 978-0-300-21562-5 (cloth : alk. paper)

A catalogue record for this book is available from the British Library.

This paper meets the requirements of ANSI/NISO Z39.48–1992
(Permanence of Paper).

10 9 8 7 6 5 4 3 2 1

Contents

Preface

This is a book about the impossibility of a Palestinian state. It has not been an easy book for me to write. Political scientists are trained to be dispassionate and objective, detached and emotionally removed from the subjects of their studies. But this book deals with the lives, histories, and destinies of millions of people, none of which have been particularly happy, and even the most detached of political scientists cannot be emotionally oblivious to the conclusions it reaches. My political science training has led me to these conclusions. And yet a part of me wishes these were not the conclusions at which I arrived. For the first time, I have written a book whose thesis and central arguments I hope will be proven wrong over time. For now, history and politics have different realities in store for Palestine.

I argue here that a confluence of developments and dynamics, both endogenous to Israel and Palestine and exogenous to the conflict between them, have rendered the establishment of a meaningful, viable Palestinian state impossible. Statehood goes beyond having such trappings of a state as a flag, a national anthem, a presidential honor guard, and even a seat at the United Nations and representation at the International Criminal Court. It also entails having sovereignty over territory designated as national and performing certain basic functions, such as the provision of services and security, in relation to a group of people who imagine themselves as part of a greater whole.

People imagining themselves as part of a greater whole is what constitutes a nation. This collective imagination, always anchored in a territorial frame of reference, is forged through a series of common bonds, such as historical experiences and folklore and national myths, which reinforce and are reinforced by traditions and heritage. Of these common bonds Palestine has had plenty, largely because of, and also despite, its tormented history. Palestine's endurance as a nation is not in doubt. What I question is the possibility of a Palestinian state.

The task of writing this book was made easier by the generous help of a number of individuals, none of whom bear any responsibility for the book's mistakes. A number of scholars, policy makers, attorneys, and activists generously shared with me their insights and their knowledge of Palestine and Israel as I sought to better understand many of the issues raised in the following pages and chapters. I gratefully acknowledge the advice and guidance graciously given to me, especially by Mahdi Abdul Hadi, Samir Abdullah, Amjad Alqasis, Sam Bahour, Hillel Cohen, Muna Dajani, Munir Fakher Eldin, Munir Ghannam, Amany Khalife, Micha Kurz, Mazin Qumsiyeh, and Maha Samman. All were instrumental in helping me gain deeper insights into the various aspects of Palestinian life and politics. In Jerusalem, Samia Al-Botmeh, Elodie Farge, and Ingrid Ross kindly pointed me in the direction of important sources. In Doha, at various stages of working on the book I benefited greatly from the capable research assistance of Kevin Mark Lee, Leena Nady, and Fatima Ramadan Sanz, all of whom helped me collect and sift through much of the material presented here. Zahra Babar, Glenn Robinson, and Eric Selbin read the whole manuscript and gave me advice that only true scholars and friends would give: thorough, perceptive, gentle, marvelously helpful. My colleagues at the Center for International and Regional Studies at Georgetown University's School of Foreign Service in Qatar provided an intellectually enriching environment in which I could work on the book. At home, my wife, Melisa, and daughters, Kendra and Dilara, tolerated long absences on research trips and the hours I spent behind the computer as I wrote the book.

I have grappled with the arguments of this book for a number of years, in fact first alluding to many of them in my 2005 book, *The Modern Middle East*. In the intervening decade or so my conviction that the book's conclusions are correct has only grown stronger, and they have been validated by developments on the ground, in Palestine and Israel, and on the diplomatic and political fronts elsewhere. I do not pretend to propose solutions here to the historically intractable conflict between Israelis and Palestinians. But I do hope that the book forms at least a starting point for new ways of thinking about the current predicament of Palestinians and, perhaps, just perhaps, for new ways of envisioning their future.

The Impossibility of Palestine

1

Introduction

This book tells the story of Palestine. The story has been told many times before. But while the story itself is not new, its retelling and its conclusions are. Palestine, this book maintains, is neither viable nor possible anymore. This lack of viability is due to developments that go beyond Palestine's mere physical and territorial dismemberment. It is on this issue, namely the growing noncontiguity of the West Bank because of Israeli settlements, that most existing conclusions of Palestine's lack of viability are based. Territorial contiguity is, of course, elemental if Palestine is to ever have any semblance of statehood. But equally significant, and perhaps even more so, are the twin and reinforcing processes of state- and nation-building, with the former involving institutional and structural dynamics, and the latter, sociological and cultural ones. Not only is Palestine territorially noncontiguous and no longer viable as a physical entity, but the very fibers and ingredients that would constitute it as a national and political whole have mutated in such a way as to make state- and nation-building improbable. The ravages of history, geography, and circumstances have combined to mitigate the possibility of Palestine reemerging as a meaningful national and political entity.

Nations tend to have remarkable resilience, adapting and surviving for centuries and millennia under the most adverse of circumstances. But when conquered and defeated, collapsing or collapsed,

1

they survive mostly in symbols and in lore, as subjective means of identity rather than as objective entities with tangible hierarchies and rhythms, social organizations, and living cultural products. Under conditions of defeat and conquest, they find themselves having to adapt and assimilate to survive, or at least having to moderate and modulate in order not to antagonize. Their essence changes in the process. They get massaged and altered not just around the edges but also in their very cores.

In the Palestinian case, the changes have been profoundly detrimental to the reconstitution of the Palestinian nation. After the signing of the Oslo Accords, the Palestinian entrepreneurial and upper middle classes in the West Bank and Gaza found themselves unwitting partners with agents and forces of the occupation. Ingathering and national reconstruction meant helping the reemergent nation grow and develop economically, and doing so was possible only through Israel. Inadvertently, nation-building became employed at the service of deepening the occupation.

A similar fate befell the state-building process. Beginning in 1994, the Palestine Liberation Organization, which up until then had conceived of itself as a state-in-exile, superimposed itself on Gaza and the West Bank and began an earnest process of developing new and additional institutions for governing Palestinian territories. But it soon became painfully evident that the newly established Palestinian National Authority was highly constrained in the scope of its powers and had at best only a small area in which it could exercise authority. Its governance purview hardly reached beyond a dozen towns and cities, and most Palestinian villages remained difficult for it to access. By enforcing law and order and running much-needed services in the small Area A it controlled, the PNA soon emerged as little more than Israel's subcontractor, a small-time administrative machinery designed to make the occupation more effective and more efficient and, presumably, more enduring.

Today, I argue in this book, the prospects for Palestine meaningfully reconstituting itself politically or nationally are nonexistent. Even the 2014 motions by parliaments in Europe—in Sweden, Britain, Ireland, Spain, and France—to recognize Palestine as a state, as symbolically important as they may be, are void of substance and meaningful consequence. The Palestinian nation lives on only in symbols and folklore and in memories proactively prolonged. But its days as a national entity are long gone by. And, as a political entity— even if the flag and the elected office and the United Nations seat meant something—a Palestinian state would still not be able to accomplish most other tasks expected of it. Israeli negotiators often argue that "there are no credible partners on the other side with whom to negotiate."[1] In reality, I argue here, these very negotiations, and whatever state-building they have fostered on the Palestinian side, have directly undermined prospects for the emergence of a viable, functioning Palestinian state.

In retelling the story of Palestine here, I have relied extensively on the works of Israel's so-called "new historians." Thanks to the pioneering works of a number of gifted Israeli historians and academics, our traditional assumptions about the Palestinian-Israeli conflict have been challenged and made more reflective of the course of events as they actually unfolded, rather than as they have been portrayed by the protagonists themselves. I draw heavily on the works of these historians in constructing my arguments here. These works have collectively helped researchers and academics to step out of the traditional narratives of the conflict that are more often shaped by prevailing political currents than by historical reality. In the construction of the new analytical framework, the contributions of the emerging counter-narrative have enabled us to more comfortably and more readily use tools that were once outside of the norm or were considered downright taboo. The earlier works of the historian Benny Morris, for example, showed that the expulsion of Palestinians from what became Israel was not a product of their voluntary departure but instead of terror operations meant deliberately to evict them from their lands and property.[2] Ilan Pappe called it ethnic cleansing.[3] Meron Benvenisti discussed the erasure of Palestinian geography and history.[4] The sociologist Baruch Kimmerling deconstructed the foundational premises of Israeli identity.[5]

These and other new historians have often been called advocates of post-Zionism, of which three varieties or meanings may be discerned. They include post-Zionism as a sociological statement, a byproduct of postmodernism and reflecting a sense of maturity and self-confidence sufficient to revise some of Israel's foundational myths; as a counter-ideology to the Israeli political spectrum's steady tilt to the right; and as a critical academic approach, through which new facts and interpretations regarding the political history of Israel and Palestine have come to the fore.[6] It is in this third meaning—post-Zionism as an academic endeavor—that I employ its conceptual and analytical tools here.[7]

By way of introduction, I need first to present some basic statistics in terms of population numbers and percentages. In Israel in 2014, the country's total population numbered 8,134,500, of whom 6,104,000 were Jews, 1,683,000 were Arabs (or Palestinians), and another 347,000 were "others." Altogether, the percentage of non-Jews was approximately 25 percent. Israel's non-Jewish population, meanwhile, was divided among Muslims (83 percent, or 1,420,000), Christians (9 percent, or 161,000), and Druze (8 percent, or 133,000).[8] Since 1948, the percentage of Palestinian Muslim citizens of Israel has increased, largely at the expense of Palestinian Christians. In 1948 Palestinian Muslims with Israeli citizenship comprised 70 percent of Israel's non-Jews, and Christian Palestinians constituted about 21 percent.[9]

Gaza and the West Bank represent 22 percent of historic Palestine, with the remaining 78 percent having become what is today Israel proper. The number of Palestinians in the West Bank and Gaza totaled 4,420,000 in 2013, with 2,719,000 in the West Bank and 1,701,000 in Gaza.[10] The Occupied Palestinian Territories house approximately 38 percent of the total global Palestinian population of about 11 million people, of whom 44 percent are officially registered with the United Nations as refugees. Five million Palestinians are estimated to live in other Arab countries, and 627,000 in other parts of the world.[11]

The general outlines of the argument I present here are as follows: The Zionist conquest of Palestine began with the assumption that the territory's existing Arab population could be "transferred" out into neighboring territories. What ensued was a process of ethnic cleansing. This ethnic cleansing took multiple dimensions—demographic, cultural, territorial, geographic, historical, symbolic—all meant to ensure the erasure of all things Palestinian from the land now designated as Israel. Over the course of time, when the process of emptying the land of all Palestinians proved impractical and unfeasible, Israel began a process of separation, apartness, meant to ensure that Palestinians were separated and segregated from Israel and the Israelis in as many respects as possible, especially physically and territorially. The gradual transition from ethnic cleansing to separation was translated into official state policy by the early 1990s, by which time Israel and Israeli identity had long become irreversible, well-secured historical realities. Parallel changes had in the meantime occurred in the Palestinian body politic that rendered its construction of a state unfeasible and impossible. The most visible and apparent manifestation of these changes were physical and territorial, with Israel's incessant settlement drive having systematically dismembered Palestinian geography and territorial viability. But equally consequential have been changes within Palestinian society itself that reinforce—if not by themselves result in—the unlikelihood that there be a Palestinian state.

Palestinian society never fully recovered from the defeat of 1948. The 1948 war destroyed and disintegrated it. Palestinians eventually did manage to put their society back together, but this time under the auspices of dispossession and dispersion, refugeedom and the struggle for liberation, the rise and fall of heroes and traitors, and hopes and endless despair of yearning for a land lost. None of these travails have boded well for the state-building process, and the confining framework of the Oslo Accords, which ended up inhibiting rather than fostering state-building, have not helped.

The general Israeli desire for the ethnic cleansing of Palestinians, meanwhile, has not gone away. As Ilan Pappe puts it, "the ideology that enabled the depopulation of half of Palestine's native people in 1948 is still alive and continues to drive the inexorable, sometimes indiscernible, cleansing of those Palestinians who live there today."[12] The depopulation of large swathes of Palestinian territory, often quietly and without much fanfare, continues on a regular basis. And, as this book argues, even more common is the drive to ensure separation and apartness. Palestine's enclavization has today become the norm.

The Failed State and the Enduring Nation

This book makes a clear distinction between the two processes of Palestinian state-building as compared to nation-building. The central thesis of the book revolves around disaggregating and distinguishing developments within and changes to the Palestinian *nation* as compared to efforts aimed at constructing a Palestinian *state*. It claims that the story of Palestine is that of *a failed state*—or, more accurately, failed efforts at forging a viable state—and *an enduring nation*. The 1948 collapse and subsequent reconstitution of Palestinian society gave rise to a national liberation movement, in the form of the Palestine Liberation Organization, which sought to accomplish two reinforcing, interrelated objectives, one explicit, the other implicit. Explicitly, it fought to supplant the newly established State of Israel and to replace it with a Palestinian state. The outcome of this explicit objective has been a failure. Implicitly, the PLO's struggle against Israel helped forge and deepen Palestinian national identity, in the process strengthening the resilience of the Palestinian nation.

The failure to establish a viable, workable state is the product of a confluence of a range of developments and dynamics both internal and external to the Palestinians. This failed odyssey, the highlight of which was the consequences of the signing of the Oslo Accords, is chronicled in the pages that follow. In a nutshell, after years of resistance and struggle, the PLO unwittingly gave up the prospects of statehood in return for municipal rule over selected Palestinian cities during the course of the Oslo Accords. Once in possession of a few cities, and that only partially, the PLO and its institutional successor, the Palestine National Authority, got stuck in a myopic political vortex in which hanging on to the limited political power they had became an end in itself. Liberation gave way to power maintenance; aspirations of statehood were replaced by those of hanging on to municipal governance. Palestinian statehood was diverted, distorted, and subverted. Israel, for its part, did what it could to ensure that Palestinian state-building efforts came to naught and remained hollow.

The cause of Palestinian national liberation has not succeeded and is unlikely to succeed in the near future. But Palestine, and more specifically the Palestinian nation, has not necessarily been defeated. The nonachievement of a meaningful, viable state should not be conflated with the "defeat" of the Palestinian cause in its entirety. As I demonstrate here, a Palestinian state may be a lost cause, but Palestine as a nation continues to live on. State-building has a symbiotic relationship with nation-building. The imaginary ingathering and reconstitution and reconstruction of the Palestinian nation, this time under the auspices of revolutionary national liberation, was the implicit objective of first the PLO and then the PNA. In this respect, in fact, the national liberation movement's implicit consequence of reconstituting the Palestinian nation has been far from failure.

The Oslo Accords had profound consequences for the Palestinian nation. Developments within this post-Oslo nation, I argue, have ironically further undermined the prospects of Palestinian state-building. This has occurred largely because of two emergent dynamics. First, a proliferation of nongovernmental organizations (NGOs) across the social spectrum, an overwhelming majority of which are funded by outside donors, has sapped the mobilizational and creative potentials of Palestinian society in the West Bank and Gaza. Second, the establishment of a Palestinian pseudo-state in the form of the PNA has fundamentally altered the makeup and orientation of the Palestinian middle classes from bastions of national liberation before Oslo to pillars of commercially motivated stability and the status quo afterward. Palestine's once universally nationalist middle class became overwhelmingly comprador in its composition and orientation, in the process developing strong preferences for trade and investment, contracts, and commercial deals. The PNA's agreements with Israel limited almost all of these Palestinian economic activities to partners only within Israel proper, therefore tying the robustness of the West Bank and Gaza middle classes directly to the Israeli economy. For these middle classes, now residing in semiautonomous swathes of territory, the imperatives of liberation and the *thawra* (revolution) gave way to those of stability and economic viability.

These changes within Palestinian society, and the overall direction undertaken by Palestinian nation-building, should not be misconstrued as the death knells of the Palestinian nation. The Palestinian nation, in fact, remains quite robust.

Before proceeding further, I need to more clearly define some of the key terms used to construct the book's arguments. The first such term is *nation*. A nation may be defined as any group of people bound together through a series of interwoven bonds, such as language, common ancestry, ethnic or racial ties, and shared historical experiences. Critically, these members of the nation also share a common territorial frame of reference as their actual or ancestral homeland. This geographically anchored conception of the nation differs slightly from those offered by Benedict Anderson and Eric Hobsbawm. Anderson has famously defined a nation as "an imagined political community—and imagined as both inherently limited and sovereign."[13] Hobsbawm has offered a similar definition, maintaining that "any sufficiently large body of people whose members regard themselves as members of a 'nation' [should] be treated as such."[14] My definition is closer to that presented by Azar Gat, who makes a distinction between a "people" and a "nation." Gat describes people as an ethnic group with a "sense of common identity, history, and fate" which "should exist even if the people does not achieve independence or other forms of political self-determination, and, hence, nationhood." A nation, on the other hand, "is politically sovereign, either as a dominant majority, *Staatsvolk*, within a national state, or as the politically central element within a multiethnic state or empire. Short of independent statehood, a people can be regarded as a nation if it possesses elements of political self-determination and self-government, or actively strives to achieve them."[15]

A number of historians and political scientists assume that for a *nation* to be designated as such it must necessarily have a *state* component to it. David Laitin, for example, defines a nation as "a population with a coordinated set of beliefs about their cultural identities . . . whose representatives claim ownership over a *state* (or at least an autonomous region within a state) from them by dint of that coordination either through separation, or amalgamation, or return."[16] He sees nation as "a product of the cultural coordination and the *claim to statehood or political autonomy* for the population that successfully coordinates."[17] This conceptualization runs the risk of confusing, or at least conflating, the two distinct phenomena of *nation* and *state*.[18] I take nation to be simply an imagined community that has a geographic and territorial frame of reference as one of its constituent bonds that tie it together in terms of lore, birthplace, and common experiences. In Gat's terminology, a nation is a people that identifies with a land although it may or may not own and control that land. Ownership and control over the land, what we commonly conceive of as sovereignty, is the purview of the state and is not a necessary component of the nation. There is, for example, a Tibetan nation— there are people who identify themselves as Tibetan—without a Tibetan state. In a similar vein, I argue that there is a Palestinian nation without a Palestinian state. I further argue that developments within the Palestinian nation have and continue to compound political dynamics, which are both exogenous to and arise from within Palestine itself, that make Palestinian statehood unlikely.

Philip Roeder has employed the concept of *nation-state* in a useful parsing of where nations and states come from. Roeder argues that while national identity formation, material greed or grievances, mass mobilization, and international recognition are all important in the formation of nation-states, the most central element for a nation-state to be formed is the nature and workings of political institutions. More specifically, he claims that "creating a nation-state is an act of institutional change."[19] According to Roeder, "new nation-states are not in the first instance the expression of society but an adaptation of existing *state institutions* to political circumstances that those institutions helped create."[20] He maintains that "the source of new nation-states has been a crisis of 'stateness'—a crisis in which residents contest the human and geographic borders of existing states and some residents even seek to create new independent states—and that this crisis typically results from the design of their institutions."[21] Almost every successful nation-state project has been associated with an existing institution, which Roeder calls a "segment-state." This institutional entity, constituting an "existing jurisdiction," forms the nucleus of a nation-state. Nation-states are brought about through "the administrative upgrade" of segment-states. "No segment-state, no nation-state."[22] Nations that have failed to form states have failed to draw on the resources of segment-states.

By now it should be clearly evident that there is often a conflation of different conceptions of *state*. At the broadest level, there is a territorial conception of state, on the one hand, and a political/administrative conception, on the other. Territorially, the term "state" is often used to refer to a country—the State of Israel being an obvious example—implying territorial sovereignty, United Nations representation, national sports teams, national holidays, and all the other symbols and accouterments that come with being a country.

But there is also a conception of state that is administrative and political. Max Weber famously defined a state as "a human community that (successfully) claims the *monopoly of the legitimate use of physical force* within a given territory."[23]

These two different conceptions of the state are seldom distinguished in discussions of a Palestinian state. When we speak of a Palestinian state, are we referring to a future Palestinian country or do we have in mind Weber's more-precise, institutionally and administratively grounded definition? If we employ Weber's definition as the matrix of analysis, then the PNA qualifies as a "state." The PNA is, by all accounts, what Roeder calls a segment-state. But, insofar as more commonly understood conceptions of state are concerned, in the form of a territorially sovereign and politically independent country, Palestine today is far from it. More ominously, the prospects for it one day becoming a state with features such as territorial sovereignty and political independence do not look bright.

Insofar as the Palestinian case is concerned, the conceptual confusion over the precise meaning of "state" may not be as unintentional and academic as it appears. Although deliberate care was made during the Oslo Accords to avoid using the term itself by both sides in the early days of the negotiations, Palestinian negotiators appear to have approached the Oslo meetings, and the endless negotiations that have followed since, with the broader, more-inclusive conception of *state as a country* in mind. The Israeli side, however, appears to have had a much narrower conception of a Palestinian state, seeing it as a mere collection of administrative organs designed to govern some but not all aspects of Palestinian society. These two conceptions of a Palestinian state—Palestine as a country versus Palestine as an administrative setup with limited purview—have bumped heads since 1993. So far, the more-limited, narrower notion has prevailed.

The failure to establish a Palestinian state has occurred despite a robust and pervasive sense of national identity among Palestinians. Palestinians may not have a state, but they do constitute a nation. And, despite Israel's best efforts at its dispersion and dispossession, this Palestinian nation is unlikely to wither away anytime in the foreseeable future.

From the earliest days, the Palestinian nation has been sustained by a number of key ingredients that have given it shape and a sense of self-identity. Some of the more central of these ingredients have included, but are not limited to, a shared language; daily life experiences and routines, such as identification with the land and farming; the works of opinion makers and identity shapers, in the form of poets, journalists, authors, academics, and activists and leaders; and, perhaps most importantly, the collective traumas of dispossession, homelessness, exile, and resistance. All of these objects, events, and experiences have shaped, sustained, and perpetuated a dynamic form of an "imagined community" through which the Palestinian nation has endured and has persevered against sustained, punishing Israeli rule. From the Ottoman colonial era to the Mandatory period, the establishment and consolidation of the Yishuv (Jewish community), the Nakba (catastrophe) and the ethnic cleansing campaigns that ensued, the "lost decade" of the 1960s, the *thawra* of the latter 1970s, the first intifada (literally, shake-up, 1987–1993), the Oslo period (1993–2000), the second intifada (2000–2004), and life in the era of the PNA—all of these events and eras have in their own way been decisive for the Palestinian narrative. All have coalesced to form the Palestinian national biography.

In addition to these defining events, which in Palestinian popular lore combine to form a coherent national narrative, the Palestinian nation continues to be nurtured through multiple forms of commemoration—the conscious works of activists, writers, and authors promulgating various facets of Palestinian identity—and collective experiences that further reinforce and reify notions of nationhood and national solidarity. As Laleh Khalili points out, "particular events are 'remembered' as the shared basis of peoplehood," whereby a commemorative and valorized nationalist narrative is constructed that shapes political strategies and aims.[24] Similarly, armed struggle, martyrdom, and funerals—acts of sacrifice and grief that are pregnant with symbolism and emotions and that foster political sympathy, solidarity, and mobilization—become indisputable affirmations of the Palestinian nation.[25] Palestinians commemorate a broad range of events, persons, and objects that signify aspects of their historical memory, experiences, and national identity. Some of the more-iconic objects of commemoration include olive trees, stone houses built in old villages, oranges, keys, framed photos of the Dome of the Rock, poetry, and embroidered dresses. Khalili's observations about the role of commemoration in Palestinian nationalism is worth quoting at length:

> Palestinian commemorations are accessible openings through which transformations in Palestinian nationalism can be examined, since in the Palestinian refugee camps of Lebanon, as in the Occupied Palestinian Territories (OPT) these footprints of memory are easily visible. In both places, images of young martyred men stare out of posters pasted on alley walls alongside photographs of murals of Jerusalem. Interior walls of almost every house carry the pictures of a young martyr, a son or daughter, a husband, a brother or sister. Schools, clinics, and even small shops are named after cities and villages left behind and destroyed in 1948. On the

margins of almost every camp in Lebanon and throughout the OPT, pockmarked hulks of semi-destroyed buildings are left standing years, sometimes decades, after the bombings that rendered them uninhabitable; they are iconic objects reminding all of the violence of war.[26]

Along similar lines, social movements, of which recent Palestinian history has seen a rich array, also reinforce common ties of nationhood and a collective sense of national identity. With common goals and social solidarities as their key ingredients, social movements are inherently empowering for those participating in them, strengthening both their collective identity and their common sense of purpose. According to Sidney Tarrow, "leaders can create a social movement only when they tap into and expand deep-rooted feelings of solidarity or identity."[27] Social movements, in other words, of which the *sumud* (steadfastness) and especially the intifada were notable examples, tend to strengthen nationalist sentiments and deepen a sense of belonging to the nation. In the 1970s and the early 1980s, for example, those in Palestinian refugee camps throughout the occupied territories and in Lebanon witnessed what came to be known as the *thawra*, whereby "peasants who were once transformed into refugees now reversed the ignominy of defeat by becoming *fida'iyyan*, the foot-soldiers of the guerrilla warfare against Israel."[28] The galvanizing consequences of the *thawra* for Palestinian nationhood cannot be overemphasized.

Perhaps even more consequential for Palestinian national identity—since it happened on the ground, within the Palestinian territories itself—was the intifada, especially in its first iteration from 1987 to 1993. The intifada represented what Tarrow has labeled as "contentious politics," denoting the strategic deployment of "a repertoire of collective action" by ordinary people, often in alliance with more-influential citizens and with changes in public mood, in widening cycles of confrontation and conflict with more-powerful elites, authorities, and opponents.[29] For Tarrow, there is a direct link between contentious politics and the sense of collective empowerment that comes from involvement in a social movement.[30] These social movements, whether the *thawra* or the intifada, are fought and carried forward in the name of the motherland, the nation's ancestral birthplace, the geographic and territorial context and the anchor of the national narrative.

The landscape of the Palestinian national narrative is vividly and compellingly portrayed in the works of a number of Palestinian artists, authors, and writers. In his ethnographic study of Palestinian musicians, David McDonald discovered that many were in reality "artist-activist-archivists" who "recognized the importance of performance in the articulation of Palestinian identity." According to Mc-Donald, "they understood that performance inscribes within the minds of participants powerful indices of national identity through shared experience and history."[31] Similarly, Palestinian poets and literary figures, both at home and in the diaspora, forged what came to be known as a "poetry of resistance" and "resistance literature," seeking in the process to proactively "contribute to the making of Palestinian culture and identity."[32] Mahmoud Darwish (1941–2008), Ibrahim Tuqan (1905–1941), his sister Fadwa Tuqan (1917–2003), and Ghassan Kanafani (1936–1972) represented but a small sample of Palestinian men and women of letters whose "committed literature" was and continues to be employed in the cause of nation-building and solidifying Palestinian national identity.[33] The cartoonist Naji al-Ali (1938–1987) used his satirical critique of Palestinian and Arab politics toward the same objectives as his fellow poets and writers.[34]

Works of literature and the arts helped frame the physical and territorial context of the Palestinian narrative. Through a confluence of these works of arts, historical episodes and traumas, collective experiences and their commemorations, an overall, somewhat coherent national narrative has emerged that is at once heroic, confident, and evocative and yet also tragic, premised on victimhood, shorn of power and protection, filled with stories of betrayal and false promises.[35] In the process, the Palestinian nation has defined and redefined itself in accordance to the sea changes and the dramatic shifts in the predicaments in which it has found itself. Khalili rightly points to the fluidity and dynamic nature of national narratives, their tone, emphasis, and selection of iconic symbols to promulgate shifting priorities depending on changing political strategies, audiences, goals, and the institutions involved.[36] For example, whereas the PLO's liberationist discourse, aimed at the broader Palestinian nation, had sought to transform national torpor and apathy into revolutionary mobilization, the PNA has tried instead to sanctify the telos of the state.[37] It so happens that the PNA is actually not a state, at least not in the sense of having meaningful independence and sovereignty, but is at best an apparatus for municipal governance whose limited jurisdiction is confined to isolated, noncontiguous cities and neighborhoods. Ironically, the very state-centered narrative that the PNA seeks to emphasize further helps to undermine the prospects of Palestinian statehood.

I take the Oslo Accords to be a "critical juncture" in the political history of contemporary Palestine. During historical critical junctures, key political leaders are confronted with a range of crucial choices before them, and whichever of these choices they adopt will have a lasting impact. "These choices close off alternative options and lead to the establishment of institutions that generate self-reinforcing, path-dependent processes."[38] Some historical "junctures are 'critical' because they place institutional arrangements on paths or trajectories, which are then very difficult to alter."[39] According to Capoccia and Keleman, "critical junctures are characterized by a situation in which the structural (that is, economic, cultural, ideological, organizational) influences on political action are significantly relaxed for a relatively short period . . . [during which] the range of plausible choices open to powerful political actors expands substantially and the consequences of their decisions for the outcome of interest are potentially much more momentous."[40]

During and because of the Oslo Accords, Palestinian and Israeli leaders made a series of key decisions that have had lasting consequences for processes of Palestinian state-building and political development. As prime examples, two such decisions included the administrative division of the West Bank into Areas A, B, and C, and the decision to allow the repatriation of a small percentage of Palestinian refugees, of which some 150,000 to 200,000 returned. Had these and other similar decisions not been made, Palestinian politics and society are likely to have looked very different today. The carving up of the West Bank, for example, as chapter 3 argues, effectively has turned Palestinian territories into a Swiss cheese–like entity in which the emergence of a viable state is all but impossible. And the returnees, as shown in chapter 4, have also unwittingly impeded the development of dynamics conducive to state-building. Given the constraints they were working under, the question of whether or not Arafat and other PLO stalwarts could have made other choices during and after Oslo is open to debate. What is certain is that the Accords set into motion a cascading series of developments whose accumulated consequences have become inimical to the establishment of a Palestinian state.

All along, the Palestinian nation has remained, under the most adverse of circumstances, adamant in its right to persevere and to endure. This endurance, and the continuous generation and regeneration of Palestinian national identity, has been masterfully chronicled by a number of scholars, among them Muhammad Muslih, Edward Said, and Rashid Khalidi, to name only a few.[41] Despite its evolution, or, more aptly, its travails, the Palestinian nation has not moved closer to its goal of attaining a state. Nevertheless, despite the elusiveness of statehood, the nation itself has continued to persevere. The Palestinian "national biography," in Khalili's words, continues to have an "enduring resonance."[42] It does not die.

One of the important reasons for the endurance of the Palestinian nation is the changing nature and objectives of the Israeli occupation since its beginning. As chapter 2 will demonstrate, the occupation's initial goal appears to have been the ethnic cleansing of Palestine and the clearing of the territory of its Arab inhabitants. But even at its peak, in the late 1940s, the twin goals of evicting all Palestinians from their lands and the erasure of all things Palestinian failed to achieve their intended results. Successive wars, especially in 1967 and 1973, saw the further expulsion of waves of Palestinians out of historic Palestine. Again, however, given their sheer numbers and the dogged persistence of many to hang on to whatever they had, the "transfer" of Palestinians out of their ancestral homeland was only partially successful. The occupation authorities then shifted tactics, first employing a policy of "occupation with a smile" in the late 1960s and the early 1970s, and then resorting to more-draconian measures after the 1973 war. Ethnic cleansing, now internationally unpalatable and practically untenable, gave way to a policy of "silent transfer," and heavy-handed military repression was complemented with an array of administrative and legal tools to dispossess Palestinians of their homes and places of residence and to displace them. By the early 1990s, this manifested itself in a policy of separation and isolation in controlled areas roughly along the border of the 1967 Green Line, namely in the West Bank and the Gaza Strip. Throughout, the very travails of Palestinians—their resistance to the occupation, their clinging to the land, their symbolic and commemorative rallying cries, their martyrs, and their legends—all became hallmarks of their national identity, the foundations of an evolving, dynamic sense of nationhood.

Despite the endurance of the Palestinian nation, the future of Palestine does not look particularly bright. Nations revolve around identity, community, and collective imaginations. But power is possessed by states, which can bestow nations with sovereignty and with protection and autonomy from other states. The birth and stunted growth of the PNA has helped to undermine the possibility of the emergence of a viable, functioning Palestinian state both now and, most likely, into the future. The Palestinian nation, robust as it is in its identity, will therefore remain at the mercy of other states, especially the State of Israel. And, as its conduct since 1948 and even before its formal establishment has amply demonstrated, Israel has shown little inclination to treat Palestinians with anything other than disdain. There is no reason to imagine a future for Palestine less bleak than its past.

Outline of the Book

In constructing my arguments, I examine Palestine's history, geography, its social composition and the social changes impacting it, and its efforts at building a state apparatus. This begins with chapter 2, which provides a historical overview of the conquest of

Palestine by settlers, the collapse and disintegration of Palestinian society, its reconstitution under conditions of dispossession and occupation for some and dispersion and exile for others, and the efforts of Palestinians at reforging a nation and building a state.

Chapter 3 turns to geography. It examines the parallel processes of territorial dismemberment of Palestine, the segregation of Palestinians from Israelis and their isolation from one another, and the various mechanisms through which the occupation takes place. In addition to and in place of the project of ethnic cleansing, one of the most viable options of dealing with "the demographic problem" was to place the mass of Palestinians within the confines of well-guarded and isolated "human warehouses" and to have someone else responsible for feeding and managing them.[43] The chapter ends by highlighting some of the aspects of life under occupation in the West Bank and Gaza.

This sets the stage for a discussion of Palestinian society, at least in Gaza and the West Bank, in chapter 4. The Oslo Accords resulted in the development of three structural consequences for Palestinian society in the West Bank and Gaza Strip. Combined, these developments have seriously undermined the revolutionary potential of West Bank and Gaza societies. First, the return of a small number of Fatah-affiliated middle-class entrepreneurs, and their organic links with the newly established Palestinian National Authority, transformed the Palestinian nationalist middle classes, once the mainstay of the liberation movement, to comprador bourgeoisie, highly supportive of the status quo and a force for conservatism. Secondly, many of the civil society organizations that had grown spontaneously during the course of the intifada gave way to nongovernmental organizations, whose primary focus became maintaining their funding streams, often from the United States and the European Union, and providing employment for urban professionals, instead of addressing community needs. The NGOization of Palestinian society helped blunt its penchant for resistance to Israeli occupation. Third, with the formal end of the national liberation movement, the failure of the promises of Oslo, and the growing chasm between religious and secularist political trends represented by Hamas and Fatah respectively, there was a steady loosening up of social commitments in the West Bank and Gaza societies. The national sense of common purpose that once united Palestinian society was now steadily replaced with more-parochial concerns and loyalties. Altogether, these developments have significantly undermined the mobilizational potentials of Palestinian society in the West Bank and Gaza. As the Hamas-Israel war of August 2014 showed, during which West Bankers also demonstrated against Israel's relentless bombardment of Gaza, the possibility of rebellion and resistance to the occupation continues to be ever-present. Nevertheless, West Bank and Gaza societies as a whole have become less likely to actively mobilize to change the status quo.

Chapter 5 focuses on efforts at state-building, beginning in earnest with the signing of the Oslo Accords. States are not created out of thin air. They have institutional antecedents, social roots and progeny, and, at times, even founding fathers. The statelike apparatus that grew out of the Oslo process had all these ingredients, none of which boded well for its evolution into a full state. But it also operated within a highly constrained framework of territorial, legal and political, and economic restrictions. What has emerged as a consequence is a form of Palestinian "self-rule" that hardly extends beyond municipal government, of which, for now at least, there is a PNA variety in the West Bank and a Hamas version in Gaza. After more than two decades, the state-building process has brought the

Palestinians of the West Bank and Gaza only added separation and apartness, increased confinement into ever-smaller pieces of land, and no closer to meaningful statehood.

The book ends with a look to the future. The road ahead, the book concludes, is not that different from the road traveled so far. Might may not make right, but it does make history. And there is nothing to indicate that Israel's might in relation to the Palestinians will diminish anytime soon or that its preferences will change. For now, the status quo is exactly what Israel prefers: continued "negotiations" and "peace process" with the PNA; the continued construction of new settlements; continued demolition of Palestinian homes and expulsion orders of Palestinians in east Jerusalem; and continued efforts at ensuring steady separation and segregation from Palestinians. Indirect control over Palestine through the PNA is more effective than direct means of control. As Baruch Kimmerling commented, "the status quo amounts to a more efficient and enabling form of annexation than any legitimate or declared sort of annexation."[44] Palestine's future, therefore, is unlikely to be different from its past.

Here I present a static snapshot of a process that is inherently dynamic and changeable. What follows is my account of where Palestine is today—the present status of its society, its perceptions of itself, its current state of affairs. My account is not meant to be predictive of the distant future, beyond perhaps how the present is likely to shape the immediate future. And the short-term future of Palestine does not look bright. My own, personal hope is that I am wrong.

2

The Lessons of History

This chapter focuses on three aspects of the story of Palestinian society—its conquest and defeat, its collapse and disintegration, and its efforts to reconstitute itself as a nation and a state under the conditions of dispersion, exile, and occupation. The chapter starts by transposing the history of Zionist settlement in Palestine onto the framework presented by the historian David Day of conquest and domination by settler societies. In his seminal study on the dynamics of conquest by settler societies and their efforts to dominate preexisting inhabitants, Day outlines the violent dispossessions and the steps generally involved from initial settlement to eventual ownership and domination of new lands. Insecurity about the land one inhabits, Day argues, has been a historical feature of all human societies. The conquest of new lands has often been in turn contested by subsequent arrivees, who try to establish firmer bonds to the land. Invariably, every community claims to be deeply rooted in the land it inhabits.[1]

The collapse of Palestinian society was followed by its fragmentation and the dispersion of dispossessed Palestinians, followed by exile for some, occupation for others, and absorption for a few others. The reemergence of Palestinian identity, and the efforts at building a Palestinian state anew and resurrecting a Palestinian nation, took place during occupation, exile, and the struggle for national liberation.

Israel has not sat idly by to see these efforts come to fruition; historically it has done what it could to ensure that a Palestinian nation does not reemerge. This chapter chronicles Palestinian political history since the early 1900s, and more specifically the travails of the Palestinian nation, by retracing the disintegration of Palestinian society and its fractured reconstruction. What follows is a story of death and stunted birth, of dispossession and exile, and what have so far been insurmountable historical obstacles to nation-building.

Conquest

The late Israeli sociologist Baruch Kimmerling identified three broad types of settler societies. In one type of settler society—like the ones found in the United States, Australia, and New Zealand—settlers brought with them exclusivist orientations. At the same time, they were sufficiently powerful to destroy the local social fabric and preexisting political institutions, and to also overwhelm native populations into near oblivion. Elsewhere, especially in Central and South America, settlers were more inclusive, gradually absorbing local populations and being absorbed by them through intermarriage. In the new states of Central and South America, the descendants of settlers tended to form the economic and political elites, while those of the indigenous populations mostly populated the lower echelons of society. In a third type of settler society—examples of which include South Africa, Rhodesia, Algeria, Ireland, and Palestine—the settler and indigenous communities developed along separate lines, maintaining their own social, religious, racial, and cultural identities. In these cases, the settlers were not strong enough, neither demographically nor militarily, to establish hegemonic rule over the large indigenous majority. French Algeria, Rhodesia, and apartheid South

Africa all disappeared, and in Ireland a peaceful settlement was eventually reached.

In Palestine/Israel, Kimmerling argued, the Israelis and the Palestinians appear to have finally decided to go their separate ways.[2] Israel, as we shall see later, is willing to live with a small population of Palestinians—no more than 20 percent—as its citizens. The remaining Palestinians should either live in the West Bank and Gaza or anywhere else. But not, under any circumstance, in Israel. If need be, they will be kept away through a massive wall. Israelis morphed from the first type of settlers, wanting to annihilate and replace the indigenous population in 1948, into who they are today, namely wanting to go their own, separate way and to disengage and distance themselves from the Palestinians as much as possible.

All too often, settlers resort to a wide variety of self-serving justifications to legitimize their conquest of new lands. Among the most prominent of these justifications is the argument that the natives have no claim to the land they inhabit, and that they were, and remain, insufficiently prepared or advanced enough to develop it. At times this logic is extended to argue that the natives have no civilization of their own and have not made any meaningful civilizational contributions to mankind.[3] In fact, for settler communities to become "supplanting societies," they usually undergo three processes: beginning with establishing legal or de jure claims to the land, then having effective or de facto ownership over it, and establishing a "moral proprietorship over the territory."[4]

Effective ownership and moral proprietorship reinforce one another, the latter often justified as bringing the "gift" of a higher civilization. From the start, Zionists wanted to make the area of Palestine a Jewish state.[5] In Zionist thinking, the "civilizational barrenness" of Palestine and its "emptiness," transposed on a firm belief in the superiority of European ideology and civilization, and reinforced by the certainty of biblical promise, were all seen as compelling reasons for the Arabs to vacate the land and make room for the superior newcomers.[6] This theme was advocated by early Zionist writers such as Israel Zangwill, who wrote: "We cannot allow the Arabs to block so valuable a piece of historic reconstruction. . . . And therefore we must gently persuade them to 'trek.' After all, they have all Arabia with its million square miles. . . . There is no particular reason for the Arabs to cling to these few kilometers. 'To fold their tents' and 'silently steal away' is their proverbial habit: let them exemplify it now."[7]

Early Zionist writings in particular constructed a narrative of Palestinians and especially the fellahin as "backward" and in dire need of the "progress" that the settlers brought with them. It was only the Zionists who could "make the desert bloom." In the process, the Palestinian landscape, and the culture and civilization it supported, was destroyed and built over by another civilization that considered itself modern and progressive, and the one it supplanted as primitive and backward.[8] The nuances of the narrative and its emphasis shifted according to the tenor of the times: disdain for the "natives" at the start of the settlement project, paternalism toward the Arabs at the height of socialist Zionism, fear and revulsion for "the murderous sons of the wilderness" once the Arab Revolt broke out in 1936.[9] But the underlying assumptions of the Zionists' superiority, and their right to redeem and develop the land, remained constant throughout. In particular, the offspring of the second aliyah (1904–1914), who considered themselves "Labor Zionists" and were ardent nationalists, believed strongly in "conquest of labor" and the victory of Jewish workers in creating a new society.[10] Today, Israeli schoolbooks reproduce a narrative that connects Jewish students to their "origins" in the Land of Israel, "as modern

Westerners who are direct descendants of the biblical Hebrews—the children of Israel."[11]

The Zionists' founding of Tel Aviv near the Palestinian city of Jaffa is telling in this regard. In 1909, Tel Aviv was founded as a specifically modern, European city to contrast with Jaffa, which was seen by the settlers as dirty, noisy, and overcrowded. The establishment of a new, modern city was motivated by three specific ideological reasons. They included segregating Jewish immigrants from Palestinians, stemming the flow of Jewish money into the hands of Jaffa-based landowning Palestinians, and bolstering Jewish prestige at home and abroad.[12] Today, Tel Aviv has grown over and has overwhelmed Jaffa, having in the process developed a decidedly cool self-image both in Israel and elsewhere.

Conquerors usually have a foundation story, a series of founding myths, that idealize and romanticize the new nation's birth. These foundation stories provide supplanting societies with legitimacy, but they do not necessarily guarantee against the supplanting society's overthrow. As Day writes, "Ignoring the long Muslim interregnum, the tenuous link to the ancient Jewish state provided the central part of the foundation story that the new Israeli state projected to the world in an effort to gain legitimacy in the face of regional hostility. Their task was made harder by the presence in the surrounding states of the hundreds of thousands of Palestinians displaced from their homeland, dispossessed of their lands, and refused the right of return."[13] As an integral part of their foundation story, Zionist settlers emphasized their background as "the chosen people," and the stiffer and more stern the Arab response, the greater the Zionists' emphasis on having divine sanction and uniqueness. Archaeology was employed to reaffirm the Israeli foundation story, "with determined efforts being made to unearth artifacts and documents from the ancient

Jewish society."[14] Zionism displayed a particular love for the cult of ancient history, the "sanctification" of places of religious significance, and a "love of the country and its landscape, enthusiasm for its vegetation, and a sense of the soil's holiness [and] truly mystical quality."[15] Israelis, in fact, tend to be more interested than other supplanting societies in the discoveries of archaeology, at least those that reaffirm the Israeli foundation story. As David Day observes, "set out in a museum display case, the remains of ancient Jewish occupation provide satisfying and seemingly incontrovertible proof of a foundation story that stretches into antiquity, while attempting to conceal the fact that other foundation stories are also attached to that land. Muslims do the same."[16] While initially not given centrality, the Holocaust was also soon woven into Israel's foundation story, giving it a potent sense of moral legitimacy.

Zionist settlers "held the Bible to be the deed to the land, the entire land of their forefathers."[17] As such, Zionist slogans included "a land without a people for a people without a land," and the Arab inhabitants of Palestine were frequently referred to as "human dust" by the early settlers.[18] Even before the formal establishment of the State of Israel, Zionism as an ideology and the Zionist ideal of "ingathering of exiles" were used for purposes of political mobilization and legitimation and for constructing the institutions of the state.[19] For both the national religious movement and the three strands of secular Zionism—General, Revisionist, and Labor—combating assimilation and preserving the uniqueness of Jewish identity were (and continue to remain) central, as is territorial expansion to the fullest extent possible. All Zionist tendencies called for unity behind the pioneers who led the reconquest and repopulation of biblically promised lands, differing only in how the land should be acquired rather than whether it should be acquired at all. To this day,

Zionism's one-dimensionality, its singular focus on territorial conquest and expansion, is the very key to its success.[20] In moments of crisis, Zionism is seen as a movement for "patriotic defense," and there is a reassertion of its core values.[21] For Israel's radical right, in fact, any thoughts of leaving the heights of "Judea and Samaria" is tantamount to moral suicide.[22]

Supplanting societies seldom welcome interface and fusion with those they have conquered. Vladimir Jabotinsky, chief ideologue and leader of Revisionist Zionists, articulated the idea of an "iron wall" of an armed Jewish garrison that would drill into the Palestinians the idea and reality of Zionist permanence and triumph. Jabotinsky was blunt in his assessment of the Arabs: "We Jews, thank God, have nothing to do with the East. . . . The Islamic soul must be broomed out of Eretz Ysrael."[23] Moshe Smilansky, another Zionist writer and Labor leader, wrote "let us not be too familiar with the Arab fellahin lest our children adopt their ways and learn from their ugly deeds. Let all those who are loyal to the Torah avoid ugliness and that which resembles it and keep their distance from the fellahin and their base attitudes."[24]

The "genocidal imperative" of supplanting societies often manifests itself in preventing symbols of identity. This translates into preventing or altogether blocking displays of a group's ethnic identity, language, national symbols, and religious or national identity. The end objective of the supplanting society is "the complete disappearance of an ethnic group from their midst."[25] Prime Minister Golda Meir, for example, for whom the Arab national movement had no legitimacy whatsoever, banned the mention of terms such as "Palestinian national movement" and "Palestinian state" on Israeli state radio and television.[26]

In most supplanting nations, the exclusivist impulse remains strong despite the fact that they seldom succeed in completely annihilating the conquered.[27] In relation to Palestine, the concept of "transfer"—sending the indigenous inhabitants of Palestine to neighboring Arab states—was shared by all shades of Zionist thought, from the Revisionist right to Labor left, and various proposals regarding transferring the Arabs of Palestine were forwarded by the Jewish Agency itself, which was, in effect, the government of the Yishuv, the settler community in Palestine.[28] Because of its political sensitivity, not all calls or efforts to promote transfer were as open and blatant. Chaim Weizmann, for example, who had been president of the World Zionist Organization and later served as the first president of the State of Israel, sought to promote the idea behind the scenes. Zionist leaders did not question the morality of transfer but rather its practicability on a large scale.[29] Although most found the idea of transfer morally problematic, they saw it as one of the only viable solutions to an intractable demographic problem; at the start of the Zionist influx, Palestinians numbered some 450,000, whereas the Jews amounted to only 20,000.[30]

Despite the prevalence and popularity of the notion among Zionist leaders, most notably David Ben-Gurion, because of its sensitivity, the Jewish press at the time failed to report on the idea of transfer or its widespread endorsement among the Yishuv's leadership.[31] Nevertheless, the idea continued to capture the Zionist imagination for some time. According to Benny Morris, "transfer was inevitable and inbuilt into Zionism."[32]

No conquest can be complete from the outset. Despite the settlers' erection of fortifications, challenges can remain for some time. Walls, in fact, may provide a "comforting sense of impregnability" to those societies that shelter behind them, but they are an imperfect and temporary means of preventing the movement of peoples across borders. As Day maintains, "where natural features were insufficient to make a border that would be impervious to alien incursions, a physical barrier was sometimes built to provide a fortified border. It might be a ditch, such as the Israelis wanted to excavate between Egypt and the Gaza Strip. More commonly, though, it takes the form of a wall."[33] In 2002, Israel began the construction of a wall to separate itself from Palestinians in the West Bank. According to Day, however, "it is likely that the Israeli wall will also fail in its attempt to define an immutable line of separation between the Israelis within the wall and the Palestinians who were pushed beyond it in 1947 and who now seek their right of return."[34]

Beginning especially in the 1920s, a state-in-the-making was created in Palestine, with multiple functions, such as defense, administrative machinery, education, welfare, health, banking and finance, and employment services.[35] To cement the resurrection of a new nation, the Hebrew language and Hebrew names were resurrected.[36] From the beginning, the distinction between Israeli society and the emerging Israeli state was blurred.[37]

The Zionists' parallel efforts at both nation- and state-building transpired within a context of weak and weakening Palestinian social and political institutions. The steady influx of settlers throughout the 1920s and the 1930s, along with the devastating consequences of the 1936–1939 Arab Revolt, only further paved the way for the rapid disintegration of Palestinian society in the immediate lead-up to and the aftermath of the 1948 war. The Palestinian Nakba of 1948 was facilitated by two parallel, almost simultaneous sets of developments, namely the deliberate and determined construction of an Israeli nation and state on the one side and the rapid unraveling of Palestinian society on the other.

The disintegration of Palestinian society was made possible by the confluence of a number of factors, not the least of which were preexisting structural and institutional weaknesses resulting from elite factionalism, the predominance of weak and underdeveloped political institutions, absentee landlordism, and an absence of effective leadership.[38] Prior to the arrival of the settlers, Palestine was a localized world, with most Palestinians engaged in subsistence farming, small-scale industries, and fruit exports; some working in the small industry that had emerged around religious tourism; and a few powerful families whose members had traditionally been involved in education, religious observance, or politics.[39] Unlike elsewhere in the Levant, where notables had lost most of their power and status, in Palestine they remained powerful intermediaries with the rest of society through institutions that were often little more than facades for family status and influence. The desire to keep their status and material wealth in the face of rapidly changing circumstances made Palestinian notables an extremely conservative social class.[40] Limited access to educational opportunities also helped maintain the status of the elite. Although there were generally positive attitudes among Palestinians, including villagers, toward education, Mandatory authorities spent little on Arab education. As a result, by the end of the Mandatory period there were schools in only half of Palestinian villages and over two-thirds of the population was illiterate.[41]

This was a society ill-equipped to absorb and respond to the shocks of massive in-migration and state-building efforts by the Zionists. Compounding matters were the devastating consequences of the 1936–1939 Arab Revolt, from which Palestinian society never fully recovered. The revolt was more a product of the frustrations of Palestinians near the bottom of the social ladder than those closer to the top, and the work, not unlike the intifada of a half-century later, mostly of a counter-elite whose efforts in the long run turned out more disastrous than productive.

The rebellion resulted in five thousand Palestinians deaths, ten thousand wounded, and over fifty-six hundred detained. In total, over 10 percent of the adult male Palestinian population was killed, wounded, imprisoned, or exiled. The revolt also left Palestinian economy in tatters, measurably worsening the economic situation of many landowners and damaging numerous businesses involved in citrus export, quarrying, transportation, and industry. By the revolt's end, Palestinian leadership was also shattered, resulting in weaknesses at both the top and the base of Palestinian society.[42] Benny Morris refers to the consequences of the Arab Revolt as "the neutering of the Palestinians."[43]

Whatever Palestinian body politic existed, meanwhile, had none of the attributes of "stateness," no international sanction or accepted context for the formulation and expression of political or national legitimation, no centralized military force, and no central national forum that could act as anything resembling a state.[44] Throughout the Mandatory period, there had been a conspicuous absence of the evolution of any meaningful Palestinian political institutions. Rashid Khalidi concludes that Palestinians "never had a chance of retaining control of their country once they were engaged in all-out military confrontation with the forces of the Yishuv."[45] In what is often called "the politics of the notable," the fractious Palestinian elites—especially the two bitterly divided notable families of the Husseinis and Nashashibis—pinned their hopes on British Mandatory authorities to keep Zionist expansion at bay.[46]

This is not to imply that a robust sense of Palestinian identity did not exist by the time Zionist settlers arrived. In addition to the elite, in fact, nonelite, subaltern elements of Palestinian society played a central, crucial role in the emergence of what can be considered a national identity. This identity—built on a number of components, such as patriotic feelings, local loyalties, Arabism, religious sentiments, and higher levels of education and literacy—had by 1922–1923 resulted in Palestinians identifying themselves as parts of a single community.[47] Combined with attachment to religious holy places, Ottoman administrative boundaries, European ambitions, urban patriotism, and opposition to Zionism, Palestinian national identity was beginning to gain widespread hold immediately prior to World War I.[48] By the middle of the 1930s, in fact, the Palestinians had generated the beginnings of a popular movement, one with a significant intellectual component and diverse notions of the future. An organization calling itself Istiqlal, or "independence," was most representative of such a development.[49] But without viable institutional expression, identity alone cannot withstand the onslaught of conquerors. Bereft of meaningful institutions, Palestine was left at the mercy first of the Zionist settlers colonizing and dismantling it, and then of other Arab leaders pretending to seek its liberation and reconstitution.

The struggle for Palestine had started in earnest long before the fateful months leading up to and after 1948. But the "catastrophe" that befell Palestine in 1948, the Nakba, would not have been possible had Palestinian society not had a number of structural features that made its unraveling and collapse easier. The conquest of Palestine, first through what observers today would not be able to label as anything other than "ethnic cleansing" and then through military defeat, was facilitated through a number of structural conditions that heightened the vulnerabilities of Palestinian society and pushed it closer to catastrophe.

Collapse

On March 10, 1948, a group of Zionist leaders met in Tel Aviv and devised what came to be known as Plan D (Plan Dalet in Hebrew) for the large-scale and forcible eviction of the Arab inhabitants of

Palestine. The plan was the fourth version of a blueprint aimed at the disruption and destruction of the Arab community in Palestine, an earlier version of which, Plan C (Plan Gimel in Hebrew), had spelled out the aims of killing Palestinian leadership, inciters, and their financial supporters; destruction of Palestinian roads and transportation, livestock, wells, and other sources of livelihood; and attacks on Palestinian clubs, coffeehouses, and meeting places.[50] While similar plans had been devised well before the war, Plan D was more comprehensive in scope and specific in details. It included a description of the methods to be used to achieve its goals: "large-scale intimidation; laying siege to and bombarding villages and population centers; setting fire to homes, properties, and goods; expulsion; demolition; and, finally, planting mines among the rubble to prevent any of the expelled inhabitants from returning."[51] Each Jewish military unit was issued its own list of specific villages and neighborhoods from this master plan.[52] Scholars have long debated whether or not Plan D was actually implemented. According to Benny Morris, "the plan was neither understood nor used by the senior field officers as a blanket instruction for the expulsion of 'the Arabs.'"[53] Ilan Pappe has a different interpretation, maintaining that the "systematic implementation" of Plan D was "a clear-cut case of an ethnic cleansing operation."[54] Even Morris agrees that as a blueprint for the expulsion of "hostile" Palestinians, in practice the plan meant the "depopulation and destruction" of Palestinian villages and communities.[55]

Ethnic cleansing operations intensified in the summer months of 1948, specifically from June to September.[56] In April, orders went out to Jewish units to clear out villages where fighting had not ceased and to evict their inhabitants, and a general atmosphere of "transfer" prevailed.[57] It was at this time when the infamous massacre in the village of Deir Yassin took place. According to the commanding officer of the Haganah Intelligence Services, "the conquest of the village was carried out with great cruelty. Whole families—women, old people, children—were killed. . . . Some of the prisoners moved to places of detention, including women and children, were murdered viciously by their captors."[58] Morris puts the number of those killed at between 100 and 120.[59]

Precisely how the Palestinian refugee problem came about has been researched and debated extensively. Morris attributes Palestinian refugeedom to war, shellings, shootings, bombings, and the fears these generated as a result. Poor leadership and the steady collapse of Palestinian society, first through the flight of the wealthy and then the departure and displacement of hundreds of thousands of others, were significant contributing factors. However, as Morris argues, "above all . . . the refugee problem was caused by attacks by Jewish forces on Arab villages and towns and by the inhabitants' fear of such attacks, compounded by expulsions, atrocities, and rumors of atrocities—and by the crucial Israeli cabinet decision in June 1948 to bar a refugee return."[60] According to Morris, "altogether about a dozen massacres occurred" during the course of the War of Independence, and those Israeli soldiers and individuals who committed crimes and atrocities, including massacres, did so believing they had "central direction and authorization" to do so by the authorities and that their actions had official sanction.[61]

As the war raged in 1947–1948 and the ethnic cleansing of Palestine picked up pace, "transfer" occurred unilaterally and without any arrangements or agreements with other countries, nor was any compensation forthcoming for the displaced Palestinians.[62] The "mini-transfers" of Arab tenant farmers throughout the 1930s and the 1940s were often cited as precedent and justification for the large-scale transfer of Palestinians out of Palestine.[63] According to Pappe,

Ben-Gurion (1886–1973), who led the Zionist movement from the mid-1920s until well into the 1960s and served as Israel's first prime minister after independence, played a central, deciding role in orchestrating the ethnic cleansing of Palestinians.[64] The bulk of the Palestinian exodus occurred over a period of twenty months, from the end of November 1948 to July 1949, with smaller appendages in the following months and years. Wealthier Palestinians left in the earlier periods, from December 1948 to March 1949, followed by mass urban flight in April and May, and then a more-wholesale exodus in the final months of the war.[65] In 1948, Palestinian society disintegrated, the Palestinians forever changed and dispersed.[66]

Already weakened, the disintegration of Palestinian society started during the 1948 war with the steady exodus of the inhabitants of the larger cities of Haifa, Jaffa, and Tiberias, and of Safad, Beisan, and Acre, and the subsequent collapse of administration and law and order, difficulties in communication and supplies, siege, and, of course, increasing and often vicious attacks at the hands of Jewish troops.[67] In both the countryside and in the cities, Palestinians were soon gripped with a sense of fear and despair. By 1949, half of Palestinian society had been uprooted. More than four hundred of the more than five hundred Arab villages were taken over by Israelis.[68] More than thirty thousand Palestinians were driven from the western part of Jerusalem alone. The ownership of more than eighteen million of the country's twenty-six million dunams shifted from Palestinians to Israelis.[69] In the lead-up to the war, the Haganah had issued plans in which the destruction of Palestinian houses was formalized as a legitimate retaliatory measure, as a result of which house demolitions became commonplace.[70] Religious and cultural sites were also targeted for demolition, and Palestinian agriculture was destroyed. Olive groves, trees, and citrus groves were neglected or were uprooted to make room for new housing developments or field crops. As Meron Benvenisti observes, "the Israelis destroyed whatever the Arabs had left that could not be integrated into their framework."[71] Some Palestinians were expelled expressly for purposes of having their homes and land taken over by Jewish settlers.[72]

The 1948 war resulted in the realization of the Zionist dream of de-Arabizing the land. More than 750,000 Palestinians, or more than 80 percent of the Arab inhabitants of what became Israel, left for exile and became refugees.[73] More than 77 percent of Palestinian territory was taken over by Israel, and 80 percent of Palestinians living in what became Israel ended up as refugees. Not only were Palestinian villages depopulated and in many instances destroyed, many were reinvented as purely Jewish or "ancient" Hebrew places.[74] Before long, the newly established Knesset created a legal framework for taking over Palestinian land.[75] Chaim Wiezmann, by then the first president of the new State of Israel, called the exodus of some 750,000 Palestinians "a miraculous clearing of the land: the miraculous simplification of Israel's task."[76] Between 60,000 and 156,000 Palestinians, depending on the sources, stayed behind and became Israeli citizens, subject to a separate system of military administration and having much of their land confiscated.[77] Nur Masalha puts the number of those who remained between 140,000 and 150,000, many of them Christian and Druze and most concentrated in Galilee.[78]

A few months after the State of Israel was officially established in May 1948, the Transfer Committee recommended to Ben-Gurion that the percentage of the Arab minority in Israel should not exceed 15 percent of the country's total population. When it was discovered that the remaining Palestinians amounted to 17 percent, the percentage was raised to 20.[79] To this day, the 80/20 percentage remains in effect; Palestinians are not allowed to exceed one-fifth of Israel's total population. A separate government directive in relation to Jerusalem seeks to preserve the ratio of the city's Palestinian-Jewish population at 28 percent Palestinian to 72 percent Jewish.[80]

Not all communities of Palestinians were targeted equally for expulsion during the war. A pro-Druze policy, for example, constrained the actions of Israeli commanders on the ground when it came to expelling them from their homes and their land. Israeli authorities saw the Druze in Palestine as useful conduits to Syrian Druze and therefore sought to woo them with favorable treatment. The policy paid off, as there were instances of collusion between Druze civilians and Zionist fighters in a few battles during the war.[81]

In 1948 and early 1949, a series of actions were taken to ensure that a return of Palestinian refugees would be impossible and inconceivable: abandoned villages were destroyed, lands and territory left behind were taken over and redistributed to Jews, and empty houses were given to settlers, leaving potential returnees with nothing to return to. These measures, all meant to ensure the erasure of Palestinian history, geography, and demography as much as possible, were reinforced by concomitant steps to solidify and further construct the necessary infrastructure and institutions of the new State of Israel, politically, militarily, economically, and, of course, demographically.[82] Combined, the dissolution of Palestine and the resurrection of Israel made the return of Palestinian refugees all but impossible in practice. The dream of return lives on; its possibility or practicality do not.

Once the war formally ended, the depopulation of Palestinian villages continued, though unlike earlier transfers, the later ones had a softer touch, with villagers being given a few days notice of the need to leave and generally allowed to take their property with them.[83] The official policy decision to bar Palestinians from returning was simply derived from what Ben-Gurion said: "I do not want those who flee to return. Their return must be prevented now." He made this statement early in 1948, as the war was beginning to pick up pace, following which Foreign Minister Moshe Sharett declared: "This is our policy: they are not coming back."[84] As with most battles, the campaign to prevent Palestinian refugees from returning assumed a life of its own on the battlefield, unleashing what Benny Morris calls "the atrocity factor" as a significant instigator of further departures and deterrence against possible returns.[85] Israeli Defense Forces (IDF) troops were instructed to "carry out harassing operations" against any refugees they suspected of wanting to return to their homes and villages.[86] As the refugees were streaming into Lebanon, for example, live fire was used to prevent any of them from returning.

Although the Arab leaders wanted to see the defeat of the Zionist experiment, they had neither the plan nor the ability to make their ambitions a reality.[87] The 1948 war witnessed at best a halfhearted effort by the neighboring Arab states to prevent the dismantling of Palestine. At their peak, the Arab forces that were sent to defeat the newly declared State of Israel were entirely comprised of expeditionary forces and numbered under twenty-five thousand, whereas the IDF had more than ninety-six thousand troops.[88] Iraqi forces, which constituted the largest of the Arab contingents in Palestine, did little more than merely occupy defensive positions.[89] Egypt, for its part, did not take the war seriously, was not well prepared for it, did not plan for it strategically or tactically, and failed to adequately supply its troops during the conflict. From the outset, in fact, the Egyptian army, Premier Mahmud Fahmi Nuqrashi, and the major political parties expressed serious concerns about the wisdom of sending troops to fight in Palestine.[90] Syria's army, meanwhile, was neither disciplined nor loyal, and was thus kept small and divided by President Shukri Qawwatli, who feared the possibility of a military coup throughout his tenure in office.[91] Syria, at any rate, was more concerned with King Abdullah's Greater Syria Plan than with liberating Palestinians.[92] Combined together, the Arab forces were unorganized and unable to coordinate their diplomatic and military moves. Not only were they internally divided, but their internal divisions were known to Israeli leaders who used the knowledge to their advantage.[93]

In the final phases of the war, as a truce was declared—between July 18 and October 15, 1948—IDF forces actually discussed the execution and completion of "cleanup" and "cleansing" operations in a number of Palestinian villages that were considered strategic or were seen as constituting security threats.[94] During this period, there was also a significant increase in the number of atrocities and acts of brutality committed against the Palestinians, including summary executions, blowing up houses with their occupants still in residence, looting and plundering, and leaving hundreds of villagers in the fields to fend for their own, without food or water.[95] Reports by witnesses, the International Red Cross, and by the United Nations recorded instances of rape.[96]

The depopulation of Palestinian geography, meanwhile, was complemented with a repopulation of Israel. Once the dust of ethnic cleansing and expulsions was settled, Palestinians added up to only 17 percent of the total population of Israel and were allowed to build and live on only 2 percent of the land, with another 1 percent of the land set aside for agricultural purposes. At the same time, between May 1948 and 1951, no less than seven hundred thousand Jews immigrated into Palestine, exceeding the number of those who were already there, and the repopulation of territory started in earnest. Many of the new arrivees were settled in abandoned Palestinian villages that were then turned into cooperative settlements.[97] Beginning in 1950, the Settlement Department of the Jewish National Fund

(JNF) was given the responsibility of deciding the fate of emptied Palestinian villages and whether they would be replaced by new Jewish settlements or Zionist forests, or something similar.[98] Although in the 1990s Israel privatized the land market and allowed for the wide-scale sale and purchase of land, the JNF's policy of "repatriating" land only to Jews remains in place, therefore excluding Palestinians from the ability to purchase land in Israel proper.[99]

Shortly after the occupation began in 1948, Palestinians in Israel, whether in Israel proper or in the Occupied Territories, started experiencing "exploitative and abusive conduct" by Israeli soldiers and authorities. Between eight thousand and nine thousand Palestinians spent the whole of 1949 in prison camps. Others were harassed, their houses confiscated, their holy places desecrated, and their freedom of movement and expression was curtailed.[100] Internal refugees, both in 1948 and in 1967, often had to pass through many "stations" before finally finding sanctuary.[101]

Not surprisingly, the "catastrophe" of 1948, the Nakba, is key to Palestinian identity and historical memory. The Nakba became a baseline for Palestinian history and for events that occurred before and after it, the marking point for passage into a melancholic existence.[102] It forever changed Palestinian history, geography, society, and sense of the self. As a result of the war, in Edward Said's words, "many families and individuals had their lives broken, their spirits drained, the composure destroyed forever in the context of seemingly unending serial dislocation."[103] Countless refugees "ended up penniless, jobless, destitute, and disoriented," and to this day "a vast collective feeling of injustice continues to hang over [their] lives with undiminished weight."[104]

For Palestinians, the Nakba was about fear, helplessness, violent uprooting, and humiliation.[105] The Nakba meant dispossession and dispersion, occupation and exile. It had brought with it the collapse of the two axes along which the special character of Palestinian society had been molded: the tension between the more self-contained, agricultural inland towns like Nablus and the more-cosmopolitan, coastal cities such as Jaffa, and the fragile balance between the notables and the society around them.[106] Not surprisingly, the "catastrophe generation" experienced ennui but, ironically, also a cultural ferment of sorts, mostly in the form of literature and songs that idealized a land lost. The poetry of Fadwa Tuqan and the literature of Ghassan Kanafani bespoke a tattered identity in need of reconstruction.[107]

Only two decades later, shortly after 1967, were Palestinian actors able to reassert themselves once again as having a viable "national movement" with a serious liberationist mission. Still two decades after that, in 1987, the national movement showed a new face, one less reflective of the predicaments and dispositions of exile and more in tune with life in what remained of Palestine. The intifada reasserted Palestinian national identity anew, this time with more of a local face, rooted in geographic Palestine, or at least in its two remaining slivers, in the West Bank and in Gaza.

Fractured Reconstitution

For some twenty years after 1948, Palestinians were too traumatized and too busy with daily life to organize and plan and to understand Israel. Hardly understanding Israel or what it was about, the only solutions offered to the Palestinian predicament were in military terms.[108] Palestinian refugees across the Arab world, meanwhile, received what Edward Said called "scandalously poor" treatment, subject to suspicion and dislike; regular reporting to the local police; curtailed educational, vocational, and social opportunities; and in a few instances even massacres—as in Sabra, Shatila, Tell el Zaatar, and Dabaye.[109] Palestinians elsewhere didn't fare much better. Jordan generally ignored the West Bank prior to its loss to Israel in 1967, as a matter of deliberate policy; it did not want to shift the center of gravity from the East Bank to the West Bank, nor did it want the West Bank's economy to improve in the farming and industrial sectors.[110] Still, Jordan's treatment of the West Bank outshined Egypt's relationship with Gaza, which at times bordered on complete neglect and abandonment. Inside Israel proper, the depopulation of Palestinian territories and their subsequent Judaization continued into the 1960s, albeit at a much smaller scale. "Soft transfers" continued with unsettling frequency.

Zeev Sternhell questions the originality and innovativeness of the generation of Israel's War of Independence, which, he claims, led decades later to the Labor Party's intellectual paralysis. For them the only operative tool was power, seeking to conquer as much land as possible. Contrary to conventional assumptions by Israeli historians, he claims, the doctrine of "constructive socialism," which the leaders of the conquest espoused, "was merely an Eretz Israeli version of nationalism socialism."[111] In fact, their ideological disposition was to subordinate the ideas and ideals of socialism to the organic unity of the whole. Class warfare was rejected for the benefit of the collectivity as a whole, and society was to be led by natural leaders chosen not on the basis of qualifications but by "sentiment, dedication, and a readiness to make sacrifices for all."[112] Not surprisingly, whereas the kibbutzim—the other ideological contribution of the labor movement and supposedly the ideal model of an egalitarian way of life—eventually petered out, constructive socialism, as a means to construct and consolidate a nation, continued to survive and to thrive. In fact, it soon became one of the conservative bastions of the status quo.[113]

As Ben-Gurion reportedly said, "we are not yeshiva students debating the finer points of self-improvement. We are conquerors of the land facing an iron wall, and we have to break through it. . . . The one great concern that should govern our thought and work is the conquest of the land and building it up through extensive immigration. All the rest is mere words and phraseology."[114]

The primary consequence of this for Palestinians was their relative silence. Bewildered at the shock of occupation at best and homelessness and exile at worst, most were focused on rebuilding their shattered lives instead of liberating Palestine. The imperative of liberation, and more importantly of asserting the rights of Palestinian national identity, of course did not cease to exist with the outcome of the 1948 war. But from the time of the formal birth of Israel until after the outbreak of the first Arab-Israeli war in 1967, because of its own circumstances and developments within the larger region, the manifestations of Palestinian nationalism were overshadowed and drowned out by the drumbeats of interstate conflict and the overpowering shadow of the Egyptian Gamal Abdel Nasser. Well into the 1950s and the 1960s, the "Palestine First" approach was still a weak and faint voice, secondary to the bravado and hubris of Pan-Arabism.[115]

But Nasserism proved no more capable of delivering Palestinian liberation, nor its own defense for that matter, than previous attempts had been able to do. Before long, the 1967 war made another 285,000–325,000 Palestinians refugees, which, similar to 1948, were once again refused reentry into Israel.[116] For Palestinians, the "catastrophe" of 1948, the Nakba, had been succeeded by nothing other than a "setback," the Naksa. The dismemberment of Palestine, meanwhile, picked up pace, this time under the auspices of the settlement movement. The movement started in earnest during the premiership of Levi Eshkol (1963–1969), who, while not necessarily endorsing the settlement policy, had no alternatives to offer in its place and in fact found it hard to counter its imperative of historic conquest and its biblical zeal. At least initially, Israelis of all walks saw settlements as a manifestation of Israel's natural, historical expansion and validation, a symbol of the Jewish people's right to their entire historical homeland. The people of Israel were finally coming back to their mythical birthplace.[117] The perception of Jewish ethnic attachment to the land west of the Jordan River became an immediate and universal aspect of Israeli political culture.[118] As Moshe Dayan said in 1969, "We came to this country which was already populated by the Arabs, and we are establishing a Hebrew, that is a Jewish state here. . . . There is no place in this country that did not have a former Arab population."[119]

Throughout the latter 1960s, the expansion of the State of Israel continued through the construction of settlements. Yigal Allon (1918–1980), the minister of labor in the Eshkol government, spearheaded the expansion policy. His celebrated Allon Plan, which included the annexation of the Golan Heights and the Jordan Valley, later became the official policy of successive Labor governments.[120] In 1968, Allon proposed the establishment of a Jewish settlement next to the densely populated Arab city of Hebron. Today, Kiryat Arba, a biblical name mentioned in place of Hebron in the Old Testament, has a population of approximately eight thousand and is a bastion of Jewish extremism. Most Israelis saw the return to Hebron as the righting of a historical wrong.[121]

From the beginning of the settler movement, the Israeli leadership has either directly supported and sympathized with it, or has been unable to resist its organized force and passion for territorial expansion and has therefore yielded to it. Neither Eshkol nor Yitzhak Rabin, for example, had much enthusiasm for Israeli settlements in densely populated Arab areas, such as those in and around Hebron and Nablus. But neither proved willing nor able to stop the settlements of Kiryat Arba and Sebastia in the vicinity of Hebron and Nablus, respectively.[122]

From 1967 on, with Nasserism in decline, for about two decades Palestinian nationalism tried to find its own footing, finding expression first in the fiery outbursts of armed struggle spearheaded by the PLO, and then the highbrow politics of diplomacy by the Arab League, the United Nations, and the Europeans. The evolution of Palestinian armed struggle was determined by three factors, namely the relationship between Palestinians and their host countries, the division between the "inside" and the "outside," and the nature of the Palestinian leadership.[123] But neither the heroics of the Fedayeen Palestinian guerrillas nor the grand declarations of international allies and friends, nor even the fiery but increasingly vacuous speeches of Yasser Arafat, were yielding results. Growth in the PLOs bureaucracy in the 1970s hampered the organization's agility and created internal bureaucratic interests, while its reliance on rents created rentier relations with its Palestinian clients.[124] By the mid-1980s widespread disillusionment had set in among most Palestinians, though those who lived under the daily burdens of occupation, who repeatedly had been promised liberations right around the corner, felt the frustration most acutely. The eruption of the intifada in 1987 in the West Bank and Gaza ushered in a new phase of Palestinian nationalism, a phase that witnessed its localization and indigenization once again, and a reassertion of its fundamentally *national* character away from a PLO whose stewards had by now spent at least two decades away from the homeland.

Whereas 1948 marked the *conquest* of Palestine, 1967 brought about the *occupation* of additional Palestinian territories. In Israel, apart from east Jerusalem, there was no consensus as to what to do with Gaza and the West Bank. Conquer, occupy, or give back?—an intractable dilemma whose answer has not yet been fully articulated more than four decades later. The default option was, and has been, occupation. In the aftermath of the 1967 war, no Israeli leader could claim that the occupation of the West Bank and Gaza lacked the moral basis of the victory of 1948. This was the start of a "new Israelism," represented by war heroes such as Moshe Dayan and Yigal Allon, a time of moral certitude, when a people persecuted in history were finally regaining their rightful place—symbolically and literally—in the community of nations.[125] When the occupation would end, or whether at all, no one quite knew. Most Israelis remained, some by choice, some by the preoccupations of daily life, unaware of what the occupation exactly meant. As long as no Israelis died, the Palestinian problem was left off the public and political agendas in Israel.[126] For most Israelis and many Palestinians, therefore, the occupation soon lost its temporary nature, assuming increasing permanence as months turned into years and years into decades.

Israel itself soon initiated a series of steps to make the occupation of additional Palestinian lands and people permanent. This was done through a variety of means, including, most notably, direct military rule over what came to be referred to as the Occupied Territories, a complex web of administrative and legal procedures ensuring economic and political dependence on Israel, and the recruitment of a large network of Palestinian informants by Israeli General Security Services, Shin Bet. Settlements, in the meantime, continued unabated. By the late 1980s, the main arterial routes in the West Bank reflected not historic roads and trade routes, but the transportation and communication needs of the Israeli state and the settlers, often bypassing major Palestinian population centers such as Nablus and

Ramallah. Israel also took control of the West Bank's water resources and integrated them into its own national water system.[127]

The post-1967 interregnum had several notable consequences for Palestinian society, especially for its truncated portions in Gaza and the West Bank, all of which created a volatile mix by the late 1980s. Three paradoxical developments stand out. First, compared to the earlier years, despite an absence of meaningful economic development in the territories, there was an impressive rise in household income and purchasing power in both the West Bank and Gaza between 1968 and 1973. This was due partly to the trickling of Israeli funds into the territories and partly due to the opening of Israeli markets to Palestinian day laborers. Due to their willingness to work for lower wages, the import of cheap Palestinian labor was also extremely beneficial to Israeli employers, thus adding an important economic dimension to the occupation (more on this in chapters 4 and 5). By the 1980s, some 40 percent of the Palestinian labor force, accounting for nearly one hundred thousand individuals, was employed in Israel as day laborers.[128] This only helped increase a general sense of helplessness and despair throughout the Palestinian community and reinforced feelings of dependence on Israel for earning a living. At the same time, Israel actively promoted the "de-development" of both Gaza and the West Bank, ensuring that local industries did not grow and that both territories remained dependent on Israel. The neglect of Gaza, discussed more fully in chapter 4, was particularly stark. According to Avi Shlaim, "Gaza is a classic case of colonial exploitation in the post-colonial era."[129]

Second, there was a sudden growth in the number of institutions of higher learning in the territories. Technical colleges were established in Hebron (1968), Tulkarm (1969), Nablus (1969), Jenin (1969), Qalqilya (1969), and Beit Jala (1970). Hebron, Birzeit, and

Bethlehem Universities were established in 1971, 1972, and 1973, respectively. Other schools and vocational training colleges were established under the auspices of the newly established United Nations Relief and Works Agency, UNRWA. Made landless by Israeli land confiscations and settlement growths, an entire generation of Palestinians pursued university education as a way out of their hopeless predicament. A corollary development was the further undermining of the traditional elite and the emergence of a younger, better educated, and more-ideological nationalist elite.[130]

This fed into a third paradox. Just as a new, more locally oriented version of Palestinian nationalism was beginning to gain hold at the grassroots level, Israel began a concerted campaign to suppress representations of Palestinian national identity. Threatened by a reinvigorated Palestinian nationalism, Israel declared all Palestinian national symbols as "inflammatory materials" and banned them, including the Palestinian flag. The PLO was declared a "terrorist organization," and hundreds of books were censored, and their very possession was considered a crime. Universities in the Occupied Territories were frequently shut down; they had been closed for four years when the intifada started.[131] By some accounts, Israel's 1982 invasion of Lebanon was motivated by an attempt to destroy the Palestinian national movement once and for all.[132]

Spontaneous disturbances by Palestinians grew throughout the 1980s, in turn paving the way for the eruption in 1987 of the intifada. In the lead-up to the intifada, random acts of violence by Palestinians and reprisals by Israelis became commonplace, as did house demolitions and the administrative detention of Palestinians. For many Palestinians, the prison experience turned out to be formative, galvanizing them for community organization and revolutionary mobilization. For those arrested, "prison was like an education."[133]

Like all revolutionary uprisings, the intifada emerged within a volatile *context*. The actual *spark* occurred on December 8, 1987, when an Israeli tank carrier crashed into a row of parked cars and vans filled with Gazan Palestinians returning from work in Israel. The crash, which resulted in the death of four Palestinians and the serious injury of seven others, was rumored to be an intentional reprisal for the stabbing death of an Israeli businessman earlier. At the time of its eruptions, even veteran observers called the intifada "the most important political development in the history of the Palestinian people so far" and a historic manifestation of Palestinian nationalism.[134] The Israeli writer and politician Meron Benvenisti called the intifada "the day in which reality broke."[135]

The intifada was made possible through the efforts of urban-based Palestinians whose affiliation and even sympathies with the PLO were, for the most part, at best tentative. As compared to the PLO's stalwarts of the liberation struggle, the new activists formed somewhat of a counter-elite that was university educated, often hailed from smaller towns or the countryside, was numerically more preponderant, and called for social as well as political transformation of Palestinian society. Within the counter-elite, authority devolved downward, thus helping to sustain the intifada over time.[136] The rise of this counter-elite was facilitated through the development of a number of structural changes, the most notable of which were a spike in Israeli land confiscations—thus making former Palestinian peasants landless and unemployed—the opening of Israeli labor markets to Palestinian workers, the increasing number of Palestinians attending newly established universities in the West Bank and Gaza, and Israel's invasion of Lebanon in 1982. Ironically, the Likud Party also attacked and sought to undermine Palestinian nationalists because of its assumption that they were too nationalistic, thus inadvertently facilitating the rise of the counter-elite.[137]

The intifada further reduced the powers of traditional local bosses and brought to the fore the activism and influence of a Palestinian counter-elite.[138] It shifted the center of gravity of Palestinian politics further away from the "outside" and focused it "inside," within the Occupied Territories.[139] The popular movement gave rise to a new form of *sumud* (steadfastness), one in which Palestinians would take active control of "as many areas of human existence as possible under occupation."[140] This was especially apparent in the reemergence of student activism and trade unionism. Its back-to-the-land movement was a central political rallying cry and a psychologically important boost for the Palestinians.[141] Especially in the early months, there was a euphoria and a sense of self-confidence in the Occupied Territories, which Israel found difficult to break.[142]

The intifada had two important consequences for Palestinian society. On the one hand, it provided a real impetus for nation-building and forged a new Palestinian identity for those who lived through it. In the 1980s, for example, a number of agricultural and health relief committees were set up by urban-based, salaried Palestinians, which, often for the first time, brought them into contact with rural Palestinians and their villages. In the first two years of the intifada, well over a hundred health clinics were established.[143] This was meant to address noticeable declines in the availability of health care in the territories: hospital beds had gone down from 2.2 per 1,000 in 1974 to 1.6 per 1,000 in 1985.[144]

On the other hand, through the intifada and because of it, Palestinian society experienced deepening Islamization. This Islamization arose out of a confluence of several developments. These included the larger regional context, which, following the Iranian revolution, witnessed a general rise in the potency and popularity of political Islam across the Middle East; a noticeable growth in the number of mosques in Gaza and the West Bank; and Israel's initial assumption that Hamas provided a welcome challenge to the authority and popularity of the PLO. Interestingly, Israel did not ban Hamas until 1989. The Palestinian intelligentsia also underwent what Glenn Robinson calls a "partial Islamization," as represented in their activities in Palestinian universities.[145] The same phenomenon that resulted in the fracturing of the support base of the Fatah in the 1980s, namely the rise of a counter-elite, also led to the emergence of Hamas as an Islamist organization tied to the Muslim Brotherhood.

Before long, a local leadership—the Unified Leadership of the Uprising, the UNLU—had developed and was beginning to direct the course of the intifada. Initially only loosely affiliated with the PLO, one of the UNLU's primary objectives was to increase the cost of the occupation for Israel. The PLO continued to retain a genuine measure of popularity throughout the Occupied Territories, despite the fact that by the early 1980s "PLO nationalism" was beginning to wane among most Palestinians.[146] However, as a sign of its growing distance from the rhythm of life in the territories, it took the PLO some time to figure out what the intifada really meant.[147] Arafat and the rest of the Fatah leadership, ensconced in Tunis after their forcible ejection from Beirut by Israel, had begun to lose touch with their constituents back in what remained of Palestine. Palestinian streets were now scenes of cat-and-mouse and spontaneous attacks directed by a counter-elite who had little in common with the PLO and its leadership of middle-aged, exiled men. Tellingly, a few months after the intifada started, Hamas announced its formation.

During the uprising, the Israeli military administration dropped its pretense of "benign occupation" and set out to humiliate and

disconnect between the outcome of Oslo and the history and reality of Palestine.[156] A severe identity crisis of sorts soon emerged within the Palestinian body politic. The new PNA regime did not trust its own society and tried to undermine the new elite through co-option, coercion, and marginalization.[157] A chasm soon began to form between the new arrivees, the so-called Outsiders, and the local activists and community leaders, the Insiders, who had cut their teeth in the intifada. The PNA soon established some eleven different security services, collectively known as the Palestinian Security Services. The "Tunisians," who exclusively formed Yasser Arafat's inner circle, had no experience with or concept of democracy, freedom, or civil society, knowing only autocracy, paternalism, nepotism, and absolutism.[158] Steadily but methodically, the counter-elite of the 1980s was cast aside, and the elite of the 1970s reasserted itself, for the most part successfully, as the claimants of the Palestinian mantle once again. Hamas held out, its rupture with Fatah culminating into civil war in 2006.

Before long, the Oslo Accords fell victim to "the tyranny of security."[159] Prime Minister Rabin's assassination by an Israeli extremist in November 1995 revealed the depth of schism in Israel over even paltry concessions to the Palestinians. His eventual successor, Benjamin Netanyahu and many of his like-minded peers in Likud, rejected the very logic of the Oslo Accords and opposed giving the Palestinians even highly constrained autonomy and truncated territories in which they could exercise a limited form of governance. Netanyahu, after all, has a "vision of the Jew as perennial target who can never entrust his security to anyone, who must surround himself with what Jabotinsky called a 'steel wall,'" and believes that making peace with Arabs is like "keeping fish in a glass bowl until they learn not to bump against the wall."[160]

It did not take long for Palestinian frustrations with the outcomes of the Oslo Accords to result in yet another uprising, a second intifada, this one far bloodier and more violent than the first. The Al-Aqsa Intifada, which erupted in 2000 and lasted until late 2004, was caused by a combination of the fundamentally flawed nature of the peace process, Israeli policies on the ground, and the Palestinian leadership's failure to meet the needs of the Palestinians.[161] In the period since the first uprising, literally all aspects of the lives of Palestinians in the Occupied Territories, save for a handful of PNA-affiliated wealthy investors, had deteriorated. Israeli checkpoints had begun appearing across Areas B and C, increasingly replaced by more-permanent structures, and significantly restricted the movement of Palestinians within the West Bank and between the West Bank and Gaza. Palestinians found themselves having less rather than more freedom and autonomy, and their lands continued being confiscated for Israeli settlement purposes with unabated vigor. The PNA was seen not just as helpless in the face of Israeli encroachments but in fact culpable in it. The freezing of PLO institutions, meanwhile, left many Palestinians outside the territories with a sense of abandonment.[162]

The outbreak of the Al-Aqsa Intifada was the last gasp of the Palestinian counter-elite. It represented their lashing out against the Israeli occupation, on the one hand, and the occupier's local conspirators, on the other. Arafat and the Fatah-dominated PNA were utterly helpless in stopping it. And yet the uprising's intense violence—with more than 140 bombings between 2000 and 2005 and more than 500 casualties—represented the desperation and anguish of the once-hopeful Palestinians. As Palestinian-Israeli violence reached levels unprecedented since 1982, a new cultural symbol of resistance emerged. The *shahid* (martyr), the suicide bomber, became the latest symbol of the culture of resistance.[163] Not surprisingly, it was at this time that Hamas's popularity reached its height, helped by a combination of the organization's ability to capture the popular

imagination through the launching of spectacular "resistance tactics," including suicide bombings, at the same time as the increasing
irrelevance and helplessness of the Fatah and the PNA. Also helping
Hamas's popularity was Israel's assassination of the organization's
wheelchair-bound founder and leader, Sheikh Ahmad Yassin.[164]

The Al-Aqsa Intifada also represented the latent collective anguish of realizing that Palestine as a viable country was no longer
realistically attainable. Israel's "last, best offer," presented to Arafat by
Prime Minister Ehud Barak on a take-it-or-leave-it basis in 2000–
2001, fell so far short of Palestinian aspirations that even Arafat—
who had earlier accepted the Oslo Accords in order to save himself
and the PLO from slipping into irrelevance—could not accept.[165]

Any doubts about the continued relevance of the Oslo Accords
were put to rest in March 2002, when Israel launched Operation Defensive Shield after twenty-nine Israeli civilians died in yet another
Palestinian suicide bombing. The largest Israeli military operation in
the West Bank since 1967, the campaign resulted in Israel reoccupying
every village, town, and city in the West Bank. During the invasion,
Israeli forces set out to methodically destroy all Palestinian institutions and infrastructures, especially during a month-long period from
March 29 to April 28, and also destroyed all administrative data and
information that the various organs of the Palestinian Authority had
collected about the population. Among the buildings that were destroyed and leveled were the Ministries of Education, Health, and
Culture, the Palestine International Bank, the Khalil Sakakini Cultural Center, and the newly built forensics laboratory in Ramallah.[166]
During the leveling of the Ministry of Education, Israeli soldiers
threw all the computers on the street and had them run over by tanks.
According to the Israeli rights organization B'Tselem, "The entire
population of the West Bank suffered as a result of the operation.

Dozens of Palestinians were killed, hundreds wounded, thousands detained, and hundreds of thousands imprisoned in their homes without food and water. Many were hurt in actions that had nothing to do with 'striking at the terrorist infrastructure.' "[167]

Under the pretext of safeguarding its citizens from the spate of suicide bombings that had marked the second intifada, in 2002 the Israeli government announced the construction of what was initially billed as a "security fence" but quickly turned out to be a massive separation barrier between Israel and the West Bank. "The Wall" is 709 kilometers long for a border that is 315 kilometers, less than half its length. Snaking through West Bank hills and towns, it is constructed so as to include into Israel proper some 10 percent of the West Bank territory.

The ultimate goal of the Oslo Accords was *separation,* with Palestinians having a number of densely populated self-rule enclaves surrounded militarily by Israel. The Wall, whose construction started in 2002 during the premiership of Ariel Sharon and which was meant to ensure the geographic separation of Palestinians and Israelis, merely gave physical and actual meaning to a process of "apartness" that had started as early as 1993 with the beginning of the Oslo peace process. Khalil Nakhleh, a Palestinian social scientist, maintains that the Likud leadership had long sought to bring about a "clean break" from the Palestinians.[168] But Likud leaders were not alone in seeking such a clean break. Rabin's ideal, enunciated as early as 1995, was separation without sovereignty. This was later accomplished in Gaza with the erection of a formidable electronic fence all around the Strip. Since a fence would be impractical in the West Bank, in 2002 Israel opted for the construction of a barrier wall.

Another major step toward separating Israel from Palestinians occurred in 2005, when Israel withdrew its forces from the Gaza Strip and dismantled its settlements there. Over the course of the previous several years, especially after the collapse of negotiations in 1999–2000, the Israeli body politic had moved steadily toward unilateralism. An absence of any viable "negotiating partner" meant Israel needed to do unilaterally what it saw fit, and "disengagement" from Gaza was sold to the public as serving the state's interests in the long term. In publicly announcing his plans in December 2003, Prime Minister Ariel Sharon assured Israelis that withdrawal from Gaza would consolidate Israel's control "over those same areas of the land of Israel [the West Bank] that will constitute an inseparable part of the State of Israel in any future agreement."[169] In other words, giving up direct control over Gaza meant ensuring further separation from Palestinians while freeing Israel from pressure, especially from the United States, to move the "peace process" forward insofar as the West Bank was concerned. As Sharon's advisor Dov Weisglas stated in an interview, "The disengagement plan is . . . the bottle of formaldehyde necessary so that there will not be a political process with the Palestinians. . . . The American term is to park conveniently. The . . . plan . . . distances us as far as possible from political pressure . . . [and] legitimizes our contention that there is no negotiating with the Palestinians. . . . We received a no-one-to-talk-to certificate . . . [whereby] the geographic status quo remains intact [and] the certificate will be revoked only when this-and-that happens—when Palestine becomes Finland."[170] Withdrawal from Gaza in 2005, meanwhile, didn't entail the Strip's freedom but its conversion into what Avi Shlaim and others have called "an open air prison."[171] It also meant a deepening and strengthening of Israel's hold on the West Bank.

The idea of separation—crucially, separation without Palestinian sovereignty—was similarly advanced by successive Israeli prime ministers. Ehud Barak, who assumed office in May 1999, advocated the construction of security zones, protected by barbed wire and fences, that would separate Palestinians from Israelis, and also the legalization of one hundred thousand undocumented workers from East Asia and central Europe to replace Palestinian workers in Israel.[172] Similarly, Netanyahu's vision of a Palestinian state is one that has no territorial contiguity, no viability, and no sovereignty.[173] As a paramount political figure in Israeli politics throughout the 2000s, and as a largely popular and powerful prime minister from 1996 to 1999 and again from 2009 on, Netanyahu has been able to give shape to his vision of Palestine, with tremendous popular approval in Israel. Today, what remains of Palestine has indeed become little more than small, noncontiguous areas that are isolated from one another and, even if combined, do not add up to a viable state. Israel assumes that all visible areas within the West Bank and Gaza can be further divided and that "this divisibility forms one of the keys to peace."[174]

Gaza and the West Bank, meanwhile, were slipping culturally and politically further away from each other. By the mid-2000s, the political manifestations of these differences had put the Islamist and secularist spectrums of the Palestinian polity on a collision course, the former based mostly in Gaza, and the latter having a foothold in the West Bank. The diminishing legitimacy of Fatah and the increasing slide toward authoritarianism and irrelevance by the Ramallah-based PNA resulted in Hamas's victory in the January 2006 elections for the Palestine Legislative Council. Arafat, long the father and face of Palestinian liberation, died besieged by Israel and under mysterious circumstances in November 2004. The following January's presidential elections resulted in the overwhelming election of longtime negotiator and Fatah insider Mahmoud Abbas. Hamas won the 2006 election by securing only 44 percent of the votes cast, but, thanks to the peculiarities of the Palestinian electoral system, was able to win a majority of seats in the Palestine Legislative Council. Pressured by Israel and the United States and soon by the European Union, Fatah and Hamas and by default the two remaining chunks of Palestine were set on a collision course. The clash came in June, leaving some two hundred Palestinians dead.

The clashes represented more than a spat between two parties fighting for relevance and over legislative seats. They signified the coming to fore of deep fissures within the Palestinian polity, discussed in chapters 4 and 5. For a time Fatah and Hamas tried cohabitation in the form of a coalition PNA government. But the punishing sanctions, which left some 140,000 people on the PNA payroll unpaid, seriously undermined all efforts at mediation, undertaken in earnest by Saudi Arabia. Amid rumors of a U.S.-backed and funded Fatah effort to attack Hamas positions from the Sinai and to oust it from Gaza, in June 2007 Hamas fighters attacked the remaining Fatah security forces in Gaza and took control of the Strip. The Gaza–West Bank rupture was now complete.

The intra-Palestinian conflict was made more acute by continuing hostilities between Israel and Hamas. In June 2006, rockets were fired into Israel from Gaza, causing minor damage. They were followed by massive Israeli retaliatory strikes on Gaza's civilian infrastructure. A tenuous truce ensued and held until late December 2008, when hostilities broke out again. In the mayhem that followed, some thirteen hundred Palestinian civilians died. Israeli casualties numbered thirteen, nine of whom were soldiers. Of Israel's nine troop casualties, four were from friendly fire.[175]

In investigating alleged human rights violations in what the IDF called Operation Cast Lead, a United Nations fact-finding mission made the following observations:

The Mission concludes that Israeli armed forces violated the customary international law requirement to take all feasible precautions in the choice of means and method of attack with a view to avoiding and in any event minimizing incidental loss of civilian life, injury to civilians and damage to civilian objects.

The Mission also finds that, on the same day, the Israeli forces directly and intentionally attacked the Al Quds Hospital in Gaza City and the adjacent ambulance depot with white phosphorous shells.

The report further found that Israeli "attacks constitute intentional attacks against the civilian population and civilian objects" and that "the conduct of the Israeli armed forces constitute grave breaches of the Fourth Geneva Convention in respect of wilful killings and wilfully [*sic*] causing great suffering to protected persons and as such give rise to individual criminal responsibility. It also finds that the direct targeting and arbitrary killing of Palestinian civilians is a violation of the right to life."[176]

Soon after Operation Cast Lead, Israel tightened its land, air, and sea blockade of Gaza, leaving illegal underground tunnels into Egypt as the Strip's only outlet. Earlier, in June 2007, Egypt had closed the Rafah Crossing, the Gaza Strip's only formal crossing into Egypt. Apart for a brief interim in 2011–2013, when the crossing was open to foot traffic, the Egyptian authorities have kept it closed. Avi Shlaim's description of Gaza as an "open air prison" is not an exaggeration by any means.

Cut off from the rest of the world except for a trickle of aid and trade deemed acceptable by Israel, Gaza's predicament has only gotten more dire since the late 2000s. From the beginning, as home to a large proportion of original refugees from 1948, Gaza's population had been more dispossessed and disoriented than that of the West Bank. Neither Egyptian authorities up until 1967 nor Israel from 1967 to 1993 sought in any meaningful ways to improve the lives of the people living in the overcrowded Strip. As far back as the early 1990s observers were warning about "increasing disablement and approaching breakdown of civil society in Gaza" prompted by a "combination of severe economic erosion, gross insecurity, rapidly deteriorating living conditions, and continued political inaction."[177]

Over the years, Gaza has experienced an even more active process of "de-development" as compared to the West Bank, brought on by land confiscations and severe water and electricity restrictions, externalization of employment opportunities and other forms of income generation, high levels of de-institutionalization, and extremely low levels of public investment in the local economy and infrastructure.[178] Despite international plans to use the infrastructure left behind by departing Israeli settlers for purposes of the Strip's development, in 2005, before leaving, the settlers adopted a scorched-earth policy of destroying the homes and agricultural greenhouses they left behind and rendering them inoperable.[179] Although after the withdrawal Israel disavowed any responsibility for Gaza, it has since only ensured that the territory does not cross the threshold of humanitarian disaster. In 2007, for example, after IDF lawyers advised against the legal ramifications of cutting off all electricity to the territory, Israeli authorities installed "current pacers" on the power grid supplying electricity to Gaza to deliberately reduce the electricity available there for consumption.[180] Similarly, while Israel has continually obstructed the work in Gaza of international relief agencies, such as the United Nations Relief and Works Agency (UNRWA), United States Agency for International Development (USAID), Oxfam, and the International

Red Cross, it has officially and practically committed to "preventing the Palestinians from crossing the threshold of malnutrition, but without moving them further away from it."[181]

As Gaza's wounds have continued to fester, the West Bank, comparatively better off, has been gripped with a political morass of its own. Following Arafat's death on November 11, 2004, new presidential elections were held in January 2005, in which Mahmoud Abbas, the incumbent prime minister and representing Fatah, won by securing 62 percent of the votes. Hamas and the Islamic Jihad boycotted the elections, resulting in only half of eligible voters in Gaza taking part in the poll. Soon thereafter Hamas's relations with Fatah deteriorated to the point of civil war, followed by an almost complete breakdown of relations between the West Bank and Gaza. Israel, of course, made certain that in addition to their political rupture, the two Occupied Territories were cut off from each other geographically and economically as well. As of 2015, the chasm between the two only keeps getting wider, driven by internal dynamics within each, on the one hand, and the larger environment, on the other, not the least of which are the occupation and Israeli policies. The two remaining parts of Palestinian territory have never been farther apart from each other than they are today, and their political, economic, and cultural distance only gets wider.

Elected for four years, Abbas's electoral mandate ran out with the formal end of his term in 2009. He has continued to remain in office ever since because of the practical impossibility of holding new elections. The Legislative Council has not done any better. The PLC, in fact, last met in 2007, leaving Abbas to govern in Area A of the West Bank, which amounts to 3 percent of the territory. President Abbas is, in effect, the mayor of Ramallah and not much more. The presidency and the whole PNA apparatus have since lingered on ineffectually and largely inconsequentially as the Palestinian-Israeli status quo continues to be perpetuated.

The status quo, of course, is far from static. Israel's hold over the West Bank becomes deeper and more strengthened, and Palestine's dismemberment continues apace. The "peace process" lingers on, with Palestinian and Israeli negotiators talking, sometimes more amicably than at other times, as the number of settlements keeps growing and Israeli presence in all corners of the West Bank deepens. Whether it is, as *Haaretz* newspaper called it, "the 'Arabs Out' government" of Netanyahu[182] or some other administration in west Jerusalem, the Palestinians of the West Bank and Gaza, PNA or Hamas, are on the receiving end of Israeli policies and agendas. They may protest and object, and Hamas or breakaways from it may even fire a small rocket or two into Israel. But they are otherwise powerless to do anything else. This has been the status quo since the mid-1990s. And it is likely to continue well into the foreseeable future.

Palestine, as we have conceived of it for so long, is no longer feasible.

Conclusion

The story of Palestine is one of conquest and dismemberment, dispersion and exile, and, for the past two decades, of efforts at reconstitution and reconstruction. In reconstitution and reconstruction, there has been little success. The conquest of Palestine started in earnest in the late nineteenth century and reached its peak in the 1930s and the 1940s. By the time the establishment of the State of Israel was formally declared in 1948, the collapse and fragmentation of Palestinian society was well underway, its physical and territorial space forever changed.[183] Palestinians were broadly divided into four general groups: those in Israel proper, carrying Israeli passports; those living in the West Bank; those living in Gaza; and those living elsewhere in the diaspora. Within each group, there are the natural diversities and contradictions of varied social groupings, further fragmenting Palestinian society. This has only made more complicated the task of rebuilding and reconstituting a nation that for decades has had to contend with the burdens of occupation, dispossession, exile, false promises, and fallen heroes.

Israel, meanwhile, has used the threat of Palestinians and their international supporters as a source of material and human-resource mobilization, engaging in what the Israeli sociologist Kimmerling called "human engineering" to forge a homogenized settler elite with a newly invented identity.[184] In the process, Israel has effectively employed a simplified and varnished version of its past, and especially its nation-building process, for purposes of solidifying internal unity and securing international legitimacy and support.[185] From Israel's perspective, the Israeli-Palestinian conflict began in 1967 and not in 1948, and therefore any agreement would necessarily have to revolve around only the West Bank and Gaza and nothing else. Nothing that occurred before 1967—especially the ethnic cleansing that accompanied the state's establishment—is open to negotiations. For the Israelis, growth in the number of Palestinians, whether a result of a return of refugees or through natural growth, is seen as a security matter and a threat.[186] Not surprisingly, therefore, Israel has done what it can to block and undermine the reconstitution of Palestinian society, especially among those Palestinians within its physical and territorial reach.

Avi Shlaim, one of the most astute observers of Israel and Palestine, maintains that the Israeli occupation of the West Bank and previously of Gaza can only be explained by the imperative of territorial expansion.[187] Territorial expansion is, of course, one of the most powerful driving forces in explaining Israeli behavior in relation to Palestinian territories. But equally important is ensuring that conditions for the reconstitution of a cohesive Palestinian national identity do not emerge. These conditions are both territorial—in terms of the physical geography in which Palestinians find themselves and articulate a collective sense of national identity—as well as cultural and symbolic. National identities are difficult to destroy. They persevere and linger even under the most adverse of circumstances. But they do change, often from within, due largely to the circumstances within which people find themselves, or because of changes in the people who claim the mantle of articulating them. Israel's efforts at blocking the emergence of conditions conducive to a resurgent Palestinian national identity have been multipronged, ranging from symbolic and cultural to political and physical. Subsequent chapters examine the compounding effects of cultural divisions and institutional and state-building failures. But the starting point, and by far the most consequential, has been Palestine's territorial dismemberment. It is to this topic that the next chapter turns.

3

The Lay of the Land

One of the key reasons for the unattainability of a Palestinian state is its physical and territorial dismemberment. While territorial noncontiguity may undermine social cohesion, it is not by itself a sufficient impediment to statehood. Many countries in the South Pacific, for example, are made up of archipelagoes that are separated by miles of ocean.[1] But in the Palestinian case what has rendered a viable state improbable is the manner in which its internal separations have come about and the consequences these separations have had. Unlike islands and archipelagoes that are commercially connected and are linked through open sea-lanes, Palestinian territories are separated from one another by a powerful military foe that over time has actively sought to restrict commercial and political ties and the transit between them. The nature and intensity of Israel's hold on the Palestinian territories has varied over the years, evidence of a lack of a coherent strategy over precisely how to handle what for Israeli leaders has become a "Palestinian problem." But the trend over the past several decades, particularly since the signing of the Oslo Accords, has been unmistakably toward one of separation and disengagement from Palestinian affairs, on the one hand, while ensuring the nonviability of a Palestinian state, on the other.

This chapter chronicles the processes and consequences of Palestine's territorial dismemberment and its subjugation by Israel.

It begins with a discussion of the means and methods by which the Israeli state has confiscated or otherwise divided Palestinian territories. Israel's occupation has been multipronged and multifaceted, involving not just military, economic, political, and administrative means but, most potently, hundreds of thousands of settlers motivated by religious and ideological or economic reasons. The chapter then moves to a discussion of the settler phenomenon, highlighting the encirclement of Palestinian population areas and their isolation from one another. It concludes with a snapshot examination of living conditions in Gaza and the West Bank.

Since its capture of the West Bank and Gaza in 1967, Israel has set into motion three parallel, reinforcing dynamics. First, it has set out to systematically dismember and erase geographic Palestine and to replace it with new realities on the ground that support its biblically inspired historical narrative. The primary objective has been reshaping geography as part of Israel's own ongoing process of nation-building.

Second, for what remains of Palestine, Israel has devised various means of control, both military and otherwise, for effecting the occupation and controlling the millions of Palestinians it suddenly found itself ruling over. In addition to massive and steady territorial expansion through the twin mechanisms of brute military force and the settlement enterprise, this also included the development of an intricate permit system and the conditioning of behavior appropriate for a conquered and defeated nation. In the process, in addition to land, Israel ensured its control over another precious commodity, namely water, and saw to it that whatever developed of a Palestinian economy only did so with heavy dependence on the Israeli economy.

Third, as a corollary to the dismemberment and control of Palestine, Israeli leaders have hived off and segregated Palestinian territories not only from Israel, but, more consequentially, from each other. After 1967, Israel gave a few rights to the Palestinians in the Occupied Territories that they had not had before, but also made sure that they were "naturalized" as *non*citizens. This was part of a larger process of "externalization" of the Occupied Territories and those residing in them.[2] Not only is the West Bank separated from Israel through an actual Separation Barrier, but it is internally divided and separated from within thanks to an intricate and deliberately positioned network of settlements, bypass roads, checkpoints, and other similar obstacles. As early as the mid-1970s, the placement of Israeli settlements in the West Bank was deliberately chosen to separate Palestinian-populated areas from one another.[3] But for Israel absolute separation from Palestinians is "a never-ending project." This preoccupation with separation both from and within the Occupied Territories has turned Palestinian territories into a "mosaic of semi-isolated spaces."[4]

Israeli leaders initially had considerable doubts about Israel's ability to hold on to the Occupied Territories and seriously entertained thoughts of not retaining them. From the beginning, the question of what to do with the territories troubled Israeli leaders, as annexing Gaza and the West Bank meant integrating Palestinians into the Israeli polity and generating a new political reality. Instead of deciding what to do, they decided on what *not* to do: neither annexation, which meant integration and the effective creation of one state, nor allowing the territories to develop their own economic and political infrastructures, which could serve as the basis of a new, second state.[5] Ever since, Israeli policies have been aimed at negating both the "two" and the "one," namely two states and two economies, and, alternatively, one political entity and one economy.[6] Not surprisingly, Israel has undertaken contradictory policies in the Occupied Palestinian

Territories at different times and has failed to devise a coherent and long-term strategy in dealing with the Palestinians.[7] The consequence of not deciding was the emergence of a dynamic and fluid status quo in which "the occupation" came to mean the steady deepening of control and penetration into Palestinian society, and, in the process, its deliberate and progressive weakening and fragmentation. Under the auspices of Israeli rule, Palestinian society was prevented from achieving even minimal levels of development or, for that matter, a viable and functioning economy. Its resources were either taken over altogether or made extremely difficult to access and develop. Gaza was taken to the verge of catastrophe and was kept there in a holding pattern, where it still remains today. The West Bank has fared only slightly better, its Palestinian areas having been effectively reduced to a fraction of what they were back in 1967 or even 1994, before the Oslo Accords formally divided it into areas of varying Israeli power and control. Today, the Occupied Territories are seen as an integral part of the Israeli regime, and control over them remains as part of one integrated control system, a component of which is the Palestinian National Authority. This control system treats the three categories of people within its orbit quite differently, with Jews, regardless of whether or not they are formally citizens of the state, free to move about anywhere and subject to the least amount of state violence and coercion; followed by Palestinian citizens, against whom the authorities use force relatively more liberally; followed in turn by Palestinian noncitizens, who have few spatial freedoms and who are frequent recipients of state coercion and repression.[8]

As soon as the 1967 war ended, the occupation authorities carried out a series of campaigns to "cleanse" the West Bank and Gaza of "nests of Palestinian resistance."[9] Israel launched a new wave of ethnic cleansing in the first days of the occupation of east Jerusalem with various methods of depopulation, such as house demolitions and arrests of those suspected of collaborating with Jordanian forces, offering relocation grants, providing free transport to the Jordanian border, and, less benignly, closing several long-established Palestinian institutions.[10] Many of the Palestinians who survived the onslaught of ethnic cleansing and stayed behind had their land declared abandoned and therefore confiscated as state property. This accounted for an estimated 40 percent of Arab land that was confiscated.[11] From the very beginning, there was an attempt to draw Israel's borders in a way that would ensure maximum territory with minimum Palestinian population.[12] Often the government would simply issue expropriation orders to confiscate Palestinian lands, leaving the residents with no recourse, taking over private property for ostensibly public purposes.[13] Between 1979 and 2002, for example, Israel declared nine hundred thousand dunam (or ninety thousand hectares) of the West Bank as state land.[14] Today, Palestinian territory has been reduced to about 12 percent of historic Palestine.[15]

Confiscation and control over land is part of an occupation regime that is omnipresent and multifaceted. It manifests itself in a variety of ways, ranging from military operations and detentions to closures and denial of one of the countless permits needed to conduct mundane daily routines. Closure or "sealing off" turns the practice of isolation and separation into one of intervention, traffic control, and disruption of everyday life. The routine of Palestinian life can be disrupted at any given moment.[16] There are especially significant restrictions on the movements of Palestinians in eastern parts of the West Bank, in the Jordan Valley, which have been effectively annexed to Israel.[17] Confinement has become a constitutive element of Palestinian life for decades.[18] As for Gaza, even after Israeli forces withdrew from it in 2005, the enclave remains part of Israel's "economy of violence."[19]

The epicenter of the occupation and of the larger conflict, both symbolically and in reality, remains Jerusalem, and it is here where the grip of the occupying power is the tightest. From 1948 to 1967 the city remained divided into an eastern and a western half, demarcated by barbed wire and soldiers pointing guns at each other. Since 1967 the soldiers and the barbed wire are gone but the divide continues. Israel remains firmly in control of the holy city, and its leaders never miss an opportunity to remind the world that Jerusalem is Israel's "eternal, undivided capital." Be that as it may, Jerusalem is also home to an estimated four hundred thousand Palestinians.[20] Israel is doing what it can to make the Palestinians' lives as difficult as possible, to encourage them to leave, and to reduce their numbers as much as possible. Western Jerusalem, overwhelmingly Jewish, is today a modern, global city, architecturally, demographically, and culturally removed from even a hint of once having been Palestinian. Eastern Jerusalem, however, remains predominantly Palestinian, its architecture and infrastructure having been frozen in time in 1967, starved of development and most accouterments of modernity. For Israel Jerusalem may be undivided. But the city's divisions, in demography and cultural universes, remain real and entrenched. "In the struggle over Jerusalem," as one of its deputy mayors once said, "there are no victors and no vanquished."[21]

This chapter maintains that as a territorial entity Palestine no longer exists. It is simplistic and naive at best and misleading and capricious at worst to assume that as a geographic and territorial entity Palestine can once again be reconstituted. Historic Palestine has been divided, dismantled, and built over beyond recognition. For slightly more than two decades, from 1967 to 1993, it still made sense to speak of a "Palestine." It was an entity with two halves, one on the western bank of the Jordan River and another a tiny strip along the Egyptian border. Even then, the settlement enterprise had made Palestinian sovereignty over the West Bank problematic and subject to qualifications. The Oslo Accords made Palestinian sovereignty over the Occupied Territories all but impossible, carving up the West Bank and ceding control over much of it to Israel and having both the West Bank and Gaza fenced off from Israel and thus unable to function as viable economic or political entities.

For decades Palestine was a nation in search of a state. Today, the very viability of a Palestine is questionable. As an "imagined community" the Palestinian nation is not about to dissipate or disappear, and it has persevered so far under the most trying of circumstances. And its continued perseverance into the future is not questionable. But an imagined community does not a country make. A country needs at least three key ingredients, namely a state, a nation, and a piece of territory. Chapters 4 and 5, respectively, examine the currents undermining the nation-building project and obstacles to the formation of a meaningful Palestinian state. In the pages that follow, I demonstrate that what remains of Palestinian territory is nowhere nearly sufficient to constitute the territorial component of a country.

Maps Drawn, Redrawn

Historically, settler colonialism has been preoccupied with securitization in order to protect the "inside" from the "outside."[22] In the case of Israel, a series of paradoxical initiatives have been undertaken in order to delineate Israel from Palestinian communities while at the same time deepening Israel's penetration into and control over what remains of Palestine. Although the Oslo Accords formally delineated the borders of Gaza and the West Bank, Israel (and the United States) did not recognize the borders and continues to colonize and Judaize the West Bank. At the same time, the physical landscape of the West Bank and its environment have been greatly transformed because of checkpoints, settlements, bypass roads, and the segregation barrier. These physical and infrastructural means—along with roadblocks, observation towers, earth mounds, trenches, and agricultural gates— are meant to ensure the fragmentation and control of Palestinian areas.[23] In a conflict where military might keeps changing the physical landscape, cartography has become a most malleable science.

One of the most common ways of asserting ownership is the naming of places. Naming, or, as the case may be, renaming, is often one of the first acts in the process of claiming. David Day talks of "naming as claiming."[24] In fact, (re)naming implies that the land was previously empty. In addition to explicit assertion of ownership, names ward off potential rivals and provide nostalgic reminders of places long since left behind or memorialized in communal lore and myth and legend. In Israel, shortly after independence, a Committee for the Designation of Place-Names in the Negev was set up whose task was "to assign Hebrew names to all the places—mountains, valleys, springs, roads, and so on—in the Negev region." In his instructions to the committee, Ben-Gurion wrote: "We are obliged to remove the Arabic names for reasons of the state. Just as we do not recognize the Arabs' proprietorship of the land, so also we do not recognize their spiritual proprietorship and their names."[25] The clandestine creation of "Hebrew maps" became a central preoccupation of Zionist operatives working with the British Mandatory authorities as early as the 1920s. From the beginning, these maps were meant to establish "facts on the ground" and to legitimize the conquest of new territories.

The whole naming exercise assumed a life of its own. Despite political pressure on its members to eradicate all Arabic names, of the 533 new names that the committee came up with, no less than 333 were either Hebrew translations of the Arabic names or Hebrew names that sounded like the Arabic original. Another 20 percent of the names came from the founders of Zion, contemporary public figures, Israeli leaders, and individuals of significance to Israel.[26] The result was often far from optimal. Many places were randomly assigned biblical-sounding names that were often inaccurate. According to one committee member: "the names that we found not only sounded strange to our ears, they are themselves inaccurate. Their meanings are unclear and many of them are nothing but random names of individuals or epithets of a derogatory or insulting nature. Many of the names are offensive in their gloomy and morose meanings, which reflect the powerlessness of the nomads and their self-denigration in the face of the harshness of nature."[27] But the names stuck, became permanent, and were steadily reinforced by new realities.

The Palestinians, meanwhile, have sought to create their own "sacred geography," but only halfheartedly and with little success. Their interests were primarily in the creation of "historical" maps, rather than contemporary ones, emphasizing loss and dispossession, fabrications and theft, rather than detailed contemporary realities. These maps were sparsely detailed, were often small in scale, and were nowhere nearly as successful as the Hebrew maps.[28] This comparatively lackluster knowledge of the land, especially when compared with the Israelis, was reflected widely in the central hallmarks of the Palestinian narrative, whose primary themes revolved around dispossession and displacement, injustice and exile, heroic struggle and return. Conspicuously lacking were themes related to the land, the landscape, and national redemption rooted in territorial (re) acquisition.[29] Although Palestinians upheld the fellahin as symbols of Palestinian nationalism—idealizing their tenacious holding on to the land, their dress, folklore, and way of living—they never quite did develop the Zionists' intimate knowledge of the land, rural landscape, or even its history.[30]

Israel, of course, has done what it can to debunk and deflate the Palestinian historical narrative and to delegitimize Palestinian symbols of national and cultural identity. There are courses in some Israeli universities today that describe and teach about "human groups" and "territorial units" before the Zionist endeavor in Palestine, as if the Arab inhabitants of the land never even existed.[31] For a time, Israel even forbade the gathering of wild thyme in the West Bank, a traditional ingredient in Palestinian cuisine, lest doing so would encourage the spread of Palestinian culture and identity.[32] Such attempts at cultural erasure have at times taken on comical dimensions. In 1994, for example, as one of its first acts, the PNA placed stickers with its emblem, an eagle, on top of Jordanian schoolbooks, whose covers featured the emblem of the Hashemite Kingdom, also an eagle, but whose head faced the opposite direction compared to the eagle on the Palestinian emblem. The books were exactly the same as before, except that their covers had a new sticker. They were distributed to both public and private Palestinian schools across the West Bank and east Jerusalem. Discovered by the Jerusalem municipality a few days before the start of the academic year, the new mayor, Ehud Barak, later prime minister, ordered all books distributed to public schools collected so that the new PNA sticker could be covered by yet another sticker, this time that of the Jerusalem municipality, which included both Hebrew and Arabic writing.[33]

More serious and consequential have been attempts at disrupting Palestinian agriculture both in an around the "seam zone" and elsewhere in the West Bank and Gaza. This has been part of a broader pattern of ensuring that a robust Palestinian economy does not get off the ground. I shall have more to say on this later in the chapter, but I do want to mention here the consequences of Israel's efforts at undermining Palestinian agriculture. In both the West Bank and Gaza, demolitions often deliberately target agricultural land, uprooting trees, bulldozing crops, and destroying greenhouses.[34] With the added restrictions on water and electricity usage, since the 1980s many Palestinians have abandoned farming, and Palestinian society has undergone a process of "depeasantification."[35] According to one World Bank survey, in fact, 68 percent of communities across the West Bank have agricultural plots that remain unused because of a lack of water, electricity, and workers, or due to land confiscations by Israel or to the general economic situation.[36] This contributed to the emergence of the counter-elite generation of the 1980s that led the intifada but was then pushed aside by the incoming Fatah elite of the PNA. Many found positions in the burgeoning PNA bureaucracy.[37] But for most others there were few employment opportunities, even if they acquired higher skills and earned university degrees. Unemployment has soared both in the West Bank and in Gaza.

Reinforcing and more prevalent than attempts at cultural erasure and economic undermining are Israeli efforts at "spatial apartheid and exclusionary zoning" of Palestinian communities.[38] This is done particularly through the construction of the Separation Barrier around the West Bank and an electric fence that envelops the Gaza Strip. The West Bank's Separation Barrier—or the Wall—is comprised of either a combination of an electric fence and other barbed-wire fences and trenches, or a concrete wall that is six to eight meters high. When completed, the Separation Barrier, which averages 60 meters in width, will be 709 kilometers long, twice as long as the 1949 armistice line commonly known as the Green Line. All land within 100 meters of the Separation Barrier are off limits to Palestinians.

The Wall is "a sophisticated geostrategic architectural machine" whose purpose is to at once ensure Israeli penetration into the West Bank and Palestinian separation from Israel.[39] In addition to creating physical separation from and within Palestinians, the Wall serves two important strategic objectives for Israel. It enables Israel to discard those areas it considers to have little or no strategic value or the ones that are densely populated with Palestinians. At the same time, it unilaterally annexes those areas viewed as strategically significant, notably the Gush Etzion and Ariel settlement blocs in northern and southern West Bank and settlement blocs and their satellites defining Israeli Greater Jerusalem.[40]

The Separation Barrier passes through some of the richest agricultural land and best underground water resources in all of the West Bank. It also cuts off east Jerusalem from the rest of the West Bank and from the cities of Ramallah and Bethlehem.[41] By one estimate it also cuts off a quarter of Jerusalem's Palestinian population from the rest of the city.[42] Its precise location was negotiated between Israeli military authorities, the settlers, and the settlement builders.[43] The party pointedly excluded from the negotiations, or any considerations of their interests for that matter, was the Palestinians, for whom the Wall has meant higher unemployment, frequent closures, and multiple restrictions.

Israel refers to the gap between the 1967 border and the actual path of the Wall as the "seam zone." The seam zone, declared a closed military area by the IDF, includes 10 percent of the West Bank's most arable land and some forty-two Palestinian towns and villages in which an estimated 60,000 people live. These individuals are often referred to as "Internally Stuck Persons." Most of the land inside the seam zone has been confiscated by the Israeli Civil Administration.[44] The remaining land suffers from insufficient water supply, and Israeli authorities prohibit the building of water cisterns. In northern West Bank, some 82 percent of Palestinian families are not permitted to access their land because it falls within the seam zone.[45] Altogether, an estimated 170,000 West Bankers are directly or indirectly affected by the seam zone, and many Palestinians living within the seam zone have been forced to relocate to elsewhere in the West Bank.[46] Only first-degree relatives can visit those living in the seam zone, but they cannot stay overnight. Most Palestinians who have farms inside the seam zone are forbidden by Israeli authorities from taking their vehicles to the farm to load their products.[47]

The very creation of the seam zone and the Separation Barrier that gave rise to it, the drawing and redrawing of maps across Israel and Palestine proper and especially in the West Bank, the placing of settlements and the bypass roads that connect them and limit the expansion of Palestinian towns and cities,[48] and the destruction and undermining of agricultural and other economic activities among Palestinians all are part of the larger phenomenon of occupation. This is an occupation that is at once as static and immovable as it is dynamic and expansive. It is multifaceted and includes multiple means of conquest and control, domination and subjugation, expansion and penetration. It is to these aspects of the occupation that the chapter next turns.

The Occupation

Insofar as preponderant methods of control are concerned, Israel's occupation of the Occupied Palestinian Territories can be divided into three broad, overlapping periods. The early occupation, from 1967 to the late 1980s and early 1990s, featured the steady intrusion of settlements into the West Bank and Gaza, backed primarily by military force and security operations. This use of force was complemented in a second period by a complex and expansive permit system after the signing of the Oslo Accords, when the construction of settlements and the confiscation of Palestinian lands intensified. This second phase continues until today. A third phase began around 2002, soon after the start of the Al-Aqsa Intifada, when in addition to the army and the settlers the colonial enterprise was reinforced by yet another component, namely private firms and subcontractors. The Israeli economist Shir Hever has labeled this current phase as one of "privatized" occupation.[49] The privatized phase of the occupation began when Israel, following the lead of the United States, subcontracted to private firms many functions ordinarily carried out by public entities, such as the security of settlements, manning checkpoints, and managing prisons. This privatization of the occupation proved most lucrative for many Israeli companies and multinational corporations.[50] The Israeli prison system, for example, is run largely by the private firm Group Four Security Solutions, and the IDF often works closely with private subcontractors providing security and other services to settlements in the West Bank.[51]

One of the most consistent features of all phases of the occupation has been the takeover of Palestinian land by the Israeli state or private individuals. Steadily, beginning in 1968 and continuing until today, Israel has continued to build eastward, first by colonizing Arab areas around Jerusalem—such as Ramot Eshkol and Ma'a lot Dafna—and then East Talpiot. In some cases Israel has built entire towns and cities from scratch. In some other cases it has taken over existing Arab cities. And in still other cases it has sought to change the demographic balance by encouraging or compelling Arabs to leave to make room for Jews.[52] At times the takeover has unfolded in a methodical, phased manner. Over the last several years, for example, the Israeli state has taken over many hillsides and swaths of land in east Jerusalem and in other Palestinian areas by declaring them as state parks and therefore state property. Then, after a few years, the state parks have been privatized and made available for public auction, but only to Israeli citizens. This way, whereas in future negotiations the state may be forced to give back state property, it cannot be forced to confiscate Israeli private property to give back to a future Palestinian state. Another example of takeover involves the Mount of Olives cemetery, for which in 1948 Israeli authorities signed a ninety-nine-year lease with the property's owner, the Muslim Waqf. In 2012, Israeli authorities simply stopped paying for the lease, and the Muslim Waqf is unable to do anything about it.

One of the more-controversial means employed by Israeli authorities to depopulate Palestinian areas is through house demolitions. These demolitions are often justified on grounds of improper construction permits or for military purposes. According to the Israeli human rights organization B'Tselem, from 2006 through November 2013, Israel demolished at least 644 Palestinian residential units in the West Bank (not including east Jerusalem), causing an estimated 3,108 people to lose their homes. Another 492 houses were destroyed in east Jerusalem in the same period on grounds of having been built without the proper permits, leaving more than 1,900 Palestinians homeless. From 2004 to 2011, some 1,754 houses were demolished in both Gaza and the West Bank for military purposes. Between 2001 and 2004, an additional 664 houses of Palestinians suspected of violence against Israelis were destroyed as punishment, a practice Israel halted in 2005.[53] These statistics present only a snapshot of a larger, ongoing process of depopulating Palestinian areas and making life difficult for Palestinians as much as possible.

Much of this depopulation has been aimed at making room for Israeli settlements. The settlement enterprise began in earnest in 1968, a year after the capture of the Occupied Territories, and it has exponentially expanded ever since. The settlement movement has gone through several phases. The first settlements, based on the Allon Plan and located in east Jerusalem and the West Bank, were meant to achieve maximum territorial gains for Israel while including a minimal number of Palestinians. From their start in 1967 up until 1977, these settlements numbered about 5,000. In the late 1970s, the settlements were seen as a means for Israel to deal with the mounting costs of social services and as a way to offer affordable housing to poorer Sephardic Jews. After 1977, when the Likud came to power, the settlement movement was given a further, ideological impetus, with the supporters of the extremist settler movement Gush Emunim seeking to populate the entire land of "Judea and Samaria." To these were added younger Israeli couples in search of affordable housing and subsidized services, significantly increasing the number of settlements in the 1980s and the 1990s. In the early 1990s, the Israeli government enlarged many of the existing settlements and established a number of new ones, under the auspices of Housing Minister Ariel Sharon's "Seven Stars Program," which was designed to connect Israeli cities and towns to settlements in the West Bank. At the beginning of 1992, just before the Oslo Accords were signed, there were approximately 247,500 settlers living in 128 settlements in the West Bank and another 3,500 settlers in 16 settlements in the Gaza.[54]

Without the Israeli state's tacit acceptance, as well as its heavy subsidization, provision of services, and extensive military protection, the settlements could not and would not exist.[55] In 2015, Hebron, for example, had a population of approximately 209,000 Palestinians, between 500 and 800 Israeli settlers, and about 2,000

IDF soldiers sent to protect them.[56] The presence of this small, die-hard settler contingent would not have been made possible without the unqualified and massive support of the Israeli Defense Forces.

The settlements, which usually grow outward and toward each other, are often deliberately placed so as to surround and separate Palestinian areas from one another, turning them into isolated enclaves.[57] As one observer has commented, "for Jewish settlers, roads *connect;* for Palestinians, they *separate.*"[58] The roads that connect settlements to each other and to Jerusalem often snake around and cut off Palestinian towns and villages from one anther. These roads are meant to be kept "sterile" and "uncontaminated" by Palestinian traffic and are protected by two-hundred-meter "sanitary margins" on either side.[59] Not surprisingly, although the settlement structures themselves account for no more than approximately 2 percent of the West Bank, their related infrastructures and roads exact control over some 42 percent of the West Bank.[60]

The settlements are an integral part of a plan to incorporate as much of the West Bank into Israel as possible while cutting off easy contact among the Palestinians and between Palestinians and other Arabs.[61] Through careful planning, Israel has connected far-flung West Bank settlements to Jerusalem through an intricate network of new settlements, expansion of existing ones, bypass roads, and other infrastructures. This has given Israel contiguous, sovereign presence throughout the West Bank and has severed and isolated Palestinian areas from one another, turning them into "small, disarticulated enclaves incapable of functioning as a viable political or economic entity."[62]

Settlements are typically built on hilltops in the West Bank and tend to be surrounded by fertile agricultural land. They often comprise modern, spacious villas with the latest amenities and include schools, recreational facilities, swimming pools, and even industrial parks. They are invariably surrounded by a variety of security-related infrastructures, such as fences, security zones, and military outposts. All of these related areas, as well as roads linking settlements to each other and to towns in Israel, necessitate the seizure of more Palestinian land. As Cheryl Rubenberg has observed, "Israel has also taken extensive amounts of land for military bases, nature preserves (off limits to Palestinians), military training areas, bypass roads, security zones, landfills, and so on."[63]

At the end of 2012, according to Israeli government sources, there were a total of 125 government-sanctioned settlements in the West Bank, not including east Jerusalem and settlement enclaves within Hebron. An additional 100 smaller "settlement outposts" were located throughout the West Bank. The Israeli organization Peace Now put the number of settlements at 137, and Palestinian sources maintained there were 239 illegal outposts.[64] These outposts, which are in reality smaller settlements, are often established with government assistance but are not officially recognized. According to B'Tselem, the settler population in the West Bank was estimated at 515,000 in 2012, growing at an average annual rate of 6 percent (Israel's overall population growth rate being 1.6 percent).[65] Overall, today's settlers represent 10 percent of the Israeli population, of whom an estimated 30 percent are ultraorthodox, 30 percent ideological, 30 percent nonideological, and 10 percent mixed.[66]

The 1968 Allon Plan called for placing settlements in sparsely populated lands of the Jordan River Valley, thus ensuring Jewish demographic presence in the farthest location within biblical Israel. This was later complemented by the 1978 Drobles Plan, named after its author Matityahu Drobles, which called for a "belt of settlements in strategic locations . . . throughout the whole land of Israel . . . for security and by right."[67] The logic of the Drobles Plan actually guided the wave of settlements that occurred in the 1990s, thus turning the settlements into an integral element of Israel's tactical control over and surveillance of Palestinians in the West Bank.

The Allon and Drobles Plans and other similar colonization campaigns have invariably been motivated by five broad, interrelated reasons driving the settlement enterprise. They include control over economic resources, use of territory as a strategic asset, ensuring demographic presence and geographic control, reasserting control over the Jew's biblically promised homeland, and having exclusive rights to the territory.[68] These interrelated dynamics give the settlement phenomenon a self-perpetuating momentum. As Azoulay and Ophir correctly observe, speed is an important feature of the "colonizing momentum" of the settlements.[69] Many settlements begin life as unrecognized, unofficial "outposts." Before long, the protection of the Israelis living there requires paved roads for the military patrols that provide security, followed by the provision of infrastructural needs such as running water, connection to the power grid, and a sewer system, often followed by a corner store selling goods to the residents, a school for their kids, more homes, and so on. In addition to military protection, the Israeli state provides the residents with educational and health services. Before too long, a new town is born. The settlement of Ma'ale Adumim is a case in point. It originally began as a workers' dormitory camp besides an industrial park inside the West Bank. In 1991 it was officially granted the status of a city, and today it constitutes one of Israel's largest settlements. As of 2014, it had a population of more than thirty-nine thousand people.

More than a mere response to the Oslo Accords, the outposts, which proliferated afterward, were meant to expand the scope of Israeli ruling apparatus, in the form of Israeli control and institutions, deep into Palestinian areas.[70] The location of these outposts and settlements are often chosen with deliberate care. Invariably located on hilltops, their location is guided by the logic of deep penetration inside the West Bank in areas with few previous Jewish residents. This has "ensured that no area of the West Bank remains Jewless."[71] After the Wye River negotiations with President Bill Clinton and Yasser Arafat, Ariel Sharon, at the time Israel's foreign minister and later prime minister, is quoted as having said: "move, run and grab as many hilltops as you can, everything we take now will stay ours. Everything we don't grab, will go to them."[72] The settlement represent "a deliberate policy of expanding one state's sovereignty into what is internationally recognized as belonging to another nation and a future state: that of Palestine."[73]

While the settlement enterprise enjoys both tacit and overt support from the state, it is doubtful whether the Israeli state could do much to reverse or to even slow down its momentum. For many Israelis, settlements represent more than just affordable, comfortable housing units in self-contained, pioneer communities. They are tangible, and presumably permanent, manifestations of redemption and reclamation, of return to and ownership over the Promised Land. No Israeli government, no matter how solid its electoral base, could possibly institute policies that fly in the face of such resonant and passionately held religio-nationalist views. In fact, after the signing of the Oslo Accords, continued settlement activity was seen as a way of ensuring Israel's political stability.[74] Today, forcibly evicting settlers from the West Bank is commonly assumed to trigger a civil war. As an alternative, it is the Palestinians who are expected to lower their expectations.[75]

Many settlers, meanwhile, exhibit high levels of violence toward Palestinians. Most of this violence manifests itself in uncoordinated attacks on individual Palestinians and their property, such as throwing stones at passersby and at Palestinian cars and buses, cutting down Palestinian olive trees at night, or throwing feces at Palestinian property. Palestinians in Nablus and Hebron are especially subject to such attacks. A 2008 United Nations report cited a "worrying trend" in the intensity and frequency of settler violence against Palestinians, often labeled as "price tag" by the settlers.[76] At times these acts of violence are more coordinated and feature bands of Israeli youths, and generally they follow actions by Israeli authorities that are perceived as harming the settlement enterprise or follow Palestinian violence against settlers.[77] For their part, Israeli security forces often ignore or overlook settler violence against Palestinians and their property, including attacks on cars and buses carrying Palestinians and setting Palestinian homes on fire.[78] Hebron's settlers, with a well-deserved reputation for ideological fanaticism and violence, often receive light sentences or no sentences at all for the violence they inflict on Palestinians.[79]

In addition to military control of the territories, Israel has devised an intricate and highly complex network of permits that govern countless aspects of Palestinian life and behavior. The permit system, at times draconian, developed over time shortly after the capture of the West Bank and Gaza, and remains in full force today in Area C and in all access points to Area A. A whole slew of "military-spatial devices" are deployed throughout the West Bank and Gaza to ensure the population's control.[80] The most noticeable aspect of the occupation until the Oslo Accords meant control over Palestinian lives, and that control manifested itself in the most extreme forms: students groups needed permission from occupation authorities to organize football and basketball matches; writers and lawyers needed permission to hold meetings; cooks were not allowed to pick thyme leaves; gardeners were not allowed to plant azaleas; teachers, lawyers, journalists, and just about everyone else were under constant surveillance; and libraries were often emptied or closed altogether and books were censored. The occupation deeply impacted and significantly changed the very fabric of Palestinian life. The rules were meant to ensure both control and, just as important, as much judicial and administrative separation as possible.[81]

Especially after October 2000, the Israeli army employed restrictions on the movements of Palestinians as a means of control, which had the added benefit of being of low cost to the army and to Israel in general. The permit system remains an important and pervasive aspect of the occupation today, and, because the occupation authorities see Palestinians as suspect until proven otherwise, any permit can be summarily revoked. Once revoked, a permit's reinstating can take a number of days and require much paperwork.[82] By one estimate, in 2012 some 101 different types of permits governed the movement of Palestinians within the West Bank or between the West Bank and Israel.[83]

While it is the eruption of violence on either side that often garners the most attention, much of the day-to-day act of occupation occurs through what Azoulay and Ophir call "withheld violence." Withheld violence is a type of normalization of separation, humiliation, being rudely interrogated at a checkpoint, delays and waiting, and being detained or blindfolded and then being released. It impinges on Palestinian lives more pervasively, and in some ways more perniciously, than eruptive violence. "By blocking movement and forcing people to loiter in the wrong place at the wrong time, withheld violence encumbers, complicates, disrupts preferences, undermines plans, maddens, wounds, infests, generates disease, and kills."[84] One of the purposes of withheld violence is to condition the behavior of Palestinians. "The Palestinians are taught how to behave when crossing a checkpoint, how to address an official in the district coordination office, how to gain benefits in detention cells."[85] In all their interactions with Israeli soldiers and other occupation authorities, Palestinians are reminded of the need for complete submission and the potential rewards of good behavior. Through a policy of prohibition and monitoring, the occupation authorities have created multiple "points of dependence" and a "normalization of submission."[86] Today, "relations of submission and obedience" permeate all realms of Palestinian life, and the Palestinians' "inferior status" is guaranteed through an articulated civil administration in east Jerusalem and the military occupation regime in the West Bank.[87] Not surprisingly, for Palestinians Israeli law sanctions rather than prevents violence.[88]

The defining feature of the occupation is a comprehensive separation of everyday life through a stifling bureaucracy, a regime of permits, and an iron grid of militarily imposed regulations.[89] I will shortly demonstrate how the Palestinian economy, or whatever of it there is, has been shaped and molded over time to serve the purposes of occupation. Insofar as judicial and administrative control are concerned, although there is supposed to be a body of regulations concerning Israeli conduct in the West Bank, the rule of law is often suspended when seen as appropriate or convenient. This is generally done in one of three ways: on-the-ground military operations, the frequent introduction of a state of emergency, and the IDF's simply ignoring the extensive judicial patchwork of laws and regulations governing the West Bank.[90] Israel does in the West Bank—and to Gaza—what it sees fit, restrained only by consideration of self-interest.

Military occupation and administrative control have affected every aspect of the Palestinian economy. From the very beginning, Israel sought to ensure the continued dependence of the Palestinian economy and prevented the development of Palestinian industries and financial institutions. It also instituted a complex system of permits for various economic transactions that could be revoked at any time. This also prevented the development of Palestinian sources of income.[91] Ironically, however, in the early years of the occupation, the Palestinian economy experienced a relative though short-lived boom. A number of reasons accounted for this burst of growth, including the "open bridges" policy of trade with Jordan and Egypt, Israeli consumers buying cheaper goods in the Occupied Territories, and increased remittances from the Palestinian diaspora in the oil-rich states of the Persian Gulf.[92] Equally important were Israeli efforts aimed at upgrading the Palestinian economy and fostering economic growth in the West Bank and Gaza. "Occupation with a lighter touch" resulted in economic growth of 15 percent in the West Bank and 11 percent in Gaza annually from 1968 to 1972.[93]

But, along with the global slump, the trend toward economic prosperity was reversed in the late 1970s and the early 1980s. This decline in the Palestinian economy was precipitated by several developments; among the most important were significant reductions in the amount of remittances coming in from the Persian Gulf states, economic difficulties within Israel itself, growth in the number of Israeli settlers and land confiscations, and an abrupt stoppage in Israeli development and other types of economic assistance to the Occupied Territories.[94] By the time of the first intifada, the Palestinian economy was already in rapid decline. The uprising left it in tatters.

The Oslo years saw a continued fall in Palestinian living standards, although, bolstered by significant investments from Europe and the United States, Israel's economy grew significantly. Israeli per capita gross domestic product grew by 14.2 percent while Palestine's fell by 3.2 percent.[95] The terms of the Oslo Accords were hardly beneficial to the Palestinian economy. As part of the accords, in 1994 an economic agreement was signed in Paris, often called the Paris Economic Protocol (PEP), which gave Israel the responsibility for collecting Palestinian customs duties in return for the right of Palestinians to continue to work in Israel. Israel has kept collecting Palestinian customs, but it has steadily worked to reduce the number of Palestinians working within its borders.[96] Before 1994, 30 percent of the Palestinian labor force in the West Bank and more than 40 percent of Gaza's worked in Israel as day laborers. Within two years, the percentage had dropped to 18 percent for the West Bank and 6 percent for Gaza.[97] Since the PEP stipulated that Israel would continue to collect customs revenues on behalf of the Palestinian Authority and then transfer over the money, the Palestinian economy in the Occupied Territories went from being labor-dependent to becoming finance-dependent.[98] On occasion, especially after suicide bombings, the Israeli government has withheld Palestinian revenues. Those who signed the PEP in 1994 assumed, in the spirit of the Oslo Accord at the time, that it would foster greater economic integration between Israel and the Occupied Palestinian Territories. Quite to the contrary, however, it brought about only greater unilaterally imposed separation and Palestinian dependence on the Israeli economy. The Palestinian economy, meanwhile, has to continue relying on revenue transfers from Israel and on international donations to function, making it unlike any other economy in the world.[99]

The Al-Aqsa Intifada left the Palestinian economy devastated as it led to drastic increases in levels of unemployment and poverty, reduced income levels, and increased income gap within Palestinians, and it made whatever was left of a Palestinian economy heavily dependent on international assistance to stave off a massive humanitarian catastrophe.[100] In the Occupied Palestinian Territories, personal income fell by 23 percent in 2002, and by another 23 percent in 2003.

By the early to mid-2000s, with the Oslo Accords all but discarded and the PNA reduced to near irrelevance in function and scope, the Palestinian economy went from bad to worse. Israel's devastating responses to Palestinian terrorism in the 2000s left an already battered economy in ruins. Between 2000 and 2002, an estimated $643 million worth of Palestinian private property and infrastructure was destroyed by the Israeli army.[101] Israel's retaliatory measures also expanded the spatial distances between Palestinian localities and their physical separation from one another.[102] By 2007, Palestinian incomes had dipped to 60 percent of what they had been in 1999.[103]

All of this has resulted in the development of a constrained and constricted, underdeveloped, and highly dependent economy. The PEP ensured that the Palestinian economy remains dependent on Israel. The New Israeli Shekel, NIS, remains the currency of the Occupied Territories, thus subjecting the Palestinian economy to monetary and financial changes occurring inside Israel as well. In 2012, Israel accounted for 66 percent of imports from and 89 percent of exports to the Occupied Palestinian Territories.[104] Israel's extensive control over Palestinian labor movements, as well as imports and exports, give a huge advantage to Israeli companies.[105] As the world's most aid-dependent region, all aid to Gaza has to go through Israel. Israel has also ensured that aid is the only thing that enters into Gaza. The PNA, meanwhile, cannot function without outside financial assistance, most of it from the United States, the European Union, and the states of the Persian Gulf. In the third quarter of 2012, for example, the PNA could not pay the salaries of public employees until after receiving a "bailout" from Saudi Arabia and the United Arab Emirates.[106]

Within the Occupied Territories themselves, there are few structural facilities and opportunities for economic development. I will highlight these restrictions in the following section, on Gaza and the

West Bank. For now, it is important to keep in mind that there are structural restrictions that severely limit the viability and development of Palestinian economy in the West Bank and Gaza. Prices remain artificially high because of transportation costs, both of people and goods, as all goods and individuals have to pass through Israeli checkpoints and are frequently delayed.[107] Few Palestinians can count on regular employment, most being daily wage earners. If they are lucky, they find employment in the PNA bureaucracy or in one of the international nongovernmental organizations that operate throughout the West Bank, as well as the few in Gaza, but even then their salaries often depend on the largesse of wealthier benefactors in the West or in the Arabian Peninsula. In 2012, overall unemployment in the West Bank measured at slightly above 20 percent, and in Gaza at nearly 32 percent. Among the young (ages fifteen to twenty-four), however, it was much higher, measuring 36 percent among males and 74 percent among females.[108]

Price fluctuations are rampant, and private investments remain minimal and are highly concentrated. The restrictive regime imposed by the occupation encourages local monopolies in the small Palestinian economy, which can in turn raise prices at whim and with little resistance.[109] Local monopolies have mushroomed, fattening the pockets of their owners, who are often affiliated with the PNA, at the expense of the rest of the population. Most other private investments, however, are kept at a minimum due to what the World Bank calls "a permanent state of insecurity" arising out of "recurrent destruction of trees, private homes and public infrastructures, as well as settlers' encroachment on private land," in addition to frequent road closures, the Separation Barrier, and permit requirements that restrict the movement of people and goods.[110] These difficulties are compounded by the PNA's chronic financial difficulties. In 2011, according to the World Bank, the PNA required $1.5 billion in budget support but received only $983 million. To close the gap, it borrowed approximately $260 million from the local banking sector. For 2012, the financial situation was even more grim. Of a budget of about $1.1 billion, the PNA was able to identify only $610 million in donor support, leaving a gap of some $540 million.[111] The bank concluded that "the Palestinian Authority continues to experience a severe fiscal crisis, which threatens to become protracted given recent and projected declines in donor assistance."[112]

Another aspect of the occupation to highlight is control over water. Insofar as Israel's occupation of the West Bank is concerned—as well as of the Golan Heights and southern Lebanon—control over rich water resources is not the cause but rather a significant source for the continuation of the occupation.[113] A 2009 World Bank report found that 80 percent, or four-fifths, of the available water in the West Bank goes to Israel.[114] The land atop the West Bank's largest underground aquifers has been taken over by Israel for agricultural purposes.[115] Water quality in Palestine, meanwhile, has severely deteriorated due to contamination from industrial and human waste as well as from settlements. An estimated two hundred thousand Palestinians in the West Bank have no access to water network connections and must rely on expensive tankered water distributed to often hard-to-reach "filling points."[116] Despite the water's poor quality, West Bank Palestinians spend on average 8 percent of their household income on water, twice the globally accepted standard.[117] Because of the comparative price advantage, availability, and quality of the Israeli water, on an annual per capita basis, Israelis consume four times more water than Palestinians do.[118] The World Health Organization recommends sixty liters of water per capita each day to maintain general health, hydration, and cleanliness. An estimated 50 percent of

Palestinians in the West Bank and Gaza survive on less than thirty liters of water per day.[119] In Gaza, water quality has reached critical levels. Gaza's underground water reserves are quite salty, and there is a lack of materials for building irrigation and water collection systems.[120] Some 90–95 percent of the water in underground aquifers in Gaza is considered unfit for human consumption.[121] An estimated 26 percent of all diseases in Gaza are water related.[122]

Water is precious and is bitterly fought over. But even more precious, and far more bitterly fought over, is Jerusalem, the city eternal. For Israelis, Jerusalem is not open to discussion. It is the eternal, undivided capital of the State of Israel. For Palestinians it is central to their sense of self and the biggest symbol of their loss and dispossession. Some, though their numbers are dwindling as the years go by, still cling to the dream that one day it will be the capital of a state of Palestine.

Divided after 1948 into a western half populated mostly with the victorious Israelis and an eastern half where many Palestinians sought refuge under Jordanian protection, Israel's conquest of east Jerusalem in 1967 was popularly seen as the truest vindication of the new country's biblical mission. After 1967, Israel faced no restrictions in east Jerusalem and did whatever it thought served its military, demographic, economic, and political interests.[123] Less than a week after the end of the 1967 war, Israel formally annexed all of Jerusalem. Soon thereafter, urban planning was employed to expand the boundaries of the city and therefore Israeli sovereignty. From that point on, Israel has made every effort to emphasize and accentuate the city's distinctively Jewish character. For the country's leaders, the planning and development of Jerusalem, whether in terms of urban planning or the simple construction of houses, is a "Jewish national undertaking," a "strategic component of a national struggle."[124]

Jerusalem's urban planners have used the two criteria of "visibility and proximity" to expand the city's boundaries: if a house is close enough to be seen from the city's border, then it is a part of the city. This kept the city's boundary expanding. Meron Benvenisti, former deputy mayor of Jerusalem, made the following observation: "In Jerusalem, of all places, whose historical site is so precisely defined, and so eternal, commissions of inquiry grant themselves—and military officers—license to inflate its jurisdictional boundaries, thereby turning its very geographical definition into a farce."[125] The expansion of "Greater Jerusalem" into ever-widening circles has been accompanied by the integration of more and more Jews into the city and the exclusion of more and more Palestinians from it.[126] Teddy Kollek, the city's mayor from 1965 to 1993, oversaw an aggressive intrusion of Israeli presence in the Palestinian areas of the city through the construction of Jewish neighborhoods on expropriated land, as codified in the city's 1978 master plan, all the while striving to have "separate development and peaceful coexistence" among Israelis and Palestinians.[127]

Israeli policy makers have orchestrated an effort to change the landscape and physical look of the city of Jerusalem, making it consonant with the desires of the Jewish collectivity. On all sides except east Jerusalem, the Haram al-Sharif (Temple Mount) has been fully enveloped by new roads and buildings. Suburbs envelope the city itself on all sides. Once compact and perched on a hilltop, Jerusalem today is unrecognizable to a traveler from the past, its map, geography, and skyline having changed beyond recognition. Over 90 percent of eastern Jerusalem today actually consists of land added after 1967.[128]

After 1967, a conscious effort was made to grow and develop the western part of Jerusalem while keeping the city's Arab, or eastern, part frozen in time. In the eastern part, zoning regulations prohibit the building of structures that are four stories or taller, and they do not permit the geographic growth of existing villages. East Jerusalem has long suffered from neglect of municipal services. There are hundreds of kilometers of missing sewers, paved roads, and sidewalks. There is no system of garbage collection; firefighting and rescue services are not up to standard; and there are frequent water shortages and electricity blackouts. Housing shortages and overcrowding are serious problems, but the municipality will not approve the construction of new homes or modifications to existing ones, both of which could well result in having the house demolished. Poverty and truancy are rampant, as is substance abuse, with few social workers to attend to the needy. Some 78 percent of Palestinians living in the Jerusalem district and 84 percent of the children live below the poverty line.[129] For residents of east Jerusalem, the municipality's provision of vastly unequal services is seen as another symptom and manifestation of the occupation, and the municipality itself as another institution of occupation.[130]

According to the Association of Civil Rights in Israel, "the cumulative effects of annexation, neglect, rights violations, and the completion of the Separation Barrier have led to an unprecedented deterioration in the conditions of Palestinian East Jerusalemites."[131] East Jerusalem lacks adequate water supply, and, similar to elsewhere in the West Bank, its residents often face water shortages. In addition to water management, there are also major issues with inadequate waste management, sewer system, and drainage. In the absence of proper garbage collection and disposal, many residents burn their trash, resulting in higher than usual rates of asthma among children. East Jerusalem schools also suffer from chronic overcrowding, crumbling infrastructure, insufficient and inadequate playground and laboratory space and supplies, and poorly paid teachers. Most pupils in east Jerusalem receive inadequate schooling. East Jerusalem is in need of one thousand additional classrooms to meet the needs of the city's Palestinian student population, and whereas west Jerusalem has sixty-six municipal prekindergartens, east Jerusalem has only six. By some counts, the dropout rate in east Jerusalem high schools is as high as 40 percent.[132] Al-Quds University, the only Palestinian university in Jerusalem, is not accredited by Israel's educational authorities, and therefore its graduates earn considerably less than comparable graduates from Israeli universities.

There is an absence of reliable and regular delivery of basic public services. Though technically undivided, the eastern half of Israel's capital remains at "the bottom of the list of priorities" for Israeli authorities and is deliberately underserviced and underdeveloped.[133] In sharp contrast to the modern, bustling western parts of the city, in many sections and neighborhoods of east Jerusalem time appears to have been frozen in the mid-1960s. Today, west Jerusalem residents enjoy sixteen times the area of parkland per person, four times the amount of sidewalks, and three times the amount of roads as compared to east Jerusalem residents. According to a 2010 survey by the Jerusalem Municipality, east Jerusalem needs $2 billion NIS ($51 million) to upgrade its infrastructure to merely a basic level.[134]

Coexistence between members of all three Abrahamic faiths today is characterized by what Benvenisti calls "geography of fear," whereby Jews and Palestinians live apart from and mostly in fear of one another.[135] In Jerusalem there are two ostensibly "normal" societies, living side by side but in completely different economic, political, and geographic universes, with quite "abnormal" relations with one another.[136] Still, the Israeli government's ceaseless efforts through law, jurisdiction, and sovereignty aimed at making east Jerusalem an integral part of Israel have so far been thwarted by Palestinian resilience and collective memory.[137]

Israel is doing all it can, administratively and otherwise, to suffocate the Palestinians of east Jerusalem and to get them to leave the city.[138] According to a 1969 report commissioned by the Jerusalem municipality, guaranteeing Jewish superiority in the city is of paramount importance.[139] Mayor Kollek did everything possible to ensure Jewish demographic superiority in the city. In February 1993, in fact, Kollek admitted to what up until that point had been an open secret, namely that since 1967 Israel had pursued a policy of restricting Arab growth in east Jerusalem by limiting the number of new homes that could be built there. This is done principally through urban planning. In fact, Israeli housing policy in east Jerusalem is all about numbers, as the Jewish presence in east Jerusalem is seen as an insurance policy against any possible redivision of the city in the future.[140]

Cheshin, Hutman, and Melamed, all well-placed Israelis, outline in detail how in the 1980s and the 1990s urban planning and zoning laws were employed to change east Jerusalem's demographic balance and to reduce, as much as possible, Palestinian presence there. Zoning laws, for example, were used to prohibit construction in Palestinian neighborhoods. In some instances, as in Kafr Akab, the neighborhood was artificially divided into two zones, with one zone being allowed to build, while the other one was prohibited from doing so.[141]

At times, attempts at reducing the population of Jerusalem's Palestinians occur more perniciously than through zoning laws. As Cheshin, Hutman, and Melamed state,

Since the time of the early Zionist movement, Jewish leaders have stressed the importance of physically staking claims to the land. The Zionists called this "putting facts on the ground," an expression which Israeli policy-makers continue to use to this day. The early Zionists were experts at putting up a "wall and watchtower" settlement under the cover of night, which Arab residents would discover the next morning. In east Jerusalem, Israel did not have to build in the dark. One new Jewish neighborhood after another has cropped up—from Ramot, Ramot Eshkol, French Hill, Pisgat Ze'ev, and Neveh Ya'acov in the north to East Talpiot and Gilo and now Har Homa in the south, again putting "facts on the ground" that the Arabs must face when making their claims on the city.[142]

Clandestine takeovers still occur, at times under the cover of darkness, especially by extremist Jewish groups who declare structures or entire towns as "religious property" over which they have rightful ownership and whose current Arab owners and residents deserve to be evicted.[143]

In December 1995, Israel instituted a policy it calls "Center of Life" in regards to Jerusalemite Palestinians. The policy basically amounts to a permanent residency permit, although Palestinians were not informed of it and only learned about its details when they went to renew their existing permits. Between 1995 and 1999 alone, some three thousand Jerusalemite Palestinians lost their right to live within the city because their residency did not meet the conditions outlined in the policy.[144] According to the Center of Life policy, for a Palestinian to maintain the right to live in Jerusalem, he or she must present confirmation of employment within the city; must have copies of at least the preceding seven years of bills in taxes, utilities, and telephone; proof of annual allotment from the National Insurance Institute; a legal affidavit from an approved attorney proving residency within the city, a legal rental contract, or conclusive proof of living with parents; and confirmation that all of his or her children above the age of six attend school within the official limits of Jerusalem.[145]

Beginning in the 1990s, a trend toward the Hebronization of Jerusalem started, whereby settlements started appearing in the middle of populated Arab areas in east Jerusalem. Previously, settlements in Jerusalem were located separately and apart from Arab areas. The development of Jewish neighborhoods in east Jerusalem is meant to ensure the cutting off of Jerusalem from the West Bank.[146] The intrusion of Jewish settlements in turn pushed up property prices. Combined with highly restrictive zoning and construction regulations, land confiscations resulted in astronomical rises in real estate prices in east Jerusalem, making housing extremely difficult to afford for most of the city's Palestinians. Between 2007 and 2011, housing prices in all of Israel increased by 53.9 percent. In east Jerusalem, however, housing prices shot up by 192.5 percent, while wages increased only by 12.5 percent.[147] Israel's attempts at demographic engineering are beginning to bear fruit, and, as early as the late 1990s, over half of the population of east Jerusalem was already Jewish.[148]

The West Bank and Gaza

It is only befitting that we end this chapter with a discussion of the conditions on the ground in what remains of historic Palestine, namely Gaza and the West Bank. As mentioned earlier, Israel initially did not know what to do about the territories it had captured, and a robust debate ensued among the political leadership over how to handle the newly acquired lands and their people. Yet the capture of the territories themselves was never in doubt. Years after the war, Israeli sources revealed that plans for the occupation of Gaza and the

West Bank had actually been in place for some time before 1967 and that the capture and possession of the Occupied Territories was anything other than a surprise.[149] Thus ensued an occupation that is approaching the half-century mark. Much has changed in the last fifty years in the international arena, with some of the countries around in 1967 no longer in existence, others having changed their political systems and national priorities beyond recognition, and a whole host of new ones having been born since. But what hasn't changed is the fundamental nature and consequences of Israel's occupation of Palestinian territories, and, in the process, both the dismemberment of Palestine as a geographic entity and the weakening of its fabric as a nation.

As chapter 2 outlined, Palestinian society collapsed in the wake of the ethnic cleansing and massive displacement that befell it with the establishment of the State of Israel. Gradually, it reconstituted itself in the three distinctive milieus within which it subsequently found itself: under Israeli rule and with Israeli citizenship, under occupation in a steadily dismembered and isolated Gaza and the West Bank, and in exile in diaspora. In the next chapter I will outline the consequences of the predicaments and the multiple divisions of Palestinian society for the twin projects of nation- and state-building. Here, in what remains of this chapter, having outlined the territorial fragmentation of the West Bank and Gaza, I will end the chapter with a snapshot of the consequences of the occupation on Palestinian society in these two remaining parts of historic Palestine.

Some 73 percent of Gaza's population is made up of refugees from 1948 and 1967 (most are refugees from 1948), while slightly more than 30 percent of West Bankers are refugees. Throughout the Occupied Palestinian Territories, the occupation regime deliberately created conditions of arrested development, battered and dilapidated infrastructure, and bare existence.[150] Two-thirds of the population of Gaza and 25 percent in the West Bank face food insecurity, and over one million Palestinians are in need of food assistance.[151] According to the Palestinian Ministry of Health, 5.3 percent of Palestinians in the West Bank and Gaza suffer from at least one form of disability, many of them in the 19–29 age group.[152] According to the World Health Organization, at least 57 percent of maternal deaths in the West Bank are preventable.[153] A 2012 WHO report warned of the possibility of chronic malnutrition and stunting among children under five in the West Bank and Gaza.[154] Many Palestinians suffer from nutrition deficiency, with an estimated 80 percent of children suffering from iron deficiency and 87 percent being deficient in zinc. Of women of reproductive age, 73 percent were iron deficient and 75 percent had zinc deficiency.[155] Levels of psychological trauma tend to be extremely high among Palestinian communities, meanwhile, as a result of the pervasive violence that surrounds daily life. Almost 50 percent of Palestinian children report personal experience of conflict-related violence or have witnessed violence.[156]

In both the West Bank and Gaza, opportunities for personal, professional, and financial and economic growth and development remain highly limited. Employment opportunities for Palestinians in Israel have also dried up significantly since Oslo, as Palestinian day laborers in the construction and agricultural sectors have been replaced by migrant workers from Southeast Asia. Many of the Palestinians who used to work in low-skilled service jobs have also been replaced by recent arrivals from Ethiopia or eastern Europe. Before Oslo, some 30 percent of the West Bank's labor force was employed in Israel. In 2012, that number had been reduced to 10 percent, including those who worked in Israeli settlements located inside the West Bank itself.[157]

By isolating Palestinian towns and villages from one another in the West Bank and by making connections and contacts—commercial, political, cultural, and otherwise—extremely difficult among them, Israel has created not just Bantustans but what the Palestinian academic and activist Mazin Qumsiyeh calls actual "human warehouses."[158] Others speak of the "'bantustanized' Palestinian population within well-guarded confines."[159] Throughout the West Bank, instead of urban sprawl, there is inward growth of Palestinian cities. Cantonization or Bantustanization ensures that Palestinians live in "manageable-sized ghettos."[160] Concentrating Palestinian communities within well-defined and well-guarded geographic limits has made their control and containment easier for the Israeli military. This often takes the form of "closures," which, as a reflexive response of the Israeli government to terrorist attacks and a frequent precautionary measure during Israeli holidays, have become a regular feature of life in the West Bank.[161]

While life in the West Bank is difficult, life in Gaza is particularly dire. In Gaza, the Zionist mantra of "maximum land, minimum Arabs" has been turned into "maximum Arabs on minimum land."[162] Even before the 2000s, the overpopulated Gaza was often perceived by Israeli leaders as a special problem, and many Israelis, both openly and privately, called for abandoning it.[163] Whereas the West Bank is subject to occasional closures by Israeli authorities, the Gaza Strip is under permanent Israeli closure. Gaza is surrounded by an electrified fence and a "security zone" that occupies a one-kilometer parameter along its length. This security zone contains 29 percent of Gaza's arable land. However, no less than 73 percent of the households near the zone live below the poverty line, compared to 42 percent in the Strip as a whole. In 2010, 50 percent of Gazans living near the security zone reported losing their livelihoods since 2000.[164]

Israel's closure of Gaza and the amplification of a process of economic de-development that had started some time ago has turned an already-impoverished region into a "humanitarian basket case."[165] "The Palestinians in Gaza," in the words of two Israeli academics, "are the abandoned people of the Israeli regime."[166]

As a powerful method of control, Israel deliberately keeps Gaza on the brink of catastrophe, pursuing "a policy of deliberate reduction" of basic goods and "a lower warning line"—or, alternately, "a higher red line"—in which deliberate scarcity is created for security purposes, and basic goods such as food products and fuel are monitored to ensure they are kept at low but not critical levels.[167] Controlled scarcity and "catastrophization" have become powerful components of controlling Gaza.[168] According to the Palestinian Center for Human Rights in Gaza, 22 percent of Gaza children suffer from malnutrition and 16 percent suffer from anemia.[169] An entire generation of Palestinians in Gaza are growing up stunted physically and nutritionally, academically and intellectually.[170] There are also acute shortages in medicine and medical care. In 2011, 32 percent of essential drugs and 22 percent of essential medical consumables were lacking in Gaza's Central Drug Store.[171]

A study by the World Health Organization found that the infant mortality rate is 30 percent higher in Gaza than it is in the West Bank.[172] The WHO warns that without humanitarian assistance, poverty in the Occupied Palestinian Territories is estimated to go up to 42.5 percent. Deep poverty, meanwhile, stood in 2010 at 23 percent in Gaza and 8.8 percent in the West Bank.[173]

Through its control of all entry gates and products entering or leaving the Strip, Israel is able to control levels of unemployment, malnutrition, income, and production in Gaza.[174] In 2007, before Israel laid siege to the territory, 5,747 truckloads filled with exports of agricultural goods, furniture, garments, and metal products left Gaza for Israel and a few other destinations from there. From the siege until 2010, on average only 56 truckloads a year found their way out of the territory.[175] Within Gaza itself there are limited employment opportunities and even fewer opportunities for economic mobility. An overwhelming majority of Gaza's industrial establishments operate either far below capacity or remain closed altogether.[176] Poverty rates in both Gaza and the West Bank remain consistently high. According to Palestinian sources, in 2011 rates of poverty in the West Bank and Gaza stood at 25.8 percent, with 17.8 percent in the West Bank and 38.8 percent in Gaza.[177] The median daily wage in Gaza is only 70 percent of the median daily wage in the West Bank, and the average wage of Gaza's workers represents only 75.5 percent of the average wage in the West Bank.[178] Gaza's infrastructure, meanwhile, remains broken and underdeveloped. In 2010, 46 percent of the agricultural land was inaccessible or unusable a year later due to destruction in Operation Cast Lead, also known as the Gaza War, which lasted from mid-December 2008 to early January 2009.[179]

Already suffering from deliberate "de-development," Gaza is subject to frequent, devastating retaliatory attacks by the IDF, whose magnitude and fury are completely disproportionate to the small, largely ineffective rockets Palestinian Islamists on occasion fire toward Israeli towns and cities. According to the Israeli Security Agency, between 2005—the year of Israel's withdrawal from the Strip—and 2012, groups and individuals in Gaza fired more than 8,700 rockets and nearly 5,000 mortar shells toward Israel.[180] This included the brief, intense weeks of Operation Cast Lead at the end of 2008 and the start of 2009. The terror that Israeli civilians within reach of the rockets must feel is undeniable.[181] But the numbers of casualties on both sides reveal lopsided levels of grief and misery.

From 2000 to 2008, B'Tselem recorded a total of 3,002 deaths in Gaza at the hands of the Israeli Defense Forces, compared to 136 deaths on the Israeli side, of whom 97 belonged to the IDF. During Operation Cast Lead, 1,391 Gazans and 5 IDF soldiers died, and from January 2009 to October 2013, 465 Gazans and 5 members of the IDF were killed by the other side.[182]

A similarly devastating scenario was repeated in summer 2014, during Israel's Operation Protective Edge, which started in early July 2014 when both Israel and Hamas started accusing each other of acts of violent provocation. In seven weeks of relentless aerial bombardment and ground assault by the IDF, more than 2,100 Gazans were killed, including 1,462 civilians, of whom 495 were children. On the Israeli side, 65 soldiers and 4 civilians lost their lives, including 1 child, as did 1 foreign national. Some 108,000 Gazans had their homes destroyed or severely damaged. This left 10 percent of the Strip's population with running water only once a day for six to eight hours, and the whole Strip was subject to eighteen hours of scheduled electricity outage. According to the Palestinian Ministry of Health, more than 10,200 Palestinians, including 3,100 children and 1,900 women, had been injured a week before the war ended. According to the United Nations, Gaza's physical devastation and the need for relief operations following the end of open hostilities was "unprecedented in the Agency's 64-year history in Gaza." The UN's Office for the Coordination of Humanitarian Affairs estimated that at the height of the conflict, 500,000 Gazans, or 28 percent of the Strip's total population, were internally displaced.[183]

According to Israeli Brigadier General Zvi Fogel, "there is no death by natural causes in Gaza."[184] The job is done instead by insufficient food supplies, inadequate health-care services, improper water sanitation, and an abundance of Israeli bombings and IDF attacks.

Conclusion

Since the capture of the West Bank and Gaza in 1967, Israel's occupation has set into motion three complementary, mutually reinforcing processes. One has been a systematic, concerted effort to depopulate, repopulate, and Judaize the land previously inhabited by Palestinians. A less-subtle and more-brutal version of the same process had occurred earlier in Palestine proper, in the form of the ethnic cleansing that occurred in the lead-up to and shortly after the official establishment of the State of Israel in 1948. Israeli authorities have devised various mechanisms, ranging from legal and administrative regulations to urban planning and zoning laws, in order to constrict the scope of Palestinian residence throughout eastern Jerusalem and the West Bank and to conversely expand and deepen Jewish presence in as many far-flung Palestinian areas as possible.

A second, complementary process has been the hiving off of Palestinian towns and cities into cantons that are isolated first and foremost from Israel and then from each other. Jews and Palestinians often self-segregate, not minding living in peace, separately.[185] But Palestinians have been forced to separate and segregate within themselves. Gaza is surrounded by an electrical fence and a security zone on three sides, and its sea line is also controlled by Israel. The West Bank is also being enveloped by a mammoth Separation Barrier, which on completion will be more than twice the length of the original Green Line separating it from Israel. The West Bank itself is divided into Areas A, B, and C, each of which have distinct characteristics. Area A includes all major Palestinian population centers. Area B includes mostly rural areas, where the PNA has civilian control and the IDF retains control over security and military matters. And Area C, under full Israeli control, includes the only area of the West Bank with contiguous boundaries. There is also the seam zone, the area in between the Green Line and the new border reality of the Separation Barrier. These territorial separations and divisions, as the preceding pages have demonstrated, are more than mere lines on a map. They have divided lives and families, neighborhoods and communities. Palestine is a society divided, a nation fragmented.

Third, there has been a deliberate process of de-development in both the West Bank and Gaza, put in place by Israel. On their own, Gaza and the West Bank are too small and underdeveloped to have viable economies and effective internal markets. As things currently stand, private investment in either place remains anemic. There are few employment opportunities and still fewer chances of upward economic mobility. Basic services such as water, electricity, and waste management are spotty at best and nonexistent at worst. Gaza cannot export anything, and its imports remain highly restricted and controlled. Food insecurity is rampant and malnutrition a real threat. The Strip teeters on the verge of a humanitarian crisis that is prevented only when and if Israel wills it.

There are a number of advantages to the assumption that the occupation is temporary. Among other things, it creates "perpetual blindness" as to what the occupation really means. It also leads to the assumption that the conditions to which the occupation has given rise can be easily addressed through ready-made solutions and remedies.[186] But the Occupied Territories aren't just occupied. They are divided, controlled, kept down. And these are only the scattered pieces in which Israel does not directly rule. The rest of what once remained of Palestine, from 1967 on, has been built over, renamed, its landscape and geography changed beyond recognition. To assume that the change is only temporary, that the geographic engineering of Palestine so thoroughly undertaken by Israel is reversible, is, at the very best, naive.

4

One Nation, Divisible

The signing of the Oslo Accords was, by all accounts, historic. After years of mutual denial, Israeli and PLO representatives formally recognized each other's right to existence and committed to ending the cycle of violence that had torn them apart for nearly a century. For Palestinians, Oslo had the additional significance of laying out the foundations of a future state by outlining its institutional features and spelling out the necessary future steps to eventual statehood. More importantly, in addition to state-building, Oslo represented a significant step toward the reconstruction of the Palestinian nation. This went above and beyond demanding the right of return for the refugees of the diaspora. It meant the deliberate reconstruction of a Palestinian national home, of one Palestine, under the autonomous rule of the Palestine National Authority.

The Palestinian euphoria was not just palpable; it was contagious. Few in the international community could simply stand by. Support and assistance poured in from all corners, often in the form of money, at times as technical help and advice. International nongovernmental organizations rushed in, and countless Palestinian ones sprang up. A new era of state- and nation-building had started. Palestine was on its way to reconstituting itself.

Two decades on, the post-Oslo national project has had three consequences. First, under the auspices of the PNA, the nation-building process has not progressed much. In fact, by all accounts, the social and cultural chasm between the West Bank and Gaza—never mind between the two and Palestinians elsewhere—is as wide as ever. Whereas Israel has ensured the physical and territorial divisions of the two remaining parts of Palestine, Palestinians themselves and especially Hamas and the PNA have pulled them politically and culturally further apart from one another.

Second, again under the auspices of the PNA, the nature and orientation of the Palestinian bourgeoisie has changed. Before Oslo, the Palestinian bourgeoisie was at the forefront of the struggle for national liberation and was the main component and constituency of the PLO. Once the PNA was established and the need for reconstructing Palestine opened up investment and other commercial opportunities, the national bourgeoisie slowly became transformed into a comprador bourgeoisie and steadily emerged as one of the primary mainstays of the status quo.[1] The national project became more of a commercial project, and Palestinian nationalism came to be increasingly conceived, at least by those with connections and investments, more in commercial and entrepreneurial terms.

Finally, the NGOs that flooded the West Bank and Gaza in the euphoric days of the Oslo Accords stayed on long after the euphoria had died down, having become sources of employment and prestige for a new cadre of professionals. They wrote briefs and published glossy brochures as Palestinian lives on the ground changed little and as Palestine's dismemberment proceeded apace. In the process, people and communities became accustomed to and in fact dependent on the NGOs, and the PNA learned to tolerate them when it realized they helped stabilize—and more significantly, depoliticize—the Palestinian population. NGOization became the morphine of Palestinian society.

Far from reconstructing Palestine, the Oslo Accords and its consequences wrecked the Palestinian nation. More accurately, Oslo further fractured Palestine.

This chapter traces the reconstruction of the Palestinian nation into broken fragments. The 1967 war, the chapter argues, deepened the chasms and differences that marked Palestinian identities scattered across different geographic locations and political systems. Masked by the imperative of national liberation, the internal divisions of Palestinian society were not reduced but further deepened with the signing of the Oslo Accords, now reinforced by tangible political stakes and competition over instruments of power. The break between Fatah and Hamas was by far the most dramatic manifestation of the post-Oslo split within the Palestinian polity. Moreover, in the years following the Oslo Accords, the composition and function of the Palestinian middle classes changed, from nationalist bourgeoisie to comprador bourgeoisie, and NGOs became more prevalent than ever before. The cumulative outcome has been the depoliticization and incapacitation of Palestinian society. Israel has done what it can to ensure that Palestine does not materialize as a country. But so too, inadvertently, have the Palestinians.

The Fractured Society

Palestinian national identity has persevered despite multiple divisions and fragmentations, first along territorial lines and then, transposed on territorial divisions, along social and cultural ones as well. That a Palestinian national identity exists, at least in the abstract for those who identify themselves as Palestinian, is not in doubt. What is more problematic is whether the ensuing chasms in Palestinian society are too deep to foster the construction—or reconstruction—of a Palestinian *nation*. Palestinian society, as the previous chapters argued, disintegrated following the ethnic cleansing of Palestine in the fateful years before and after the creation of the State of Israel and the "silent transfer" of Palestinians ever since. The reconstruction of Palestinian society, and with it Palestinian national identity, occurred under conditions of dispossession, exile, and fragmentation. While this reconstructed identity has certain basic common denominators, it is not clear whether these commonalities outweigh the divisions.

For Israel, Palestinian national identity is more threatening than popular, localized identities in the West Bank, Gaza, and elsewhere. Israel has been especially sensitive to the continued presence of Palestinian national identity in Jerusalem, seeking to institute a variety of means and processes to contain and reverse it as much as possible. In addition to the Center of Life policy, Israeli authorities have banned Palestinian NGOs, civil society organizations, and institutions from operating in Jerusalem.[2]

But the effects of Israel on Palestinian identity go beyond the implementation of specific policies. They have consequences for the larger context of Palestinian existence and experience. The Israeli occupation has brought about a complete change to the Palestinian fabric of life. In addition to profound changes to the Palestinian landscape, physical geography, and urban environment, it has blocked economic development and has dismantled some social institutions and eroded the authority of others.[3]

The Palestinians, meanwhile, cling to the memory of a "paradise lost." For them, collective perceptions of a grave historic injustice committed against them, as well as hopes of "return," are key ingredients of what it means to be Palestinian. The Nakba remains a powerful aspect of lived experience for all Palestinians, as do themes such as "rootedness" and "Palestine as Paradise."[4] Another aspect of Palestinian life is the continuous state of emergency in which they live.[5] Not surprisingly, there is a tendency to romanticize life in Palestine before it was dismembered.[6] It was not accidental that when new nationalist leaders came to the fore of the liberation movement in the 1970s, they began de-emphasizing the divisions and contradictions of Palestinian society for the sake of national unity.[7] In an effort to preserve and strengthen national unity, PLO officials and the Palestinian intellectual community struck an alliance, resulting in what the author Fawaz Turki called "a pact with the devil."[8] They were aided in their efforts by the spectacular nature of their attacks and their perceived heroism among refugee-camp Palestinians, on the one hand, and Israel's draconian and disproportionately harsh responses, on the other. The Palestine Liberation Army's campaign of armed resistance in Gaza from 1967 to 1971, and Israel's reprisals— mirroring the Gaza rocket attacks and devastating Israeli responses of the 2000s—were emblematic of the need to cast aside societal tensions and divisions in favor of the revolutionary struggle.[9] But divisions, predating the collapse of 1948, continued to persevere and became magnified in the lead-up to and especially after the signing of the Oslo Accords. While the Oslo Accords did not completely remove Israel as an outside enemy against which Palestinian factions needed to present a united front, they also did raise the stakes in the domestic competition over position, resources, and the very future of the national movement. Thus the contradictions and internal tensions of the national movement—and therefore of Palestinian national identity—became harder to mask.

There were multiple divisions within Palestinian society prior to 1948, regionally among northerners and southerners, hill dwellers and plainsmen, nomads and settled population, urbanites and villagers, and Muslims and Christians.[10] In 1947–1948, with the collapse of Palestinian society, Palestinians were divided into four main groups. Fewer than half remained in their original houses: 160,000 in Israel, 350,000 in the West Bank, and between 70,000 and 100,000 in Gaza. Another 750,000 or so refugees were scattered in the Gaza and the West Bank, Lebanon, Syria, and Jordan.[11]

There was even less unity and cohesion among Palestinians in the immediate aftermath of the war, and tensions remained high for some time between refugees and nonrefugees. From 1948 to 1967, there was little discussion of a Palestinian national entity or a united society, and Palestinians were often seen as dispersed refugee groups.[12] After 1948, in fact, Palestinian political space was determined by each host country, and popular grassroots patriotism was transformed into protonationalism.[13] From 1948 to 1967, during which time Palestinian nationalism was overshadowed by the larger, overpowering forces of pan-Arabism emanating out of Cairo and Damascus, each of the scattered Palestinian groups developed distinctive patterns of social, political, and economic organization.[14] The two remaining chunks of Palestinian territory—Gaza and the West Bank—were separated from one another, and there was little or no interaction between them. It was only after 1967 that there was some freedom of movement between the two.

The 1967 Naksa, or "setback," turned out to be a catalyst for the rebirth of Palestinian nationalism, this time with greater focus and more-concentrated purpose. Refugee life and exile had resulted in the breakdown of the power of the old economic and political elites in the 1960s and in the emergence of the professional middle classes as the new leaders of the Palestinian national movement. This new middle-class leadership became especially effective in mobilizing support and giving widespread popularity to national liberation ideals in refugee camps in nearby countries and in the West Bank and Gaza. This trend gained particular strength especially after 1967, as manifested in the use of the terminology, rhetoric, and slogans that were employed in the service of the national struggle.[15] By the 1970s, the Palestine National Council represented a quasi leadership of the Palestinian people. Within a decade, by the 1980s, as "occupation with a smile" had turned into hardened military rule, Palestinian universities had emerged as centers for interpreting the occupation's common meaning.[16]

By the time the first intifada broke out in December 1987, a more locally conditioned Palestinian identity had begun to emerge and gain hold in the Occupied Territories, centered in the cities and neighborhoods of the West Bank and Gaza and shaped by the lived experiences of daily life under occupation. The new nationalism took by surprise both Palestinian intellectuals and the leadership that had seen itself exiled and scattered to lands farther and farther away from Palestine. Although Fatah and the PLO soon imposed themselves on the new nationalist movement and sought to portray it as representative of the aspirations of Palestinians everywhere, by now neither the unifying forces of the intifada nor the direction provided by the Fatah-dominated leadership were sufficient in overcoming some of the deep chasms that distinguished Palestinians societies across the globe. The eventual direction of the Oslo Accords, what some Palestinians saw as the hijacking of the fruits of the intifada by the PLO "Tunisians,"[17] only exacerbated the manifold divisions that had emerged within Palestinian society over the preceding decades.

Palestinians in diaspora are united by the fact that their parents or grandparents were forced to leave Palestine and that they cannot return to their ancestral homeland and birthplaces.[18] No matter how powerful and compelling, though, memory alone does not compensate for the challenges of maintaining a transnational Palestinian political and cultural identity in the face of exile and dispersion over generations. Both during and after the intifada, Palestinian nationalism only partially masked the wide variety of vastly differing experiences and circumstances in which Palestinians live. As Ahmad Khalidi commented as far back as 1995, "The experience of the refugee camp of Beirut is as remote from that of the middle classes of Ramallah as is that of the militant in Gaza from the intellectual in New York. These are not merely normal differences between different social and economic orders, as in any society; rather they are disparate histories that have been aggravated vastly by the difficulties of communication and interaction imposed by the occupation, and by the obstacles to basic freedoms throughout the Middle East (such as the freedom to speak, move, or merely to subsist in peace)."[19]

Palestinian identity has been fragmented by the brute force of Israeli military power. Today there are five main categories of Palestinians, each with their own subcategories. They include Palestinian citizens of Israel; Palestinians in east Jerusalem with Israeli permanent residency; Palestinians in the West Bank, with West Bank identity cards; Palestinians in Gaza, with Gaza identity cards; and Palestinian refugees. In the West Bank, there are subcategories of those who live in Areas A, B, C, and the seam zone.

Refugee-camp society, meanwhile, developed distinct features from country to country.[20] According to a 2012 poll by a Bethlehem-based NGO, generations of exile have strained the identities of Palestinians in Jordan, Lebanon, and Syria the most. Only in Syria does a vast majority, close to 70 percent, identify themselves as Palestinian, with the next highest group, some 15 percent, viewing itself as Palestinian-Syrians. In Lebanon the percentage identifying themselves as Palestinian goes down to 52, with another 10 percent considering itself as Palestinian-Lebanese; 5 percent identify themselves as "Palestinians with Lebanese Documents." In Jordan, where the social and political assimilation of Palestinians has been the highest, only 10 percent identify themselves as Palestinian, and an equal percentage as "Palestinians with Jordanian Documents," with 50 percent identifying as Palestinian-Jordanian.[21]

Of the diverse Palestinian communities around the world, those who by accident of history or by design have found themselves inside historic Palestine—namely Palestinians with Israeli citizenship, those in Gaza, and those in the West Bank—deserve particular attention. Each group is separated from the other by an array of physical, economic, social and cultural, and political differences. At the broadest level, Israeli Palestinians are generally better off financially and tend to be better skilled, followed by West Bankers, and then lastly by Gazans, most of whom come from refugee backgrounds. Different experiences and predicaments have bestowed on each group a different worldview.[22]

Since 1948, Israel has tried to cut off the West Bank and Gaza from each other as much as possible. Economically, the connection between the two is very limited, and products from one are not allowed into the other. At the social and cultural levels, there is still a vibrant level of interchange, as people from the two territories, in the words of one of my Palestinian informants, can and at times do "meet in third countries."[23] But occasional trips abroad or staying in touch via social media do not come anywhere near sustained and meaningful commingling and interface over time. Gaza and the West Bank have had multiple differences for well over a century, among the most prominent of which are geographic, sociocultural, and economic.

These differences have only been exponentially magnified under the weights of trusteeship and rule by different masters—that is,

Egypt and Jordan—occupation and colonization by Israel, internal dismemberment for purposes of Israeli rule and for the sake of settlements, and isolation from one another and from the larger world. Even Israel has attached different levels of importance to the two territories, effectively annexing large swaths of the West Bank, which it considers as biblical Judea and Samaria, but altogether abandoning Gaza in return. For many Israelis, the reconquest and re-Judaization of Judea and Samaria is central to the ongoing project of colonizing Palestine. Not surprisingly, Israel has done all it can since 1967 to stunt any form of Palestinian development in the West Bank and Gaza, culturally, economically, and of course politically.

The spread of schools and universities in the 1960s and the 1970s did little to smooth out emerging cultural fissures within Palestinian society. To begin with, the education of Palestinian schoolchildren about their own history and background has remained, both before and after Oslo, highly incomplete and problematic. Up until 1994, Jordanian textbooks in the West Bank and Egyptian ones used in Gaza were heavily censored by the Israeli authorities. The word "Palestine" was removed, maps deleted, and anything deemed nationalist was excised. Infrastructure was also highly dilapidated, and there was no investment in infrastructure since 1967.[24]

The skewed and incomplete nature of the information taught in Palestinian schools did not necessarily change after limited autonomy turned the Palestinian curriculum over to the PNA. Today, Palestinian textbooks do not tackle unresolved political issues, do not provide maps of Israel or Palestine (since the final shape of borders is yet to be decided), and generally reflect the Palestinian narrative of natives in conflict with colonial settlers after the 1948 Nakba.[25] In Gaza, Hamas has sought to promulgate its own "official history," which spuriously credits the Muslim Brotherhood with a continuous and preeminent role in the liberation struggle for the past seventy years.[26] Throughout the 1970s and the 1980s, meanwhile, Palestinian institutions of higher education became highly politicized, with students usually supportive of one of the main formal Palestinian political groupings under the PLO umbrella—Fatah, Popular Front for the Liberation of Palestine (PFLP), Democratic Front for the Liberation of Palestine (DFLP), the Communist Party—or the Islamic tendencies.[27] Instead of functioning as institutions for the spread of national ideals and the growth of social cohesion, in many ways, in fact, Palestinian educational institutions inadvertently heightened social chasms.

The differences in the overall backgrounds of the leaders of the PNA as compared to those of Hamas leaders are revealing. Whereas many Fatah leaders had their houses in Palestine intact after the 1948 or 1967 wars, most Hamas leaders were refugees in Gaza, and many hailed from the countryside. Many had had their villages razed from the map by Israel, and most had acquired university degrees in engineering or the hard sciences.[28] Gazans, therefore, who have historically had less to lose, have been on the whole more vociferously and militantly opposed to Israeli occupation.[29] Gaza, as might be expected, has generally been more difficult for Israel to control as compared to the West Bank.

Since 2006–2007, the cumulative effects of occupation and separation in Gaza and the West Bank have been compounded by bitter political and ideological rivalries by the two governing bodies dominant in each territory: Hamas in Gaza and the PNA in the West Bank. The ensuing strains on Palestinian national identity and on the construction or reconstruction of a Palestinian nation are difficult to overlook. In the same 2012 poll cited earlier, only 67 percent of Gazans identified themselves as Palestinian, with 23 percent identifying themselves as Gazans.[30] More than 10 percent of Gazans believe it is not important to develop social ties with the West Bank, and another 10 percent have "neutral" feelings on the matter.[31]

More than twenty years ago Sara Roy observed a "reemerging animosity and psychological divide" between the populations of the West Bank and the Gaza Strip.[32] Since that observation was made, the divisions and animosity, and mutual isolation from one another, between the Palestinians of Gaza and the West Bank, has only grown in depth and magnitude. Few organic ties have emerged to draw the two territories closer to one another, and political and institutional linkages between them have been remarkable in their failures.

If Gaza and West Bank Palestinians have far-reaching differences with one another, they have even more profound differences with Palestinian Israelis. Since 1948, the Palestinians who remained in Israel have consistently found themselves in an ambivalent, often difficult position. Long subject to military administration because of their suspect loyalties to the very notion of an Israeli state, in Israel they are officially referred to as "Arabs" as part of the state's efforts to erase as much of Palestinian identity as possible. The educational system promotes Israeli patriotism among Palestinian children, representing the Israeli system as democratic without referring to their own secondary status.[33] In March 2011, the Knesset went so far as to pass a law, which has since come to be known as the Nakba Law, that bans the funding of any schools or public institutions that reflect on the establishment of the State of Israel as a *nakba,* a "catastrophe," for the Palestinians.[34] Israeli attempts at identity erasure notwithstanding, the Palestinian Israelis' sense of Palestinianness gets agitated depending on the ebb and flow of the conflict and the larger context within which they find themselves. Consistently, however, they are scrutinized carefully by the Israeli state and are subject to discriminatory treatment at multiple levels.

The position of Palestinian Israelis was particularly precarious from 1948 to 1967, with a majority feeling uncertain and ambiguous about Israel. Subject to a fierce military regime, Palestinian Israelis were left without intellectual, cultural, and economic leadership, living in very deprived conditions.[35] The 1967 war had a reintegration effect for many, but most continued to feel psychologically and socially pained about their separation from other Palestinians and continued to identify with the cause of Palestinian nationalism.[36] This feeling of ambivalence continued into the 1970s and the 1980s, kept in check through the heavy scrutiny of the Israeli state. Although Palestinian Israelis felt sympathetic to the intifada, they did not join the rebellion in large numbers. Nevertheless, they did feel its repercussions in terms of increased Israeli vigilance and suspicion.[37]

By the 1990s Palestinian Israelis self-identified themselves as a distinct and cohesive group but different from other Palestinians. Nevertheless, the relative dissolution of the boundary with the West Bank and Gaza provided the basis for the recreation of a Palestinian identity.[38] In many ways, the construction of the Separation Barrier in 2002 was meant to reassert boundaries between both Jews and Palestinians and also Palestinians on the inside and outside, thus ensuring the fragmentation of Palestinian identity and preserving Israel's Jewish majority and character.

Today, Palestinian Israelis number slightly more than 1.5 million. They are themselves divided into various groups. Approximately 82 percent are Muslim and 9 percent are Christian, and another 9 percent Druze. An estimated 170,000 of the Muslims are Bedouins, residing mostly in the southern Negev (Naqab) Desert region or the northern Galilee.[39] Treating each group of its Palestinian citizens differently, the Israeli state has given preferential treatment to the Druze, then the Bedouin, then Christians, and finally non-Bedouin

Muslims. The state has sought to politicize the identities of the Druze, the Bedouin, and the Christians while at the same time trying to depoliticize Muslim identity. This divide-and-rule policy has had some success, especially in relation to the Druze, albeit unevenly. Largely through the work of their co-opted leaders, the Druze often consider themselves a community, even a nation, separate from Palestinians.[40]

It is important to note that, except for a small, elite group of co-opted individuals, Palestinian Israelis are subject to systematic, structural discrimination in Israeli society. Although 20 percent of Israel's population, Palestinian Israelis constitute 53 percent of Israel's poor families, earn on average 57 percent less income than Jewish Israelis do, and live in thirty-six of the forty towns with the highest unemployment rates. Palestinian workers are paid on average 29 percent of a Jewish worker's salary.[41] A large number of Palestinian Israeli men aged forty-five to sixty-five drop out of the labor market, thus increasing poverty and dependence on welfare and state services.[42]

The decidedly inferior status of Palestinian Israelis within Israeli society has not translated into a uniform or unambiguous political and national stance toward the question of Palestine. According to Peleg and Waxman, a vast majority of Palestinian Israelis want to remain active and loyal citizens of Israel.[43] But a 2012 poll by the Palestinian NGO BADIL found that 34 percent see themselves as "Palestinians with Israeli citizenship," and for a vast majority, "Palestinianness" is their primary identity.[44] At the same time, however, paradoxically, the rates of voter turnout for Palestinian Israelis in national Israeli elections has not been significantly lower than that of Jewish Israelis. Excluding the 2001 elections, which took place within the violent context of the Al-Aqsa Intifada, the average Palestinian turnout for Israeli elections from 1949 to 2009 stood at 74.4 percent.[45]

In the 2013 Knesset elections, it was 56 percent, defying expectations of lower turnout.[46] Wanting to simultaneously belong to the two worlds of Israel and Palestine, Palestinian Israelis appear to have developed collective hybrid forms of behavior, like voting for Knesset candidates or hanging Israeli flags in villages with no roads or running water.[47] Yet in some Israeli football matches, Palestinian Israelis have been seen to wave the Palestinian flag.

Palestinian scholars and NGOs often argue that the Palestinian Israelis' identification with Israel is only in terms of citizenship and that they lack any symbolic identification with Israel or what it stands for.[48] Alienation from Israeli public culture, they claim, has resulted in a strengthening of Palestinian and Arab culture among the Palestinian population of Israel. Palestinian Israelis consume Israeli culture only for instrumental purposes. This is especially represented through their means of communication and their media consumption.[49] That may well be the case. But instrumentalist use of Israeli citizenship or cultural products have not translated into tangible and sustained efforts at disengagement from Israel and reengagement with Palestine. In 2006–2007, in fact, a number of Palestinian Israelis issued a series of "vision documents," or "constitutions," that outlined their ideal vision of Israeli society and the state, proposing far-reaching changes to the existing social and political orders and outlining a series of changes. All of these documents, interestingly, demanded changes *within* rather than outside the Israeli social and political frameworks.[50] BADIL's own poll in 2012 found that even with no physical barriers between Palestinian Israelis and Jerusalemite Palestinians, social connections and ties between the two groups usually do not take place.[51]

Part, if not much, of the ambivalence of Palestinian Israelis toward the Palestinian question may be their almost complete disregard by the PLO, and by other Palestinian leaders, of voices that ought to be considered in any peace deal with the Israelis. Israel's Palestinian population is completely ignored in all events, discussions, and accords related to the peace process. This is largely because "the Palestinian problem" is seen by Palestinian leaders in terms of demands for statehood—that is, sovereignty over territory and instruments of rule—rather than as a matter of striking equality between the various ethno-national groups.[52] Consistently, the Palestinian leadership—before, during, and after Oslo—has eschewed tackling or even considering the issue of those Palestinians left in Israel. This avoidance appears to be because of the profoundly challenging issues involved in settling their nationality questions, and, perhaps, because of fears of the rejection the Palestinian Israelis' would-be liberators may experience. If the vague and imprecise poll by BADIL is any indication, the Palestinian leadership was well-advised to leave alone the issue of Palestinian Israelis, at least for now.

To sum up, three broad sets of causes have brought about the fragmentation of Palestinian society over the last sixty-five years or so. One has to do with the force of circumstances, with dispersed Palestinian communities finding themselves in separate territories, in different geographies, and under different sociopolitical systems of rule. Whether made refugees in 1948 or 1967, or having left historic Palestine since then, generations of exile or immigrant life are bound to have consequences for assimilation and integration into host societies, changed preferences, and divergent outlooks. Related to this is each community's own internal dynamics of change. Societies change not just because of outside environmental factors—that is, where they find themselves and the influences that are brought to bear on them—but also due to the initiatives of their own leaders, the deliberate or inadvertent changes and directions of their own institutions (schools, religious establishments, families, intellectuals, and the like), and the path dependencies that shape and influence social change. Contingency and agency work in tandem with structural factors to foster indigenous or exogenously generated change to societies, including Palestinian society.[53]

Finally, and perhaps most consequentially, there are the deliberate changes that the State of Israel has set out to make in Palestinian society. Whether through its design of the school curriculum that is taught to Palestinian Israelis or its Center of Life policy in east Jerusalem, or the curfews and closures it places on Palestinian towns and communities,[54] or the countless other means through which it seeks to expand its control over and erasure of all things Palestinian, Israel continues to influence the rhythm of Palestinian life and shape the nature and degree to which it changes. Throughout this book I have highlighted some of the more-obvious and more-blatant Israeli efforts at Palestinian social engineering—settlements, closures, expulsions, encirclement, and the like. But such efforts are not always newsworthy campaigns and occurrences. Conquest and occupation unfold at every level, every day.

One of the more-subtle ways, for example, in which Israel seeks to expand its control and surveillance of Palestinians is through recruiting collaborators, one of the consequences of which is the further fragmentation of Palestinian society. Collaborators are meant to collect information and sew mistrust among Palestinians.[55] According to a study by the Palestinian Academic Society for the Study of International Affairs (PASSIA), most of the recruited collaborators were found to have committed some type of moral transgression and are therefore susceptible to blackmail by Israeli authorities and by other collaborators.[56] A number of means are used to recruit collaborators, among them promises of easing economic pressures or reducing prison sentences, financial inducements, blackmail, career promotion, and entrapment.[57] Israel's recruitment of collaborators intensified after the Oslo Accords, when Israeli authorities felt they had reduced access to some of their resources.[58] In fact, under the terms of the Oslo Accords, the PNA is barred from prosecuting collaborators.[59]

The Politics of Social Change

The struggles of daily life among Palestinians has been well documented and analyzed by a number of scholars and observers.[60] What has been less studied is the composition of Palestinian classes, especially in the Occupied Territories, and the broader consequences of social change for these classes in specific and for the larger Palestinian polity in general. While the impact of Israeli policies on Palestinian society has always been profound, it became particularly acute after the 1967 occupation, and especially so in Gaza and the West Bank. The occupation was a major shock not just to the newly occupied territories but also to Israel. Partly out of necessity and partly to foster development in the territories, Israel opened up its economy to both territories, enforced a customs union, and kept bridges with Jordan open but established a permit system to regulate and control the flow of Palestinians in and out of the territories. Israel maintained the "open-bridges policy" in order to facilitate the Palestinians' continued departure from the territories. There were some public-works projects that allowed for economic development, and, as Israel's economy grew at the same time, the West Bank and Gaza also benefited as well.

The West Bank's economy had already stagnated under Jordanian rule, suffering from a policy of discrimination and deliberate underdevelopment in the industrial and agricultural sectors, in turn prompting the emigration of some 170,000 West Bankers between 1950 and 1967.[61] Kept deliberately small under Hashemite rule, the industrial bourgeoisie remained extremely weak, suffering from limited capital and unable to compete with Israeli industrialists.[62] Gaza had fared even worse under Egyptian rule. The open-bridges policy notwithstanding, Israeli rule did little to improve the economic lot of the West Bank and Gaza. In fact, the economic dependence of both territories on Israel deepened throughout the 1970s, and recession in Israel or a slump in its housing market had significant consequences for uncontrollable rises in unemployment in the Occupied Territories.[63] By 1973, 90 percent of the imports into the Occupied Territories were from Israel, while only 2 percent of imports into Israel were from the West Bank and Gaza. In terms of the types of exports, the Occupied Territories exported mostly agricultural products, but their imports from Israel were largely manufactured and industrial goods.[64] Palestinian agriculture, in the meantime, shifted toward satisfying the Israeli market. By 1973, Israel absorbed some 39 percent of the agricultural products from the Occupied Territories, up from 18 percent in 1969.[65]

Investments in industry remained minimal throughout the 1970s. Estimates of the sclerotic size of the working class in relation to the workforce varies from 12–15 percent in the West Bank to 8–12 or –13 percent in Gaza.[66] Labor wages remained low in all sectors, especially compared to wages in Israel. By 1973, the average wage of an Israeli was 65 percent higher than that of a Palestinian in the construction sector, 80 percent higher in agriculture, and 100 percent higher in the industrial sector. Overall, Israeli labor earned twice as much in wages as Palestinian labor did.[67]

At the opposite end of the scale, thanks to heavy state subsidies, Israeli producers enjoyed considerable advantage over their Palestinian counterparts, who had no such subsidies from which to benefit. Palestinian manufacturing and production remained anemic and highly underdeveloped, and the Palestinian economy became almost entirely driven by and dependent on imports. Prices for most basic goods, meanwhile, remained high as a result. Bread and other basic foodstuffs, for example, were significantly less expensive in Israel than they were in the territories.

Significantly, Israeli rule modified rather than radically altered Palestinian class composition and class relations.[68] Israeli occupation gave rise to some classes and altered the composition of others. The working classes, for example, especially those in the agricultural sector and those working as wage laborers, increased both in relative and in absolute numbers, by the mid-1970s constituting about 48 percent of the Palestinian population. The petite-bourgeoisie was divided into a more-traditional group comprised of merchants, keepers of small shops, and artisans, and a more-modern group made up of teachers, administrators, foremen, technicians, and the like. An estimated 18 percent of the economically active West Bankers and 25 percent of Gazans belonged to the petite-bourgeoisie.[69] The class pyramid included a small group of merchants at the top, followed by a few capitalist farmers, then workers, and wage laborers at the end. In the West Bank, many of those in the professional middle classes who could not find employment emigrated. In Gaza, however, emigration did not provide as great an escape valve as it did in the West Bank.[70]

It was around this time that an increasing number of Palestinian day laborers began working in Israel. Most of the wage laborers came from the countryside and had become victims of the depeasantification process that had started as early as the 1950s and the 1960s. This was an inherently negative process. As refugees, many former agriculturalists lost their ability to use their skills as farmers but were ill equipped to become absorbed into the industrial labor force, turning instead into "a dislocated unskilled proletariat."[71] Because of its own contraction, the Palestinian agricultural sector had also lost its ability to reabsorb daily wage laborers.[72]

As the previous chapter demonstrated, the presence of Palestinian day laborers in Israel has dropped significantly since the signing of the Oslo Accords. Nevertheless, they still constitute a sizable portion of the Palestinian—especially West Bank—labor force. Hired by the day, the Palestinian laborers that work in the settlements or in Israel proper lack basic labor protections and privileges and constitute a segregated ethnic minority.[73] Following pressure from Israeli employers, the authorities opened up the domestic labor market to migrant workers from Asia and Africa in 1989, and since then there have been increasing moves to replace Palestinian laborers with imported workers from Thailand, Philippines, Sri Lanka, Nigeria, and some of the poorer states of eastern Europe, such as Bulgaria and Rumania. This has made Israel one of the world's leading employers of noncitizen labor. That this contradicts the very foundational tenets of Zionism as reliant on "only Hebrew labor" to help "the healing of the Jewish nation" seems not to matter to policy makers and others keen on ensuring the maximum disentanglement of Israel and Israelis from Palestine and Palestinians.[74]

Looking at Palestinian society in Gaza and the West Bank in the 1960s and the 1970s, three major social trends were discernible. They included an increase in the number of Palestinians living in cities and larger towns as a result of the de-peasantification of the population; a softening of vertical social barriers and achievement of upward mobility, thanks to greater educational and administrative opportunities; and the growing significance of refugee settlement patterns derived from the host countries.[75] These trends converged to result in the emergence of a new elite in the 1980s, the development of which was further facilitated by significant increases in the number of university graduates. Interestingly, the new middle class that emerged in the 1980s approximated the middle class that had emerged elsewhere in the Arab world in the 1950s and the 1960s and which had acquired political power in Egypt in 1952, in Syria in 1963, and in Iraq in 1968.[76] Similar to elsewhere in the Arab world, the new Palestinian middle class also brought about the political mobilization of Palestinian society.[77]

Some of the changes taking place also had unsettling consequences for those involved. Throughout the 1970s and the 1980s, due to the social changes that developed because of economic and employment opportunities, family ties were strained and class consciousness emerged.[78] Large segments of the Palestinian population were cleaved from their social moorings and were open to recruitment into new forms of social relations and new organizations. Old patterns of identity broke down, new ones developed, and new patterns of political behavior emerged.[79] Disillusion with the status quo prompted many of the new professionals to look to political and organizational alternatives, and many established or became active in nongovernmental organizations. As the decade of the 1980s wore on, a number of professional associations emerged, especially in the medical and agricultural fields, all loosely affiliated with one of the PLO factions. These associations were purposefully political, sought to establish ties with social constituents and mobilized them, were meant to function as component parts of a future state, and, often for the first time, brought the urban-based professional classes into contact with refugee camps and with the rural population.[80] It was within this context that the intifada took place.

The intifada's "back to the land" movement initially led to impressive increases in Palestinian agricultural output. But the uprising's most significant consequence was psychological, giving Palestinians a strong sense of empowerment.[81] As it turned out, neither the agricultural gains of the intifada nor its uplifting psychological consequences lasted that long. As the foot soldiers of the first intifada and its principal revolutionary force, in the 1980s and the 1990s the Palestinian middle classes were also quiet vibrant in the heady days of the uprising. But this vibrancy was not to last long. The restrictions of movement and the steady disentanglement of Palestinian commerce from Israel that resulted from the signing of the Oslo Accords put increasing pressure on the Palestinian middle classes. Since then, many have seen their purchasing power eroded, at times even finding themselves among the lower classes. Oslo, in fact, introduced fundamentally different and new dynamics into Palestinian society, setting into motion new processes of social change, this time with their impetus and sources centered more within the Palestinian polity.

Of the consequences of the Oslo Accords for Palestinian society, three merit further analysis. They include the transformation of the middle classes from national into comprador bourgeoisies, a loosening of the fabric of life and social commitments, and the NGOization of society.

The establishment of the Palestinian National Authority significantly impacted the formation of classes across Palestinian society in the West Bank and Gaza. This was especially the case with those perceived as the elite, especially political elite. Once the PNA was established, Palestinian elite formation was made possible by multiple changes in traditional patterns of social relations, occupational and socioeconomic changes, organizational dynamics, and the emergence of formal PNA structures.[82] While the PNA's membership did not necessarily represent the broad spectrum of Palestinian society, it did show that there were multiple paths for inclusion within the political elite. Elite formation in contemporary Palestine cannot be understood mono-causally but must be approached in a holistic and nuanced manner. The Palestinian elite is fairly heterogeneous, made up of different elite types that are overlapping, and there are multiple potential lines of elite cleavage.[83]

The signing of the Oslo Accords was also followed by a return to the West Bank and Gaza of a number of wealthy Palestinians from the United States, Europe, and the Persian Gulf states. Approximately 150,000–200,000 Palestinians returned home after Oslo was signed.[84] Along with PLO operatives and their families, the influx of these two diaspora communities back into the West Bank society changed the very fabric of life in the West Bank. These returnees began constituting a new Palestinian middle class, one that had a critical difference with the traditional middle classes. Whereas Palestinian middle classes had been the bearers of the nationalist mantle since before 1948, and were therefore instrumental in articulating nationalist goals and agendas, the new middle class was in large part commercially minded.

Now that the two-state solution was supposedly within sight, and nation-building was the order of the day, the new middle class saw its national duties in commercial and economic terms. As such it was commercially oriented, interested more in economic activities instead of political activism. Its primary concern was the creation not of revolutionary upheaval meant to bring about the liberation of Palestine, but rather of a stable and secure environment suited for investment and commercial activity. This middle class is interested in consumption, wealth accumulation, and investment opportunities.

It is an economically and commercially dependent class with an entrepreneurial spirit and the disposition of investors rather than one steeped in the tradition of the national liberation struggle. Its disposition, and its preference for the status quo, were much closer to that of the new Fatah and the PNA, now bastions of institutional power, rather than the middle-class–based revolutionaries of yesteryears plotting the liberation of Palestine. As such, they forged and retained extremely close relations with public institutions, so much so that at times they became both titans of industry and captains of political and administrative power. What economic growth has taken place has been at the individual level, with the former middle classes having now become nouveau riche, while the rest of society ekes out a living. Large villas and opulent mansions today dot the Ramallah landscape as markers of the West Bank's newly wealthy.

The returnees with some financial resources became mid-level capitalists. A few with considerable means became wealthy investors, especially in the banking sector, cement and construction-materials production, phone companies, and supermarket chains. Given the particularities of West Bank economy, the new members of the bourgeoisie invariably invested in infrastructure and related industries. Big companies started operating alongside small and medium-size industries. Since then, they have had to rely on Israeli middlemen for supplies and on Israeli authorities for import-export permits. For many Palestinian investors and industrialists, their natural partners, with whom they can trade, have been Israeli exporters. Today, Israeli products and consumer goods, imported by Palestinian merchants— from soap and shampoo to processed foodstuffs and other daily necessities—dominate the Palestinian market. Drawn together by common interests, both Palestinian importers and Israeli exporters are interested in stability and a secure environment conducive to trade and investment. Not surprisingly, the new bourgeois class is commercially minded, not politically or nationally minded. The middle classes, meanwhile, have found more consumer goods available for purchase, although their purchasing power has not risen commensurately, having therefore to finance their new lifestyle through bank loans and mortgages. This has been compounded by the physical growth of Ramallah as Israel has cut it off from east Jerusalem. Both the size and powers of the middle classes have shrunk, in fact, while a new class of oligarchs has appeared.

To the newly rich have been added a handful of established industrialist families, one of the most notable being the al-Masri brothers, Munib and Sabih. Sabih's empire includes Paltel cell-phone company and PADICO, the Palestine Development and Investment Company. Munib is known alternately as "the Duke of Nablus" or the Palestinian Rothschild. In 2013, he was estimated to be worth some $5 billion, with investments across the West Bank as well as in Jordan, Saudi Arabia, and elsewhere.[85]

At the same time as changes were occurring to Palestinian economy and society, the very fabric of Palestinian life began getting looser, less tightly knit. Before Oslo, the experience of occupation had made Palestinian community closely knit. There was a much greater sense of community, of community-based self-help and civic-mindedness, and a sense of common experiences as victims of outside occupation. This was particularly the case during the intifada. Starting with the establishment of a nascent PNA, a much looser societal fabric emerged, one that continues to exist today. The "externals" altered the relative cohesion of West Bank and Gaza societies. They came back with capital and with preexisting connections to the PNA, which they put into immediate and extensive use for their newly established enterprises. With the externals leveraging their capital and their privileged access to the PNA, the internals suddenly found themselves at a disadvantage.[86]

From the very start, PNA operations were geared toward guaranteeing and expanding the privileges of wealthy Palestinians.[87] In the 1990s, individuals affiliated with the PNA were reported to have made millions of dollars from such monopolies.[88] In the words of a Palestinian lawyer in Ramallah, "your political leader is the same person who is selling you things and is raising prices on you."[89] Today, the economic power bases and the wealthy classes are all linked to the PNA, having turned Palestine into a two-class society. A few Palestinian oligarchs own major companies in water and electricity, telecommunications, food processing, and construction materials, and all are connected directly to the PNA. Many of the PNA's high-ranking and influential leaders are themselves owners of major Palestinian companies. By one count, trade in eleven essential commodities— flour, sugar, oil, frozen meat, cigarettes, live animals, cement aggregate, steel, wood, tobacco, and petroleum—is controlled by individuals affiliated with the PNA.[90]

Much of the PNA's largesse was funneled into the West Bank, more specifically to wealthy West Bankers affiliated with it. In the meantime, the PNA's increasingly blatant authoritarianism, coupled with the uneven development it was fostering in the West Bank as opposed to Gaza, was deepening an ongoing political and ideological rift between the two regions throughout the 1990s and the early 2000s. Islam has long had deeper roots in Gaza society due to the efforts of the Egyptian Muslim Brotherhood. There had been an especially noticeable growth of Islamic tendencies and sentiments across Gaza and the West Bank as far back as the early 1980s, and Islamist students had also made impressive gains in Palestinian university associations.[91] The PNA's initial popularity in Gaza was as ephemeral as it was meteoric. By the 1990s, as the next chapter more fully shows, it had already lost much ground to Hamas.

Gazans had long suffered disproportionately from the perniciousness of the occupation. As far back as 1993, shortly before the PNA was formally established, the researcher Sara Roy warned about "civic disintegration" in Gaza. Higher levels of violence as a routine aspect of daily life, a lack of apparent possibilities for social mobility, and a way out of the morass were resulting in "increasing disablement and approaching breakdown of civil society in Gaza" and "widening societal divisions and internal fragmentation never before seen inside the territory."[92] Gazans, she observed, suffered from "extreme psychological exhaustion" due to the continuing deterioration of their living conditions, the erosion of their economic well-being, and the gross insecurity in which they live.[93] "There is, in Gaza," Roy wrote, "a profound sense of finality, of having nowhere to go and nowhere else to look."[94] As we saw in the previous chapter, after more than two decades into supposed Palestinian self-rule, the predicament of the Gazans has changed little. If anything, it only has taken a turn for the worse. According to a 2011 study, 85 percent of Gazan children have seen homes raided; 42 percent have themselves been beaten, and 55 percent have seen their fathers beaten by Israeli soldiers; and 60 percent suffer from severe to very severe post-traumatic stress reactions.[95] The consequences of Israel's summer 2014 war on Gaza have wreaked even more havoc on the lives and daily routines of Gazans.

Whereas in the 1990s the PNA's composition and policies shaped the political economy of the West Bank, in Gaza this was done by Hamas after the group assumed full control over the territory in 2006. Once in power, Hamas changed the shape of the Gazan economy in important ways. Within less than a decade, the traditional private sector was almost entirely destroyed. The few industries that survived Israel's crushing closures were subsequently destroyed by Hamas policies. The economic sanctions imposed on the territory by the United States and the European Union following Hamas's electoral victory hit the private sector and the entrepreneurial classes especially hard. Gaps in personal income and gross domestic product between Gaza and the West Bank grew exponentially as a result of the sanctions on Gaza.[96] Hamas soon moved to establish its control over the "tunnel economy" that subsequently appeared. Gaza's private-sector entrepreneurs used to import essential and sought-after goods, such as petrol, cement, and medicine, from Israel. At peak levels, these imports amounted to some $1 billion from Israel and $.5 billion from the West Bank.[97] But the closure of Gaza to trade and commerce after 2006 brought with it the collapse of the Strip's merchant classes. Trade, when it happens, is now oriented mostly toward Egypt. What remains of Gaza entrepreneurs today are those affiliated with Hamas. Smugglers, operators and other beneficiaries of the tunnel economy, distributors, and members of the Hamas bureaucracy have become the strongest elements of the Gazan economy.

Hamas itself has benefited directly from the tunnel economy. Not only is there a passage tax, Hamas directly controls the flow and distribution of goods and directs them to merchants and shop owners affiliated or sympathetic to it. This has given rise to a wealthy counter-elite made up of some five hundred rumored millionaires.[98] While the West Bank–based PNA is closer to wealthier investors and the upper middle classes, Hamas is assumed to be closer to the petite bourgeoisie. Nevertheless, Hamas's broader ability to create sustainable employment opportunities in the long run, especially for high school and university graduates, remains unclear, as does its ability to deliver such basic services as health care, education, travel, and civil affairs.[99]

Writing in the late 1980s, before Hamas was born, the author David McDowall wondered if the Muslim Brotherhood, Hamas's parent organization at the time, was more interested in establishing an Islamic state than liberating Palestine.[100] That Hamas is indeed a national liberation organization has by now been proven beyond doubt. But, after nearly ten years of rule in Gaza, it has so far failed to establish viable economic or, for that matter, political institutions that could foster long-term development. All this has taken place within a backdrop of comprehensive Western sanctions and Israel's chocking blockade and its controlled catastrophization.

The West Bank is in a slightly better predicament, but not by much. The Bantustanization of the West Bank has destroyed the possibility of a Palestinian national economy, has increased economic dependency on Israel, and has perpetuated the fragmentation of the Palestinian labor market.[101] In each of the two Palestinian territories, in the West Bank and Gaza, the middle classes are different and have their own features and priorities, but they are subject to largely the same sorts of pressures, whether emanating from Israel or from domestic authorities. Prior to Oslo, the middle classes, and within them the intelligentsia, were important in fostering debate and discussion and generating a social movement. Whether private-sector or public-sector employees, they were at the forefront of the national liberation movement. But today most have been politically marginalized. Many have been co-opted into the burgeoning administrative institutions of rule, while others are scrambling to maintain their middle-class living standards. For the lucky few, commerce continues to remain an option, at times lucratively so, but almost exclusively with Israeli merchants and institutions. They have, in effect, become unwitting accomplices in the occupation.

Many Palestinian importers complain about having no choice but to deal with Israeli middlemen in order to be able to import goods into the West Bank. The Palestinian and Israeli business communities are intimately linked to one another, and therefore, indirectly, so is the Israeli business community with the PNA. Many Palestinians often jokingly dismiss the PNA as "a subcontractor for the occupation." Dark as it may be, the humor does have some truth to it.

The Palestinians' options are not that varied. The PNA is generally seen as a source of largesse, Gaza as a religious police state, and parental authority as increasingly irrelevant. The few who keep on fighting see diminished support.[102] East Jerusalem middle classes are not much better off. Many cannot find employment in Jerusalem and therefore have to work in the West Bank, thus losing their "Center of Life" in Jerusalem and having to move to the West Bank in hope of better employment opportunities. Younger Palestinians, the post-Oslo generation, are especially discouraged and disenchanted by politics, seldom speak Hebrew or know much about Israel, want to migrate, and have weaker bonds to Palestine.

Young Palestinians feel let down by the Tunis generation.[103] They see and experience how "an old order atrophies while a new one cannot be born."[104] Reflecting on the anguish of Palestinians, Fawaz Turki writes: "The Palestinian Everyman feels betrayed by his leadership, his movement, his dreams. There is a vacuum in his life that he cannot fill. . . . There is no way out of, around, or through his existential ennui. And since he cannot turn a deaf ear and a blind eye to the riot and humiliation heaped on the cause he has believed in for so long, he is whistled clean of any will to live."[105] Turki's passage is from the mid-1990s. But his words are just as valid today as when they were written nearly two decades ago. In public-opinion polls in 2013 and 2014, anywhere from 70 to 79 percent of Palestinians saw no chance for the establishment of a Palestinian state within the next five years. There are also pervasive fears of insecurity in both territories. Nearly 50 percent expressed fear that they or a family member may be hurt or have their house destroyed and their land confiscated by Israel.[106] Few hold positive views about their living conditions. In 2013, fully 84 percent of Palestinians polled offered a negative evaluation of conditions in Gaza and 70 percent had a negative evaluation of conditions in the West Bank.[107] If the poll were to be conducted after the summer 2014 Israel-Hamas war, the level of pessimism and resignation would no doubt be much higher.

Into the abyss have stepped NGOs and civil society, seeking to rescue, with their well-meaning Western funders, and to rebuild Palestine. With feverish excitement, they saw their task as pulling Palestine out of its morass, filling the gaping holes in services left by the occupation, and helping Palestine in its march toward nation- and state-building. Before long, they proliferated in numbers and in function, having taken over much of life in Palestinian society. As one Palestinian activist I interviewed remarked, "the NGOs feed off the donors, and the donor system is a great place for business. But donors also hijacked civil society, moving it away from the national agenda and to a technical agenda instead."[108] Before long, we started witnessing an NGOization of Palestinian society.

The NGOization of Palestinian Society

Associational life expanded considerably throughout the Occupied Territories in the 1980s and the 1990s, its growth accelerated by the exigencies of service delivery, on the one hand, and international donor support, on the other.[109] Oslo exponentially increased donor money, which created new classes and categories of professionals. This in turn helped the proliferation of NGOs, which provided employment for a specific segment of middle-class Palestinians, who could read and write in English. The NGOs provided a welcome alternative to civil service employment, which often offered no more than minimal middle-class pay and mundane office jobs. At least initially, the NGOs were effecting change, or appeared to be, and therefore were generally seen as contributing agents to the process of nation-building.

The petering out of the national liberation movement also helped the proliferation of NGOs. After the signing of the Oslo Accords, most Palestinian parties and political activists who were not affiliated with either Fatah or Hamas pulled out of politics and slowly transformed themselves into NGOs. The PLO's former left wing took advantage of donor support for NGOs and, despite political marginalization by the PNA, became active in the NGO arena.[110] According to one survey, 37 percent of NGO activists were members of a political party at some point. Only 24 percent of NGO employees continue to be formally affiliated with a political party, and only 16 percent actively.[111] In the 1990s and the 2000s, a process of devolution of politics took place, whereby many politically minded individuals either founded their own NGOs or became NGO employees. Today, therefore, the multiple political parties and associations that were once a vibrant feature of the Palestinian landscape have transformed themselves into NGOs. Many still have political ideologies and tendencies but no avowedly political agendas.

Palestinian NGOs fall into two broad categories. There are a number of NGOs that focus on service delivery, especially in the areas of agriculture, health care, and education. A second group focus on awareness and advocacy, focusing on issues such as the rights of prisoners and refugees, settlements and land confiscations, civil rights and access to services, and other similar issues. Whereas the first group of NGOs often work closely with the PNA and with larger, international funders, such as the World Bank and the European Union, the second group often receives smaller amounts of funds from more diverse funders and frequently relies on funding for their annual, or even month-to-month, operations.

The West Bank has long had one of the richest associational landscapes in the Middle East. As far back as 1999, some 20 percent of the population was involved in associational life.[112] Since the signing of the Oslo Accords, however, the politicization of Palestinian civil society has resulted in polarization and inconsistencies in patterns of civic engagement. With the establishment of the PNA, many Palestinian NGOs felt that their autonomy was threatened and many NGO activists gave up in frustration. Those associations supportive of the PNA have been beneficiaries of security, prestige, credibility, legitimacy, media exposure, and visits and endorsements by high-ranking foreign officials.[113] Since the early 1990s, in fact, civic associations in Palestine have tended to be polarized along the two poles of those that are pro-PNA and those generally opposed to it. Pro-PNA patrons draw resources that reinforce the benevolent image of the PNA, and they pass it on to their clients. Those not in the "in-crowd," however, urge their clients to be skeptical of the PNA and caution against approaching the PNA's corrupt institutions. Because of their closer proximity to governing institutions, pro-PNA associations often offer better and more material benefits, and, consequently, they tend to be numerically greater and often enjoy more popularity.[114]

Service NGOs are most frequently found to be active in areas where the PNA's capacity is weakest and its institutions face obstacles in implementing policies and objectives.[115] Insofar as service delivery is concerned, Palestinian service NGOs actually often fill a noticeable gap in the delivery of some essential services in both Gaza and the West Bank. According to a 2006 report by the World Bank, a breakdown of the percentage of services by NGOs in some areas poorly attended or unattended by NGOs was as follows at the time of the survey:

Agriculture	53
Hospital beds	32
Primary health-care centers	29
Psychological counseling	25
Vocational training	25
Health-care training	21
Preschool services	21
Rehabilitation	19[116]

Additionally, some 40 percent of poor Palestinian households relied on health-care services provided by NGOs, with the remaining 60 percent using the services of UNRWA health clinics. Significantly, the report found that the target constituency of service NGOs are generally happy with the quality of the services they receive and appreciate the professionalism of their staff, the upgraded facilities, and their better resources.[117]

Although in many instances NGOs help fill critical gaps in Palestinian society and fulfill much-needed services, their proliferation across the social spectrum has had several adverse consequences, both politically and socially. To begin with, the spread of associational life has done little to encourage the emergence of a democratic Palestinian political culture. Contrary to what is often assumed to be the case in Western democratic settings, in Palestine, patterns of civic and community engagement, political knowledge, and support for democratic institutions tend to be inversely related to levels of interpersonal trust. According to the findings of Amaney Jamal, "in centralized clientalistic settings, associations that support the regime will exhibit higher levels of interpersonal trust and lower degrees of democratic forms of civil engagement. Conversely, associations not linked to the regime will hold lower levels of interpersonal trust and higher levels of democratic civic engagement."[118] In pro-PNA associations, individual interests were secured and advanced through clientalistic ties to the government.[119] These associations are hardly democratic, nor, as constituent components of civil society, do they act as agents of democratization. In associations in which there is strong support for democratic institutions, there is a lower rather than higher level of interpersonal trust. Members of pro-regime associations tend to be more trustful, presumably because they are drawn together through clientelism and patronage, and exhibit lower levels of support for democratic institutions and lower levels of civic engagement.

One of the problems with Palestinian NGOs, especially those that are issue-focused and advocacy-driven, is that they often operate in a social milieu that is largely disconnected from the rest of Palestinian society. Historically, up until Oslo, Palestinian NGOs were large, mass-based organizations that aimed to mobilize large cross sections of Palestinian society. Examples included charitable associations and labor, students', or women's organizations. Many started to decline in the early 1990s. Funding played an important but not singular role in turning mass movements into an NGO community of elite professionals and politically autonomous institutions.[120] The post-Oslo NGOs are different in discourse, form, leaders, focus, organization, and, of course, sources of funding. They are frequently small, urban-based, and donor-dependent, focused on specific, often micro-issues and are run by urban-based elites. Especially after the second intifada, a "globalized Palestinian elite" emerged, tied more closely to global actors, such as international NGOs and donors, than to local actors and constituents. Informed of global issues, they support the peace process.[121]

Far too frequently, the NGOs are themselves staffed by Palestinians who hardly represent Palestinian society. As one study noted, NGO employees are "yuppies": 71 percent of NGO employees are young (seventeen to thirty-seven years old), 76.5 percent are urban, and they are professionals (90 percent have academic degrees, 41 percent have undertaken further training courses).[122] As such, NGOs and the type of work they do tend to appeal to a particular mind-set. Here is a recurring description of the appeal of NGO work in the occupied territories: "NGOs are among the few workplaces perceived to operate according to professionalism. They have thus become desirable workplaces for a new generation of middle class professionals who view NGO employment as a career path to more-lucrative salaries and more-prestigious jobs in international organizations. Speaking English, dressing well and maintaining a nice office are all part of this new culture."[123] Islah Jad observes that "many NGO activities are held in fancy hotels, serving fancy food, distributing glossy materials, hiring 'presentable' young people to help organise the event or the activity."[124]

Moreover, as Jad explains, NGOs rely on modern communication methods to get their message out, such as conferences, social media, workshops, and publications—globalized tools rather than local ones. "These methods may not be bad in themselves, but they are mainly used to 'advocate' or 'educate' a 'target group,' usually defined for the period needed to implements the 'project.' Here the constituency is not a natural social group; rather it is abstract, receptive rather than interactive, and the 'targeting' is limited by the timeframe of the project. This temporality of the project and the constituency makes it difficult to measure the impact of the intervention."[125] This turns the organization's mission into a "job" rather than something based on conviction and voluntarism. Often times, well-meaning young Westerners who intern at the NGOs based in east Jerusalem and the West Bank—especially in Ramallah—often seem more eager and enthusiastic about the mission of the NGO with which they are affiliated than are the NGO's local employees. They are believers in the mission of the NGO—they have often studied the work of NGOs and more closely believe in the gospel of "capacity building," "sustainability," and civic empowerment—as compared to employees for whom NGO work is mostly a source of employment. In the process, and alongside routinization, a "magic bullet syndrome" emerges that leads both the NGOs and their funders to declare work on various projects a success. A "project logic" takes over, defining goals and social change in terms of progress toward the never-ending peace process.[126]

While most employees of NGOs are young, they are often led by an older generation of Palestinians, mostly in their fifties and sixties. Many of these NGOs are like their personal fiefdoms, more as sources of employment and as something respectable to do, rather than as true grass-roots organizations meant to address specific needs and fill local vacuums. These NGO leaders may be internationally recognizable and with access, but that does not necessarily translate into local effectiveness.[127] Empowered by high levels of education, professional qualification, access, and a mastery of development "lingo," NGO leaders often have a tendency to patronize the others.[128] More commonly, they lack a unified strategy to achieve local goals.[129] Being project-focused and dependent on funding, the prospects for most NGOs to create change beyond narrowly defined target groups is, at best, uncertain.[130]

Perhaps even more detrimental has been the growing dependence of NGOs on international funders and, concomitantly, the growing sense of helplessness and dependency on the part of Palestinian community activists and organizers. The capacity of NGOs to raise local funds is severely limited. Meanwhile, in receiving international funding, the NGOs all too frequently face uncertainty, unpredictability, and lack of transparency.[131] According to a 2011 study by the Rosa Luxemburg Foundation in Palestine, on average 80 percent of NGOs' budgets come from foreign donors, mainly in the European Union and the United States. Donor assistance to Palestinian NGOs went from $48 million in 1999 to $257 million in 2008, further deepening dependency on international funders.[132]

The large sums of money committed to development projects in the Occupied Palestinian Territories by agencies such as UNICEF, United Nations Development Programme (UNDP), and USAID unintentionally strengthened individuals rather than communities and unrealistically raised expectations and created dependency relationships.[133] NGOization has resulted in the spread of "values that favour dependency, lack of self-reliance, and new modes of consumption."[134] Becoming aid-dependent can serve to entrench a self-image of uselessness to society. But suddenly cutting off aid can be even more harmful, as aid at least prevents catastrophe and keeps disaster at bay.[135] A similar development had occurred throughout the 1980s, when the multitude of services provided by UNRWA in the fields of health, education, and relief had increased greatly. Given that the administrators of the aid were generally Western professionals and that the recipient refugees had no say, this had created "a profoundly damaging sense of dependency" on continued assistance and the general operations of UNRWA.[136]

This is not to imply that Palestinian NGOs are always passive recipients of external influence, at the mercy of donors. At times they have the power to manipulate, renegotiate, and legitimize donor agendas. They are part of a "globalized elite" and therefore often engage their donors on terms advantageous to them.[137] Nevertheless, the international NGOs have changed the focus of the Palestinian national agenda. Prior to the Oslo Accords, Palestinian civil society was nationally driven. But from the 1990s onwards, donors began insisting on "the correct political conditions" for funding, thereby depoliticizing Palestinian NGOs.[138] Since the World Bank and other donors want to "depoliticize" humanitarian donations, complying NGOs often inadvertently strengthen the forces of the market economy at the expense of political institutions and regulations.[139] In the Palestinian context, "the donor role became to underwrite the occupation and the political stagnation on the ground."[140]

NGOization has fostered dependence. Across Palestine today, many individuals and entire communities have become reliant on Western or Western-funded NGOs to provide a whole variety of services or various types of microfinancing. NGO service delivery has bred dependence. A number of NGOs chase funding opportunities and therefore modulate their activities accordingly, adopting the universal NGO language that is appealing to funders but lacks relevance and meaning to the local context. In the process, a dominant language, an NGO discourse, in fact, has emerged that is perfectly suited to securing repeated funding but is devoid of any meaning or substance insofar as prevailing or emerging conditions on the ground are concerned. Local actors and NGOs use terms such as "empowerment," "transparency," "capacity-building," "dialogue," "peace," and "confidence-building" with great mastery because these are what Western funders want to hear and because they are generally seen as notions central to progress in resolving the conflict. In the meantime, the erasure of Palestinian identity in east Jerusalem, across the West Bank's Area C, and throughout Israel proper continues unabated; the size and infrastructural and institutional depth of settlements continues to expand; restrictions on the movements of Palestinians becomes tighter; and Palestinian areas become more isolated from one another.

Proliferation and professionalization has not necessary resulted in the NGOs' greater accountability or transparency to those other than their funders. Although most Palestinian NGOs tend to have professional staff members, the selection of their directors often lacks transparency and is noncompetitive, reinforcing a general image that they are run by and are the preserve of a small, Western-oriented elite.[141] The World Bank found that most Palestinian NGOs are more concerned with "vertical accountability" to their boards, their foreign funders, or the PNA than with "horizontal accountability" to their constituents and the communities they serve.[142] An earlier study of sixty Palestinian NGOs, conducted in 2001, found a marginal role by their boards, top-down decision making across the board, little participation by employees or the "target group" in decision making or setting priorities (due to passivity or lack of competence), and an internal governance structure that was "a mirror reflection of the Palestinian political system based on individual decision-making, patronage and clientelism." Internal procedures and dispute settlement within the NGOs were done in "a way far away from the rule of law."[143]

In some ways, Palestinian civil society took a very different turn in Gaza than the one it took in the West Bank. In each territory, associational life generally reflected the pervading social and cultural landscapes, a life that was more overtly religious in Gaza as compared to the West Bank. Most Gazan civic associations and home-brewed NGOs, therefore, tend to be Islamist in their outlook and orientation. Not coincidentally, Gazan NGOs by and large tend to have more-robust and more-meaningful ties with the social actors they target than do many of the NGOs in the West Bank. In fact, whereas after Oslo the PNA sought to absorb the youth into the security forces, Hamas focused on the creation of a religious and cultural framework within which community development would take place. The ensuing personal identification was a result of involvement in community and civic affairs rather than employment in the bureaucracy.[144]

During periods of weakness, civic activity became the key to the Islamist social institutions' self preservation.[145] These institutions are popular, particularly in Gaza, because they "provide islands of normality and stability in a sociopolitical context of chaos, dislocation, and pain." Moreover, because of their work at the grassroots level, they were effectively creating "a cultural private sector that felt familiar and safe to Palestinians in an otherwise rapidly evolving, confusing, and oppressive environment."[146] Hamas clearly taps into and benefits from the religious orientation of these Islamist civic associations. But it does not have a clear political input into their operations or their ideology.[147]

Clearly, the prevalence of associational life in general and NGOs in particular has had profound consequences for Palestinian politics. More specifically, NGOization has, paradoxically, created a sociopolitical environment that has become supportive of—or at best apathetic toward—the PNA and its authoritarianism. Prior to the Oslo Accords, associational life gave Palestinians a voice and the vision to end the occupation.[148] In the pre-Oslo era, often for purposes of self-protection and in order to circumvent restrictions imposed by Israel, Palestinian political factions frequently disguised themselves as social organizations, often with as many as four organizations in any locale devoted to the same issue (women, sports, students, and so on).[149] During the Oslo years—from 1993 to 2000—the social sector emerged as a key actor in seeking accommodation and negotiation with the dominant, largely secular institutions and arrangements of the PNA.[150] But, as it turned out, instead of being a source of checks and balances on the PNA, Palestinian NGOs have inadvertently emerged as a source of stabilization for the ruling system.[151]

Several developments account for the paradoxically supportive relationship between societal NGOization and PNA authoritarianism. To begin with, the World Bank reports the existence of a generally positive cooperation between the service NGOs and the PNA.[152] The two have a mutually reinforcing, beneficial relationship with one another. Service NGOs get support and assistance from the PNA to perform some of the functions that PNA institutions are meant to provide—especially in the areas of health care, education, and skills training—which in turn alleviates some of the pressure on the PNA. Insofar as issue-driven and advocacy NGOs are concerned, early on in the 1990s the PNA developed a multipronged strategy to silence, co-opt, and marginalize them. As soon as it could, the PNA began monitoring associations, demanded access to a portion of their funding, and started playing a more-visible role in associational life itself.[153] It created "local" institutions to compete with NGOs for World Bank funding, accused many human rights organizations of being foreign agents and of acting against the "national interest," and even arrested and imprisoned some well-known human rights figures.[154] Before long, associations saw their role as one of either supporting the PNA or, alternatively, trying to get around its authoritarianism.[155]

But the NGOs themselves have helped foster an environment that is conducive to authoritarian perseverance. The dynamics of state-building in the post-Oslo period brought about a fragmentation of NGOs rather than resulted in the formation of "sustainable networking."[156] In postconflict circumstances, in their effort to address glaring shortcomings in service delivery, NGOs can aid in the de-governmentalization of the state and therefore inadvertently work to undermine state-building.[157] This has partially occurred in the Palestinian case, albeit under different conditions, whereby NGOization has transformed the Palestinian national agenda from a struggle for self-determination into a project for donor funding.[158] Following the economic devastation of the Al-Aqsa Intifada, international economic assistance went from 5:1 in favor of economic development to 7:1 in favor of crisis management. Humanitarian aid in turn reduced the Palestinians' own productivity.[159] But it also brought a measure of "professionalization" into Palestinian NGOs by forcing them to learn how to play the funding game, pushing them to adopt the correct jargon and ensuring that they were compliant with the criteria of donor agencies. This was taking place against a backdrop of "global war on terror" and hypervigilance by U.S., EU, and UN funders not to finance groups designated as terrorist organization by the United States or Israel. Professionalization, in sum, turned the NGO movement into one of the mainstays of the status quo and a source for the further demobilization and depoliticization of Palestinian society.[160]

"The road to hell," the saying goes, "is paved with good intentions." NGOs mean well, and more often than not they perform critical functions that states cannot or will not perform. Across the Arab world, for example, including in Palestinian territories, a whole variety of NGOs have emerged that deal with women's issues, such as health, legal literacy, education, income generation, and rights advocacy.[161]

But there are also unintended consequences to the work and especially proliferation of NGOs, especially as they cease being components of civil society and instead turn into ordinary organizations chasing Western funding. In these cases they actually begin to undermine their very own mission and vision, helping maintain social and organizational fragmentations and, in the process, also the political status quo. In the specific case of the women's movement, in Palestine (and elsewhere in the Middle East) NGOization has not necessarily resulted in empowerment but has actually had a negative impact on the mobilizing potentials of mass-based women's organizations.[162]

In Palestine, NGOization has helped sustain and has reinforced depoliticization. The NGOization of Palestinian society has made it far less political, and the leadership of the NGOs tend to be averse to and detached from mainstream politics.[163] With the increasing ascendance of the PNA and Fatah, and also Hamas, most politically minded Palestinian middle classes exchanged direct political party activism for involvement in NGOs and grassroots organizations. And the NGO language they speak is more for the sake of securing funding rather than affecting social change or rebuilding the Palestinian nation.

Conclusion

Nations are not formed or destroyed easily. They are forged through centuries and generations of common experiences, glued together through common lore and a sense of common belonging, an "imagined community" of individuals who, like their ancestors, feel bound to a piece of territory, or at least its idea, through shared symbols, experiences, means of communication, and meanings. As such, neither internal divisions nor statelessness are by themselves sufficient to bring about a nation's demise. Even under great adversity, nations endure.

But contexts and conditions do matter, as do leadership and internal developments, in making some nations more cohesive than others, more amenable to some developments than others, more dynamic and spirited than others. The same nation may also exhibit different features and symptoms over time depending on its leadership and its circumstances, its internal forces, and the different contexts in which it may find itself at different times.

The Palestinian nation has experienced its share of drama over the past several decades. In the late 1940s and again in 1967 it went through processes of ethnic cleansing. It experienced dispossession, dispersion, and exile. In the 1970s it saw revolutionary armed struggle, *thawra,* as a means of overcoming tradition and embracing modernity.[164] By the 1980s it had discovered the efficacy of grassroots activism and associational life, "shaking off" the occupation at the street and local neighborhood levels in the West Bank and Gaza. Euphoria set in in the 1990s as the intifada forced Israel to concede self-autonomy and a blueprint for eventual statehood through the Oslo Accords, followed by violent anger and frustration a decade later, when promises of peace and sovereignty brought only more-constrained circumstances, political authoritarianism, continued geographic separation, and stultified and self-serving leadership both at the official and the local levels. Today, two decades later, anger has given way to resignation, and hopes for a better future are replaced by desperation to hang on to the little that is there.

Today, the Palestinian nation endures. But just barely.

5

The Travails of State-Building

In January 2008, Ahmed Qurei, known as Abu Ala', who had served as the prime minister of the Palestine National Authority from 2003 to 2006, outlined the vision of a Palestinian state: "a state that has adequate land space that is geographically contiguous and is able to absorb all civilians of whom refugees are a part. Such a state will have the respect of its neighbors and will have full control of its own water resources, borders and holy places. It has also to be capable of developing its own economy."[1] A longtime Fatah operative with impressive revolutionary credentials, Qurei's realistic assessment was no reflection of the reality of Palestine as it exists today. Instead, he was outlining the essential ingredients a Palestinian state would need if it were to succeed, ingredients that Qurei and other PNA stalwarts have failed to produce since the Oslo Accords were signed. Today, more than two decades after the first handshakes took place and negotiations started, the reality of a Palestinian state remains as elusive and remote as ever. As previous chapters have shown, Palestine's geography is torn and truncated, and its nation is fragmented and scattered. This chapter focuses on Palestinian state-building, a process and a project, as we shall see, in as much disarray and as stalled as the other facets of Palestine's life.

There are two essential components to state-building: institutional engineering and political consolidation. Revolutions and wars of national liberation afford actors the opportunity to create political institutions anew and to outline their nature, functions, and interrelationships with one another in a constitution. These institutions are then consolidated both domestically, in relation to society, and internationally, in relation to other states. Put differently, institutional engineering entails creating institutions and outlining their power relationships to one another and to society, often, but not necessarily always, in a constitutional document. Political consolidation involves the operationalization of those institutions over time, not always according to plan, but in a way that gives the new power arrangement resilience over time.

Palestinian state-building and all it entails has been taking place within the context of ongoing negotiations with Israel, which started in 1993 and which as of 2015 continue to unfold. But negotiating with Israel has not been an easy feat. The Palestinian "negotiating team," made up almost entirely of Fatah insiders, has been negotiating in the belief that the other side remains interested in a Palestinian state of some sort as an eventual outcome of the talks. Palestinian negotiators appear oblivious, either out of conviction or willful ignorance, that for the Israeli government the negotiations are a low-cost means of maintaining a dynamic status quo of expanded settlements and increasing truncation of Palestinian territory. Thanks to leaked transcripts of the negotiations, we now know that beginning in 2008, Palestinian negotiators were willing to give up all settlements except for one in east Jerusalem, and in 2009 they were also willing to give up on the Palestinian right of return save for ten thousand refugees and their families.[2] Saeb Erekat, the chief Palestinian negotiator, is quoted as having said in January 2010: "what is in that paper gives them the biggest Yerushalaim in Jewish history, symbolic number of refugees return, demilitarized state. . . . What more can I give?"[3] But the more the Palestinians have conceded, the less they have received in return.[4] More than two decades after the signing of Oslo, the Israelis and Palestinians are still defining what the core issues are.

For the Palestinians, negotiating with Israel has also meant having to contend with the heavy hand of the United States. This has ranged in everything from convening the meetings and setting the agenda at a minimum to going so far as to drawing up suggested maps and listing actual villages and neighborhoods to be given to one side or another. To say that the United States has consistently taken Israel's side in the conflict is to state the obvious, a point of pride in U.S. foreign policy since the earliest days of Israel's establishment.[5] What is worth bearing in mind is that the American factor has also been an important dynamic in the Palestinian state-building process, not just geographically and territorially, but also institutionally and politically. It is well known, for example, that the United States has consistently refused to take a strong stand against Israel's continued expansion of settlements, merely calling it "unhelpful."[6] According to released transcripts of meetings between Israeli, Palestinian, and American negotiators in the mid- to late 2000s, U.S. officials consistently sought to compel Palestinian negotiators to moderate their demands on the issue of settlements.[7] In addition to influencing the overall direction of negotiations, American officials have sought to shape the very contours of Palestinian institutions. Palestinian state-building has not just unfolded under conditions of occupation. It has occurred within the context of overt and direct interference by both Israel and the United States. In 2004, President George W. Bush was viewed as having gone so far as to endorse Prime Minister Ariel Sharon's minimalist vision of what a future Palestinian state would look like.[8]

The institutional foundations of what a Palestinian state-entity would be were laid in the Oslo Accords, the terms of which were overwhelmingly if not entirely determined by Israel. Institutional path dependence then kicked in, and the PNA's evolution assumed a life of its own, resulting in institutional proliferation. But neither the weight of the occupation nor the consequences of regular outside interference—whether directly or indirectly through donor dependence—have since been far from the PNA's operations. In November 2008, for example, a senior U.S. official is quoted as having pointedly said that "the new U.S. Administration [of President Obama] expects to see the same Palestinian faces [President Mahmoud Abbas and Prime Minister Salam Fayyad] if it is to continue funding the Palestinian Authority." A year later, Secretary of State Hillary Clinton was equally blunt: "Abu Mazen [that is, President Abbas] not running in the election is not an option—there is no alternative to him."[9]

Consequential as outside factors have been, Palestinian statebuilding, or lack thereof, has been equally a product of domestic factors indigenous to the PNA and intra-Palestinian politics. Present at birth, Arafat and his "Leadership" cadre oversaw the creation and proliferation of multiple institutions and the increasing empowerment of some over others. Law-and-order mechanisms were established, a parliamentary body was set up, ministries were created, and laws were enacted. State-building, momentous and historic in scope, was well underway.

But, as this chapter shows, such was not to be. I argue here that when the Israelis couldn't derail the Palestinian state-building process—and try they did, ceaselessly—the PNA did it itself. In fact, one may go so far as to argue that the process was doomed even before it got off the ground. The new Palestinian order had a hard time effecting a smooth and incremental transition from being a revolutionary movement to becoming one of a "state" and a civil society.[10] The PLO's liberation struggle had earlier resulted in a process akin to state-building, which had led to a proliferation of offices and the use of nationalism as a legitimizing instrument. But because the PLO did not actually have a territory to govern, and because of the international and regional milieus within which it found itself, the ensuing state-building process was highly distorted.[11] Arafat had steered the national liberation movement with great skill, but also with a fair amount of manipulation and maneuverability, protecting it as much from internal splits as from outside control and international machinations. The habits and practices he picked up along the way stayed with him in the post-Oslo period—Arafat was no Mandela— and reverberated through the institutional growth and operations of the PNA.

The PNA, of course, and its internal dynamics and travails, went above and beyond the personality and preferences of Arafat. There were deeper structural forces that shaped the contours and evolution of the growing Palestinian polity. Those revolutionary and national liberation movements that endure and survive internal and external challenges, as the PLO had done, are meant to destroy, not to construct, and their aims are overthrow and capture rather than the construction and governance that follow victory. Successful revolutionaries are gifted in the art of revolutionary struggle, not necessarily in the intricacies of state-building and governance that follow their ascent to power. As a national liberation movement engaged in armed struggle, the PLO had in the process grown wary of administrative, civilian, and social organizations needed to form a state. From the very beginning, this did not bode well for the process of state-building in Palestine.[12]

Mostly unaware of the PNA's limited authority and purview, Palestinians of the West Bank and Gaza initially greeted the PNA with considerable enthusiasm, many seeing it as an emerging state.[13] Not everyone was equally enthused, but there were, after all, no viable alternatives to the PNA, Fatah, or Arafat. Imperfect as it was, the state-building process retained enough mass popularity, at least initially, to keep the PNA's critics at bay.[14]

But, as is so often the case in Palestinian history, the moment of enthusiasm was just that—a moment. The facade did not take too long to unravel. Given that most senior appointments went to the PLO's top cadre that had been based in Tunis, it soon appeared as if the PNA was engaged in "state-building from the outside."[15] According to the Palestinian social scientist Khalil Nakhleh, all talk about state-building was (and remains) a myth perpetuated by the PLO and the PNA. Palestinian state-building, he argues, died at birth.[16] Within less than five years of the signing of Oslo II, by 1999, it became clearly evident that the Israeli-Palestinian accord had been nothing but a temporary agreement. In the meanwhile, Arafat insisted on giving the PNA the trappings of the state. He adopted the title of president (*al-rais*) and dropped his long-held designation of chairman (of the PLO). The PNA instituted an honor guard, flew a flag, and composed a national anthem, and the red carpet was spread for visiting dignitaries. Ministries were established, and a Palestine Legislative Council was inaugurated. But in reality the ministries had no meaningful power, and the PLC, whose functions were spelled out in detail in the Oslo Accords, was meant more as a gathering forum for purposes of discussion and consultation rather than an actual legislative body. Nakhleh's dark assessment, in sum, is not far off the mark.

This chapter chronicles Palestine's halting steps toward state-building, beginning with its efforts to devise political institutions and to articulate workable arrangements between them. This started through institutional engineering and the drafting of a constitution, consolidating power and making political institutions functional and relevant in relation to one another and to Palestinian society, and exercising, as much as possible, a limited form of sovereignty and whatever autonomy there was to be had. But state-building processes go beyond merely devising institutions on paper or even issuing permits and enforcing laws. They are also deeply political processes embedded in the interactions between a nexus of state organs with social forces and dynamics, on the one side, and the state as an actor of some agency with other states, on the other. This chapter shows that the state-building process in Palestine has been fraught and deeply skewed, a product as much of its own missteps and internal dysfunctions as the stifling context within which it has unfolded. Today, twenty years after Palestinian state-building started in earnest, the resulting outcome—the Palestine National Authority—is no more than a mere administrative machinery for the limited governance of a few urban clusters and some scattered rural communities. It is neither efficient nor democratic, with little legitimacy and widespread assumptions of corruption and nepotism. Spinning its wheels in seeming futility, the PNA has made the realization of a viable Palestinian state a more-distant rather than a more-realistic possibility. Not surprisingly, today a deep political morass grips Palestinian society.

Institutional Engineering

Institutional engineering in Gaza and the West Bank has involved several key, interrelated ingredients. They include, in roughly chronological order, the Oslo Accords; the actual creation and establishment of institutions; attempts at constitution-writing; the efforts, modi operandi, and priorities of Yasser Arafat and his close coterie, known as the Leadership; the largely abortive work of the Palestine

Legislative Council; the rise and nature of the Palestinian security forces; and the nature and efficacy, or lack thereof, of the Palestinian judiciary. As foundational seeds of a Palestinian state, these combined elements came to determine the overall nature and direction of PNA institutions, their relationship with one another and with West Bank and Gazan societies, and the overall extent to which the PNA was or was not consolidated.

The Oslo Accords constituted what may be called a "critical juncture." A critical juncture, as mentioned in chapter 1, is a historical turning point, "a major event or confluence of factors disrupting the existing economic or political balance in society. [It] is a double-edged sword that can cause a sharp turn in the trajectory of a nation."[17] Critical junctures present leaders with an opportunity to make choices that have lasting consequences and that constraint the range of subsequent choices available in the future.[18] As such, the Oslo Accords laid out the foundational premises of state-building in Palestine. But, as we have seen, the scope of such an endeavor was exceedingly small and narrow. The institutional arrangement that emerged out of the Accords—the Palestine National Authority—was heavily restricted in what it could and could not do. Even at the initial signing of the Oslo Accords, PLO insiders themselves were aware of the formidable challenges they would face, especially insofar as their ability to represent and defend the rights of Palestinians were concerned.[19] Even these insiders appear to have known that the foundations they were laying were wrong-footed from the very beginning.

Apart from the institutional limitations they contained for Palestinian self-rule, there were several consequences to the way the Accords were presented to the Palestinians. According to the social scientist Khalil Nakhleh, there were no attempts to explain Oslo to the people, as if people were irrelevant. "It was a deal to allow Oslo elites to come back, as if it weren't a concern of the people. The agreement was never explained or defined except in the broadest of terms, much less being put to a popular test through a referendum. The general assumption was that it was leading to a two-state solution. It was never explained that the West Bank would be divided into three areas and that one of the areas, C, comprising 64–65 percent of the West Bank, would be off limits."[20] Instead, the myth of statehood was being sold to the Palestinians, who, after decades of occupation, were only too eager to believe in the heroic diplomacy of Arafat and his comrades. Arafat's eagerness to call himself president (al-rais), have an honor guard, and to assume for the PNA the trappings of the state gave Palestinians the impression that the fledgling authority was indeed a state or at least a state-in-the-making. But these cosmetic trappings were only skin-deep, with little or no substantive significance. The facts on the ground soon started pointing to a very different reality. The Oslo Accords, as one Palestinian entrepreneur put it, were soon seen as a platform to create a security cooperation between the Israelis and the Palestinians and, as much as possible, to outsource the occupation through the PNA. Oslo, in reality, had a "security only" agenda.[21]

The Palestinian state-formation process started in earnest in 1993 but was halted with the Al-Aqsa Intifada of 2000 and then reversed and suffered setbacks with Israel's reoccupation of the West Bank in 2002. The series of state institutions that evolved from 1993 to 2000 contained a number of paradoxical features.[22] Palestinians started asking questions around 1999, as the deadline for the so-called final-status negotiations approached and it became clear that a two-state solution was nowhere within reach. This was exacerbated by Ariel Sharon's statement that if there is ever a Palestinian state, it will be within only 10 percent of the West Bank.[23] Within this context, unlike the first uprising, the eruption of the Al-Aqsa Intifada in September 2000 was proceeded by far more planning than the earlier one. This intifada was directed as much against the Palestinian leadership as it was targeted at Israel. Whatever hope for a Palestinian state remained was effectively dashed in 2002, when Israel reoccupied the West Bank after a series of Palestinian suicide bombings. The reoccupation did much to dismantle, or at the very least to set back, the process of institution-building by the PNA.[24] By then the foibles of the Oslo Accords and the internal decay of the PNA had become painfully apparent for most Palestinians.

A big part of the problem, as we shall see shortly, was the person of Yasser Arafat, who was in many ways the PNA's founding father. During the liberation struggle, Arafat had been able to keep decision making within the PLO relatively independent and autonomous. With relatively consistent success, he was able to fend off or even to neutralize the multiple pressures that were brought to bear on the organization by various international and regional actors. But when it came to the PNA, he largely failed to enable institutions so that they would outlast and outlive him. Within the PNA, decision making, delegation of authority, and staffing and personnel decisions all remained highly personalized and were made only by Arafat. Only after Arafat's departure from the scene did many of the PNA institutions that had been established earlier assume much significance.

Moreover, the return of the PLO under the rubric of the PNA brought with it many of the tribal practices that had marked the politics of the organization in its years in exile. Not only did Fatah refuse to share power with Hamas, it refused to share power within the PNA.[25] As president of the PNA and head of the PLO, Arafat used his dual position to outmaneuver his critics.[26] Arafat picked cabinet members based on factional quotas rather than considerations of merits or qualifications. He would often ask PNA ministers to hire relatives or friends of those who asked him for employment. "Arafat's concern was to place people. He didn't say 'no' and most recruitments were based on loyalty."[27] He used ministries as gifts and as means to strengthen his base of loyal supporters.[28] As a result, the PNA civil service grew astronomically, but without a commensurate growth in effectiveness or efficiency. Public services still lagged, and the delivery of even the most basic service, such as securing a driver's license, often took a frustratingly long time.

Part of the problem lay in the fact that there was no governance precedence in the Occupied Territories. In addition to the occupation authorities and their regulations, there had, of course, been a variety of local administrative mechanisms that had grown, or been imposed, in relation to local needs and demands. But in many respects the PNA still found itself having to fill multiple administrative and governmental vacuums. This made it necessary for the PNA and especially Arafat to make and interpret the day-to-day rules of governance.[29] One of the first tasks, therefore, was to draw up a constitutional document, a "basic law," that would outline the fundamentals of a political system and serve as a signpost for its operations. Thus ensued the first iteration of the Palestinian Basic Law, which was "perhaps the most carefully-crafted and liberal constitutional document in Arab history."[30]

Palestinian constitution writing had actually occurred on a number of previous occasions—in 1948 and 1988—and the exercise was repeated again in 1996 and 1999. Nevertheless, Palestine still does not have a recognized constitutional framework, and the leadership remains ambivalent about pursuing it further.[31] Arab constitutional thought and legacy often exercised great influence—not always positively—on various drafts of the Palestinian Basic Law.[32] There was an attempt to remedy this with the drafting of another document in 2003, this one far more detailed and with a more-diffuse executive power. But even the 2003 draft failed to meaningfully liberalize the PNA's emerging preference for centralized power. When it suited him, Arafat simply ignored constitutional limitations on executive authority.[33] To this day, the relevance of constitutional development to Palestinian politics remains questionable.[34]

Efforts at institutionalizing the PNA through the Basic Law notwithstanding, the process of institution-building soon assumed a dynamic of its own. The PLO cadre, and especially Fatah insiders, moved in quickly to establish dominance over emerging PNA institutions. As early as the late 1990s, Palestinian observers were writing the obituaries of storied Palestinian liberation organizations, such as the Popular Front for the Liberation of Palestine (PFLP) and the Democratic Front for the Liberation of Palestine (DFLP).[35] Soon after the formation of the PNA it became obvious that it directly overlapped with Fatah, and at times the PNA cabinet was hardly distinguishable from the PLO Executive Committee.[36] Fatah dominance was further ensured by the fact that several prominent independent Palestinian personalities refused to join the PNA's twenty-four-member cabinet, while a number of ministers, frustrated by their lack of power and authority, threatened to resign.[37] PNA ministries, meanwhile, went from fourteen in 1994 to twenty-three in 1996, and thirty-three in 1988. At some points there were more than seventy-five public bodies answering to Arafat.

Dislocation, dispossession, exile, and loss of identity encouraged an obsession with rhetoric and symbols at the expense of effective or even functional organizations.[38] And symbolism was one of Arafat's strong suits. But for governance and decision making, he also relied on a small inner circle of trusted allies, which came to be known as the Leadership (*al-qiyadah*). The Leadership was a little-understood cabal around Arafat that met and made key decisions. Its membership expanded and contracted at different times and supposedly included the heads of the various factions within the PLO, as well as other notable "Tunisians." According to Nakhleh, it acted as a control mechanism for Arafat. There was no independent decision making on the part of the Leadership, but rather it was simply a rubber stamp that validated the decisions made by Arafat. Arafat's control over the Leadership was cemented through patronage. The status and wealth of members of the Leadership depended directly on their position within the PNA and in relation to the person of Arafat. Their salaries, officially furnished cars, mobile phones, allowances, and the many other perks of office all depended on their perceived loyalty to Arafat.[39]

The arrangement naturally lent itself to both the reality and perceptions of nepotism and corruption. From the very start, in fact, the PNA faced charges of corruption, leading to widespread dissatisfaction among Palestinians, especially those in Gaza.[40] At the very least, under Arafat the PNA's operations often featured strong elements of both patrimonialism and neopatrimonialism, with the former relying on the dispersion of resources and privileges to buy political legitimacy, and the latter overlaying the informal social structure of patrimonialism with the formal and legal structures of the state.[41] Significantly, Palestinian neopatrimonialism is not simply a product of tradition. Rather, it is an outgrowth of social change, attempts to manage political fragmentation, and efforts aimed at addressing immediate political and organizational imperatives.[42] According to Rex Brynen, neopatrimonialism in the Palestinian polity had earlier emerged within a context of inadequate charismatic leadership, multiple social and political divisions, and the need to use resources and the granting of privilege in order to hold together a dominant political coalition.[43] The strong neopatrimonial undercurrents of Lebanese politics had further reinforced neopatrimonial tendencies within the Palestinian movement during the PLO's years of exile in Lebanon.[44] There had also been considerable incentive within Fatah to use patronage to mobilize supporters and to counteract centrifugal forces within the PLO and the broader national movement.[45] These same patterns found their way into the PNA.

In addition to neopatrimonialism, a number of other political dynamics also soon took hold within the PNA. In the formative 1993–2000 period, for example, the process of state formation did not witness a corresponding increase in state tax collection or meaningful accountability of the state to the electorate.[46] Prior to Oslo, a viable Palestinian political opposition never really existed, and if it did, its mandate revolved around specific issues. The concept of opposition had no space within the PLO system. Because of this, once the PNA was formed, neither the PNA nor the opposition knew how to relate to the other nor to operate in the new political environment.[47] The PNA soon started engaging in routine violations of human rights, often detaining opponents for perceived infractions. Before long, the Authority was accused of resorting to torture and clamping down on free expression and on the media. The PNA's authoritarianism continues to this day. Ambiguity over what is and what is not politically permissible has also resulted in considerable self-censorship among many Palestinians subject to PNA rule.[48]

It is worth bearing in mind that in Palestinian politics, two deep structural problems inhere, one being the authoritarian political context within which it operates, and the other the purely administrative nature of PNA institutions as necessitated by the extent and pervasive nature of Israeli occupation.[49] The PNA's ability to pursue a menu of policy alternatives is limited by a variety of structural factors, such as the fact that its budget comes mostly from abroad, by pressure from the United States, by the structural realities of Israel's occupation, and by pressures coming from multinational institutions such as the World Bank and the International Monetary Fund.[50] This was exacerbated by the fact that Israel's control over West Bank economy and diplomacy, as well as control over the movement of labor and goods, became much more formalized and extensive after the Oslo Accords.[51]

To environmental and exogenous restrictions imposed on the PNA were added a host of internal contradictions. The system that was set up contains tensions and facilitates the emergence of parallel authorities that can use institutional resources to exercise negative power in order to balance each other out.[52] Administrative confusion and paralysis were quick to set in within the PNA shortly after its formation.[53] Whatever governing and administrative capacity the PNA had acquired in its early years were completely destroyed by Israel during the course of the Al-Aqsa Intifada.[54] Much of the lost capacity has been recouped since, but the preexisting contradictions and constrictions have continued. Neither its institutional path dependence since, nor deliberate tinkering to it have addressed or ameliorated the PNA's inherent tensions and contradictions. One of the most significant of these contradictions is the division of executive power between the offices of the president and the prime minister. The presidential-parliamentary system facilitated the emergence of a condition of "dual authority," which in turn led to the Fatah-Hamas rupture along institutional lines.[55]

Initially, PNA insiders appear to have genuinely believed that negotiations with Israel will ultimately result in the establishment of a Palestinian state. But within a few short years of its establishment, the Authority's institution-building efforts suffered one blow after another. Compounding the shock of the Al-Aqsa Intifada was Israel's 2002 reoccupation of the West Bank. Arafat, increasingly frail and physically besieged in his compound, spent the last months of his life simply trying to hang on to what had been achieved. From the very beginning, the Oslo process had been characterized by a disregard for deadlines.[56] By November 2004, when Arafat died, the premises and promises of the Oslo Accords were also long dead. By then, even the election of the popular Mahmoud Abbas as the PNA's new president in January 2005 could not reverse the slide in the Authority's popularity. A year later Hamas decided to take part in the elections that were held for the Palestine Legislative Council, and garnered more than 44 percent of the vote compared to Fatah's 41 percent. Gaza's break with the West Bank was not long in coming. As Gaza–West Bank tensions continued to simmer amid an international boycott of Gaza, in June 2007 Hamas forces took over Gaza and dismissed Fatah officials. What had begun as an attempt at institution-building had ended up in a small-scale civil war and Palestine's further fragmentation.

In June 2007, in an attempt to inject new life into the process of institution-building, Abbas appointed former finance minister Salam Fayyad to the premiership, a post in which Fayyad remained until June 2013. Fayyad's tenure in office is often considered one of intense institution-building on the part of the PNA. The most urgent task was seen as the empowering of national institutions in order to reverse the deterioration of their role in the decision-making process.[57] In reality, however, Fayyad only succeeded in polishing some institutions and breathing life into a few others. But he did not, and could not, succeed in establishing new ones.[58] Insofar as the development of Palestinian institutions is concerned, some have indeed experienced limited progress. Many others, however, have continued to undergo regression since they were first established.[59]

One of the institutions that experienced progressive atrophy soon after its establishment was the Palestine Legislative Council. From early on, in fact, the PLC failed to achieve its two main objectives of executive oversight and enacting substantive legislation.[60] Much of the reasons for this marginality revolved around contextual and structural dynamics beyond the control of the PNA or the PLC itself.[61] From the beginning, both Israel and Arafat were opposed to elections for the Palestine Legislative Council and did what they could to undermine it.[62] Israeli authorities went so far as to frequently harass elected deputies and often blocked those residing in Gaza from attending PLC meetings in Ramallah.[63] Moreover, within the PNA structure itself, PLC members had no leverage, and Arafat simply ignored them when he felt like it. The PLC's repeated efforts to institutionalize procedures that would help buttress democracy were also repeatedly blocked or undermined by Arafat.[64] Arafat saw himself as a member of the PLC and at times even sat in the speaker's chair.[65] While the PLC won some initial symbolic battles against the PNA in the early days, the executive branch soon started simply ignoring the PLC—ignoring requests for information, ministers not showing up for their sessions, and so on—and some PLC deputies were even attacked by the security forces at one point inside the PLC building.[66]

For its part, the PLC sought to increase its capacity and capabilities but kept losing control and influence within the PNA, making noise without affecting policy.[67] The Palestinian media also largely ignored the PLC and often failed to cover the spirited debates inside the chamber.[68] The PLC remained marginal so long as it was business as usual within the PNA, thus guaranteeing Fatah's near-complete political hegemony. But, insofar as the Fatah-Hamas competition was concerned, the PLC did remain a potentially important institution to compete over. Thus, when Hamas decided to field candidates in the 2006 PLC elections, Fatah was put on notice. And the electoral defeat handed to Fatah was punishing: of the 132 seats contested, 74 went to Hamas and only 45 to Fatah. The election results pointed to a significant Islamization of Palestinian society.[69] But, even more so, they showed levels of popular disenchantment with Fatah and the PNA in general. Hamas's victory was as much a protest vote against Fatah as it was a result of Hamas's promise to clean up the corrupt establishment and to deliver results.

Similarly constrained has been the functioning of the PNA's judiciary, which has had to grapple with several structural difficulties since its establishment. In particular, the judiciary often lacks physical protection and does not have adequate facilities and court buildings, and court sentences are rarely effectively implemented. The existence of armed factions and militants has kept the Palestinian judiciary weak, leading to the emergence of an alternative judicial system. In fact, dispute resolution through means other than the judiciary have become commonplace, especially in cases of the security services, whose exact legal jurisdictions are often not quite clear.[70] The legacy of the past also continues to loom large on the Palestinian judiciary. Prior to the PNA's establishment, the West Bank and Gaza had a confused mélange of legal systems, with Egyptian law predominant in Gaza, Jordanian law in the West Bank, and leftover Israeli Emergency Laws from the pre-Oslo period in both Gaza and the West Bank.[71] When it was established, similar to a number of other nondemocracies in the Arab world, the PNA laid down an authoritarian legal framework. To give itself a freer hand and greater maneuverability, the PNA kept in place the military orders that had been issued by the Israeli occupation authorities from 1967 to 1994, reviewing them individually to determine which ones to keep and which ones to abandon.[72]

For over two decades of its operations, the PNA has yet to adequately address a number of shortcomings within the judiciary. The judiciary continues to be plagued by personal and institutional rivalries, and the security services continue to operate outside the law while also interfering in politically sensitive cases.[73] Restrictions on the judiciary, and a concomitant concentration of power within the executive, continue unabated. In fact, the PNA's inability to devise and implement a coherent policy has resulted in a number of extrajudicial killings of suspected collaborators by vigilantes.[74] Due to backlogs and perceived inefficiency, the PNA has gone so far as to enhance and formalize alternatives to the court system, thereby further undermining its autonomy and independence.[75] Under the premiership of Salam Fayyad (2007–2013), courts in the West Bank became more efficient and more widely used, but political interference in their operations and their decisions continued.[76] To this day, the judiciary continues to be the stepchild of the PNA.

The institution that is not a stepchild is the police force. The formation of the PNA was soon followed by a proliferation of different security forces, all armed and all with wide-ranging powers.[77] From the start, the incorporation of the Palestine Liberation Army into internal security structures hampered the democratic impulse of the PNA and strengthened the likelihood of a democratic deficit.[78] Arafat had to deliver on security, but in the absence of other institutions was reluctant to see his security chiefs become too powerful or popular. He therefore set up multiple police agencies, giving the police-to-population a ratio of 1:75, one of the highest in the world.[79] Reliable estimates on the size of the Palestinian security forces are difficult to obtain. In the West Bank, they are generally estimated to number around 23,000–24,000. There is a roughly equal number of Hamas paramilitary forces in the Gaza Strip. The West Bank is also thought to have an additional police force of around 8,000.[80] There are multiple security agencies under the PNA umbrella, all of which further reinforce the centralization of authority.[81] Soon after its establishment, the PNA also established a State Security Court designed to handle politically sensitive cases. The SSC was "audacious and brazen" even by the ruthless authoritarian standards of the Arab world, often passing summary sentences and silencing PNA and Arafat critics with ruthless efficiency. During the Al-Aqsa Intifada, the SSC was brutal in punishing suspected collaborators.[82]

One of the central premises of Oslo, namely the notion of "security first," led to the centralization of the PNA's executive and therefore increased the potential for militarization at the top.[83] The PNA has taken steps to guarantee the militarism of the police force rather than preventing it, by deliberately blurring the lines between responsibility for civilian policing and internal security.[84] More than 97 percent of the PNA's security-services personnel are thought to be affiliated with Fatah and are loyal to Fatah leadership.[85] Not surprisingly, the Palestinian security sector tends to be highly politicized and remains under the dominant political control of Fatah, suffering from what some have called a "feudalization of institutions."[86] Despite their growth in numbers, however, the security forces often lack professionalization and even adequate training. According to one estimate, some 99 percent of members of the Palestinian police force initially lacked knowledge of policing.[87]

In the security sector, the PNA continues to face a number of structural difficulties, including recruiting and training personnel, defining ranks, and setting salaries and bonuses. More importantly, the Palestinian leadership has not devised a comprehensive security vision, often confusing the needs of the state with those of Fatah.[88] Although the security sector remains one of the most robust of the PNA institutions, the degree to which it has facilitated the PNA's institutionalization remains uncertain. Its seemingly uncontrollable growth and expansive powers have helped undermine the PNA's legitimacy, and, by virtue of their function, they have been at the forefront of the Hamas-Fatah split. Whether and to what extent they help or hinder Palestinian state-building remains to be seen.

Combined, the PLC, the judiciary, the security forces, and Arafat and his Leadership cadre constituted the institutional infrastructure of the PNA and, along with it, the emerging foundations of a potential Palestinian state in the future. The ensuing process was highly skewed in favor of the executive and the security forces, steadily strengthening the dominance of Fatah at the expense of other political tendencies and groups. As Fatah was painfully reminded in January 2006, however, institutional dominance did not necessarily mean political legitimacy or electoral popularity. As the emerging system went about consolidating itself—that is, making itself operational in relation to social actors and groups—its institutional features and the environment within which its emergence was occurring both had consequences for Palestinian political life and state-building. It is to an examination of these dynamics that the chapter turns next.

Political Consolidation

The institutional development of the PNA has had a number of consequences for Palestinian society in Gaza and the West Bank, of which four stand out. First, the PNA has directly influenced the political economies of both Gaza and the West Bank, particularly at the macro level in terms of trade, taxation, employment, and the general size and economic health of the various classes. Second, as a supposed state-in-the-making, the PNA has directly shaped Palestinian perceptions about politics and political institutions. Rightly or wrongly, Palestinians widely perceive the PNA to be corrupt and inefficient. This has directly led to a third development, namely the empowerment and resilience of an anti-Fatah political front in the form of Hamas. Fourth and finally, political economy, assumptions of corruption, and the longevity and operations of Hamas, especially in Gaza, have combined to turn the PNA from a would-be state into an administrative organ that is feared and tolerated, not one that is seen as the hope of the future. Not surprisingly, the state-building process has been stalled and has not moved forward.

As we have seen, state formation in Palestine has been severely curtailed by external constraints. By far one of the biggest constraints has been in the evolution, or lack thereof, of Palestinian political economy. By controlling Palestinian fiscal revenues, Israel sought to ensure that if a Palestinian state ever emerged, it would be a client one. Palestinian leaders, for their part, accepted Israeli control over the economy.[89] Nowhere is this more apparent than in the signing and enforcement of the Paris Economic Protocol, the PEP, which Israel and the PNA signed in 1994 as part of the Oslo Accords. Meant to last only five years when it was signed in 1994, the PEP has regulated economic interaction between Palestine and Israel ever since. The protocol represents "an unbalanced power structure" as "Israel can allow itself noncompliance with the [agreement] without having to fear negative repercussions."[90] The PNA's calls for renegotiating the PEP have been repeatedly rejected by Israel.

The PEP has turned out to be one of the most consequential aspects of the arrangement between Israel and the PNA. Foundational as it was, the PEP failed to strengthen Palestinian sovereignty and instead ceded to Israel control over labor movement, trade, economic integration, and, indirectly, macroeconomic policy making.[91] The Protocol has greatly constrained the economic viability of the PNA, and is open-ended enough to allow Israel to contain the Palestinian economy. The PEP gave Israel tax-collection authority and severely restricted the scope of trade for the Palestinian economy by prohibiting the PNA from negotiating its own trade agreements. Moreover, the possibility of a Palestinian currency was ruled out.[92] According to the PEP, Palestinian value-added tax (VAT) cannot be more than 2 percent lower than the Israeli VAT, and the difference between fuel prices cannot be greater than 15 percent. When VAT and fuel prices change in Israel, they therefore also have to change in the West Bank.[93]

The Protocol also stipulated that Israel would collect customs duties on all goods exported to Palestinian territories. But Israel only placed duties on goods directly imported from abroad by Palestinian companies, not on goods that were first imported to Israel and then from Israel to the Palestinian territories, which, for security reasons, comprised the bulk of the imported goods. Moreover, Israel would often transfer to the PNA only a third of what it collected from Palestinian customs.[94] In 1995, a year after the signing of the PEP, this amounted to some 6–7 percent of the Palestinian gross domestic product.[95] All import charges that came to Palestine indirectly via Israel were paid to Israel but were not always refunded to the PNA. The annual loss of revenue represented 78 percent of the refunded amount in 1997.[96] Additionally, the PEP gave Israel control over most if not all commodities entering Palestine.[97]

The PEP not only promoted an Israeli monopoly over Palestinian trade, but it also created Palestinian monopolies and provided the PNA with access to rents. This in turn enabled the PNA to foster the rapid growth of a politically dependent Palestinian middle class. This growth was facilitated by the expansion of the PNA and the growth of NGOs. By some accounts, the percentage of the Palestinian middle classes doubled from 11 percent before the signing of the Oslo Accords to 22 percent after its creation. If self-employed artisans and shop owners are also considered, the percentage goes up to 30–40 percent of the total employed.[98] But this is a middle class whose status depends overwhelmingly, if not entirely, on its relationship with the PNA and the salaries and contracts it receives from the Palestinian Authority. Significantly, these same restrictions, seizures, and extractions that limited autonomous Palestinian economic activity also made it impossible for a politically independent Palestinian national bourgeoisie to emerge within the West Bank.[99]

Initially, when the PNA was established, there were a number of optimistic scenarios about its economic development. Some observers went so far as to call for the PNA's transformation into a developmental state that would facilitate conditions for rapid and far-reaching infrastructural and economic development. But it soon became obvious that several factors impeded the potential emergence of the PNA as a developmental state, the most important of which included territorial fragmentation, the leadership's use of state resources for purposes of factional patronage, and an absence of full control over policy making.[100]

For its part, the PNA has pursued a dualistic economic policy, on the one hand fostering statist economic policy, while on the other hand also promoting private investments, especially by individuals high up within its own bureaucracy.[101] As of 2014, the PNA had approximately 160,000 civil servants on its payroll, including in the security services. The PNA also transfers around 45 percent of its budget to Gaza for salaries of public employees, providing medical and health-care services and improving education. In return, Gaza's contribution to PNA revenues went from 28 percent before the Hamas takeover in 2007 to 2 percent after the takeover.[102] Nevertheless, the PNA remains responsible for the salaries of some 77,000 civil servants and security officers on the public payroll in Gaza. Moreover, a majority of the 90,000 families that get direct cash transfers from the PNA are located in Gaza.[103]

A number of other structural factors also constrict the potential growth of the Palestinian economy. From the very beginning, Israel ensured the sustained vulnerability of the Palestinian economy by control over its finances and tariff revenues. Checkpoints within the West Bank allowed Palestinian labor mobility to be at the mercy of Israel.[104] The Al-Aqsa Intifada, meanwhile, resulted in a drying up of foreign investment and brought the Palestinian economy close to collapse.[105] The West Bank–Gaza split and the contraction of the Israeli labor market to Palestinian day workers have added additional burdens to the PNA. Some thirty thousand employees of the PNA security forces in Gaza continue to get paid although they are no longer working.[106] There are also few and finite domestic sources of income for the PNA. As a quasi state, the PNA has had no access to its own natural resources.[107] Direct taxes account for only 7 percent of the PNA's revenues, and, perhaps largely as a result of its close nexus with wealthier Palestinian industrialists, especially compared to the situation in Jordan and Egypt, the Authority has levied low corporate taxes on Palestinian corporations.[108]

Assuming that the establishment of monopolies would facilitate large-scale investment in infrastructural projects and accelerate economic development, the PNA made a calculated political decision to encourage the establishment of monopolies. Monopoly owners in turn protected their interests by forging close financial ties with PNA officials.[109] The emergence of some monopolies was a rational reaction to the consequences of the PEP.[110] As a result, the PNA became not just a source of employment but indeed of wealth for many officials with connections. In the early 2000s, PNA officials were believed to control approximately twenty-seven monopolies, including steel, wheat, meat, wood, paint, building materials, livestock feed, cement, flour, fuel, gravel, cigarettes, cars, computers, TVs, and household appliances.[111] Some even created monopolies for their children, wives, aunts and uncles, and other relatives. In addition to blatant nepotism, there have been persistent rumors of protection money and bribes meant to oil the wheels and speed up contracts and the other procedures involved.[112]

Despite its limited wealth generation, the PNA has failed to devise rent-management strategies that would enhance the economic and political viability of the state.[113] Initially, to strengthen Arafat's hands in dealing with his adversaries and to make the Oslo Accords stick, Israel deposited part of the official tax remittances into a special account controlled only by Arafat and his closest advisors.[114] Although Israel at times denounced the secret accounts of the Palestinian Leadership, it was fully aware of them and denounced them only when it suited its purposes.[115]

The president in turn used these rent revenues to consolidate his position, often at the expense of the middle classes. These rent handouts ranged from access to offices and official cars to VIP cards and appointments of party cadres to public office.[116] Arafat is long gone. But the political economy of rent-dependence on which his authority and that of the Leadership rested continues to this day.

Significantly, the PNA's economic failure goes beyond its inadequate management of rent revenues. More fundamentally, because of Israel's policies of land confiscation, closures, sieges, and its intensification of colonization activities, the PNA has been unable to produce a developmental vision based on cooperation with Israel. Nor, because of its dependence on donor money and international financial assistance, has it produced a developmental vision based on resistance to and struggle against Israel.[117] This might be easier said than done, since the Palestinian economy remains "totally dependent on Israel for its electricity, international communications, fuel, almost all of its cement and more than 40 percent of its water."[118] More consequentially, the PNA remains heavily dependent on donor aid for its fiscal sustainability, receiving some $1.5 billion in budget support in 2010 alone.[119] Since its establishment in 1994, in fact, the PNA has not been able to have fiscal viability without donor support.[120] Donor support for employment-generating schemes unwittingly allowed for the bloating of the bureaucracy and the spread of rent-seeking and patronage practices.[121] Not surprisingly, the Authority has been running a chronic budget deficit for a number of years.[122] In the long run, PNA fiscal sustainability is highly unlikely unless there is a political settlement.[123]

The Palestinian economy remains in shambles. Between 2010 and 2011, for example, real wages in the West Bank fell by 3 percent, and Gaza continues to remain in recession. Between 2009 and 2012, meanwhile, prices in Palestine increased by 13 percent.[124] To most Palestinians, their economic predicament is as much a product of PNA failures and corruption as it is a result of Israel's occupation. Overwhelmingly, the PNA is seen by Palestinians as corrupt and made up of a small, isolated elite. Among Palestinians, there is a perception that the PNA suffers from widespread corruption, routinely abuses the rights of Palestinians and arbitrarily curtails their liberties, and is used for the personal interests of specific individuals.[125] In 2012, fully 50 percent of Palestinians expressed dissatisfaction with the performance of President Abbas in office.[126]

Perceptions of corruption within the PNA have been strengthened by the vast extent of structural deterioration and the massive and unnecessary increase in the number of employees on the PNA's payroll.[127] In a 2012 poll, 71 percent believed there was corruption in the PNA institutions of the West Bank, and 58 percent of Gazans viewed the public institutions of Hamas as corrupt.[128] According to a report by Transparency International, also issued in 2012, while perceptions of corruption remain high among Palestinians, few actually experience petty bribery. Nevertheless, corruption in sectors with monopolistic features remains a major concern.[129] In particular, the forms of corruption that had characterized the PLO—most notably nepotism, favoritism, and political allegiance—continue to remain in the PNA. *Wasta* (nepotism), not unlike elsewhere in the Middle East, remains by far the most pervasive form of corruption within the PNA.[130]

To rectify its image problem and combat instances of corruption, in recent years the PNA has made significant improvements in areas such as the rule of law, government effectiveness, regulatory quality, and control of corruption. However, suspicions of corruption, particularly widespread among Palestinians in the early years of the Oslo, continue to remain strong.[131] These suspicions are not altogether misplaced. Reforms in the areas of land management, transparency in licensing, and access to public information have largely stalled.[132] The use of government vehicles for personal purposes remains a problem.[133] Some university presidents are said to run their universities as if the university were "a family feudal possession."[134]

Hamas capitalized on these widespread perceptions of PNA corruption to enhance its own popularity. Over time, with the increasing irrelevance of other opposition parties, Hamas was left as the only viable alternative to Fatah. There are currently eight political factions or political organizations in Palestine. They are, to the left of the Palestinian spectrum, the Popular Front for the Liberation of Palestine (PFLP), the Democratic Front for the Liberation of Palestine (DFLP), the Palestinian Democratic Union (FIDA), and the Palestine Peoples Party (PPP). The religious parties include Hamas, Islamic Jihad, and Hizb ut-Tahrir. And then there is Fatah, which has also lost much of its legitimacy as a once-popular revolutionary organization. A bastion of resistance before the Oslo Accords, it has now become dependent on PNA salaries, paid mostly with donations that come from the United States and the European Union.

The secular opposition has no clear program and faces a deep organizational crisis.[135] Whereas the PFLP and the DFLP opted for "contained opposition" in line with the PLO system, Hamas and Islamic Jihad were not bounded by traditional limits and pursued goals that were fundamentally different from those of the PNA in relation to Israel.[136] In recent polls, Fatah and Hamas are just about equally (un)popular. Both have an approval rating of about 34–35 percent in the West Bank and Gaza.[137] Part of this lack of popularity rests on assumptions of corruption on the part of both parties. But equally important appears to be the fact that all Palestinian political factions, both on the right and the left, appear to have lost touch with their respective constituents. More specifically, they seem unaware of important shifts within their electorate. For example, there appears to be increasing support for nonviolent activism, and 26 percent of Palestinians say they would support a one-state solution.[138] But Palestinian political factions are far from endorsing anything remotely similar.

Besides the PNA and Fatah, Hamas deserves special attention. It would, of course, be a mistake to assume that Hamas operates in a social and political vacuum. As we have seen, the twin demands on the PNA of ensuring Israel's security and instituting a system with a democratic resemblance were incompatible and often led to its institutional paralysis, thus facilitating the rise and popularity of Hamas.[139] This popularity occurred within a context of growing religious sentiments among many Palestinians prior to the outbreak of the intifada. From 1967 to 1987, there was a significant growth in the number of mosques in the Gaza Strip and the West Bank, therefore increasing support for the Muslim Brotherhood.[140] Once founded, Hamas was deliberate in its efforts to institutionally tap into popular religious sentiments. In the post-Oslo period, in fact, in the face of attacks from the outside, from Israel, and from the inside, coming from the PNA, Hamas concentrated on institution-building, especially at the grassroots level.[141] After the second intifada, when the Palestinian nationalist movement split into a populist nationalist strand represented by Fatah, and a populist Islamist strand represented by Hamas, Hamas was well positioned to make its move.[142]

Hamas's political ascendance needs to be understood within the context of the occupation and changes to Palestinian nationalism. Whatever its Islamic underpinnings, Hamas is essentially a nationalist organization.[143] There have been three phases, or faces, of Palestinian nationalism, corresponding to the pan-Arabist movement of the 1950s, the secular nationalism of Fatah of the 1970s, and Hamas's religious nationalism of the 1990s and the 2000s. Each nationalism started out with maximalist goals of reclaiming all of historic Palestine but had to modify them under the impact of overwhelming Israeli power. The apparent failure of each phase of nationalism was followed by the ascendance of the other. The movement of Arab nationalism, as heralded and headed by Gamal Abdel Nasser, gave way to the more nationally focused Palestinian nationalism of Fatah, followed by the religious nationalism of Hamas.[144] As Sara Roy argues, "Hamas's fundamental impulse is political and nationalist, not religious, which has accounted for its pragmatism and flexibility."[145]

Although tense from the start, it took some time for Fatah-Hamas relations to degenerate into open conflict. Regardless of how much it was harassed or its members were jailed, Hamas initially refused to see the PNA as the enemy, largely because of its adherence to Palestinian nationalism.[146] It was only after the Hebron massacre of February 1994 that open clashes between Hamas and the PLO erupted.[147] With Hamas's victory in the 2006 PLC elections, the United States and Fatah tried to shift power away from the PLC to the executive under the presidency of Mahmud Abbas.[148] Reflecting the PNA's lack of institutional depth, this was soon a moot point, as the Fatah-Hamas break resulted in a complete rupture between the West Bank and the Gaza Strip.

After Hamas's takeover of Gaza in June 2007, its security force, the Al-Qassam Brigade, transformed itself from an underground guerrilla organization into a uniformed military force designed to protect Gaza from outside attacks and augmented its military arsenal. It upgraded the tunnel system used to smuggle weapons from Egypt, and reinvigorated the Al-Qassam Brigade's command and control structure.[149] Ironically, Hamas's efforts to solidify its rule over Gaza were aided by the sharp reaction its victory elicited from the United States, the European Union, Israel, and the PNA. For its part, Israel has sought to restructure Palestinian politics through its "assassination policy" in order to facilitate the rise of Palestinian moderates at Hamas's expense. By one count, in the mid-2000s, Israel was killing on average two Hamas activists every week.[150] But the killings, coupled with the ensuing destruction of Gaza, have only perpetuated Hamas's popularity.

The United States' and European Union's withdrawal from Gaza further significantly reduced their leverage over Hamas. According to a 2008 report by the International Crisis Group, the policy of isolating Hamas and sanctioning Gaza has backfired and is politically "bankrupt," having resulted in a further consolidation of Hamas over the Strip.[151] This is despite the facts that not everyone within Hamas supported the takeover of Gaza and that the move exacerbated tensions within the movement.[152] Nevertheless, despite its comparatively reduced level of popularity as a result of the takeover, Hamas has since established an effective monopoly over the use of force in Gaza.

Hamas has a short- and a long-term program. In the short term, the organization seeks to bring about change and reform to Palestinian institutions, such as the security sector and the bureaucracy and also in the area of Palestinian finances and economy. In the long term, Hamas's goal is to foster the Islamization of Palestinian society through especially the educational establishment and by fostering Islamic cultural practices. Hamas's vision of Palestine's future consists of only one state, one that is Islamic. In the interim, it sees the possibility of a "truce" with Israel, but only for tactical purposes and until it can regain all of Jerusalem as the capital of Palestine.[153] Hamas has readied itself for the active promotion of *hudna* (armistice) with Israel, whereby it would retain long-term claim to all of historic Palestine and Jerusalem as well as the right of return. For many Palestinians, this is an attractive alternative to the PNA's compromising stance.[154]

Given the dire predicament of most Gazans and the ready potential for the growth of Salafi jihadism, Hamas has emerged as a bulwark against further radicalization and social breakdown in Gaza.[155] A number of factors underlie the potential growth of religious militancy and radicalism in both the West Bank and Gaza. Although

Hamas's roots in the Muslim Brotherhood movement bring the organization closer to mainstream political activity, its decision to take part in the 2006 PLC elections alienated some of its more-extremist members and facilitated the potential growth of jihadist tendencies in the Occupied Territories. The existence of an organizational vacuum for opposition is also important, as are the manifold failures of the PNA to address regressive slides in many areas of Palestinian life over the last several years.[156]

For an increasing number of Palestinians, Hamas's rejection of PNA accommodationism does not go far enough. The Muslim Brotherhood has long viewed the *reform* of Arab society as a primary task, and only then, once properly Ismalicized, is society sufficiently prepared for jihad. Hamas's success was initially facilitated by its concentration on incremental reform of social and cultural values.[157] Given the steady deterioration of living conditions in Gaza and the worsening of Palestinian life in general, it is not clear to what extent and for how long Hamas's incremental approach will continue to hold sway among a people with increasingly less to lose.

Hamas's precarious popularity in Gaza is mirrored by a similar predicament on the part of the PNA in the West Bank. For most Palestinians in the West Bank and Gaza, the establishment of the PNA was the first opportunity they had to observe the PLO leadership at work. They quickly realized that PNA leaders were not as pristine as they had generally assumed and that the quality of the Leadership left a lot to be desired. These negative perceptions were reinforced as Oslo's failure became increasingly more evident, and the PNA was seen more as an outsourcing security organ rather than a meaningful form of authority.[158] According to a 2010 poll, 40 percent of Palestinians go so far as to support dissolving the PNA.[159] Sam Bahour, a public intellectual and political activist based in

Ramallah, estimates that Hamas and the PNA each have support among approximately 20 percent of Palestinians, with the remaining 80 percent being largely politically apathetic. The young remain by and large skeptical of both Hamas and the Fatah, seeing both as means of elite enrichment and as "gimmicks."[160] Fatah was unable to win the April 2013 municipal elections, losing ground to independent candidates, who scored a number of victories. Given a choice, most people would vote for neither Hamas nor Fatah, but would instead prefer freelance, nameless independents. The young are especially skeptical of organized parties and their platforms, weary that their aspirations will once again be hijacked.[161]

Within this context, it is all but meaningless to talk of a Palestinian democracy. In a 2010 poll, 65 percent of Palestinians in Gaza and the West Bank feared expressing criticism against the PNA, and a similarly high number, 66 percent, feared criticizing Hamas's authority in Gaza.[162] In 2012, 67 percent of Palestinians felt they lived in an undemocratic system.[163] As Anne Le More stated back in 2005, "the PNA regime was built with international funds at the cost of democracy, transparency, accountability, the rule of law and respect for human rights. Not surprisingly, although it has survived, it has today lost much of its legitimacy and popularity."[164] The warning back in 2006 by Ziad Abu-Amr, a PLC member, has today turned out prophetic: "If this experience of democratization fails, the Palestinians will have lost an historic opportunity to establish a new democratic entity. It also could mean the diminishing of international sympathy and support for the Palestinian quest for democracy and statehood."[165]

From early on, a number of prominent Insiders were warning about the erosion of civil liberties and the PNA's resorting to undemocratic practices.[166] The PNA had turned into an authoritarian governing mechanism by 1999, a condition that has more or less continued up until today. Palestinians today live in an environment of little democracy and accountability and of weak institutions.[167] Writing in 2010, Nathan Brown's conclusions may be blunt, but they are spot on: "Palestinian democracy has simply come to an end in both halves of the PA. The president's term has expired, the parliament's term is also expired, no new elections are in sight, elected local officials selectively dismissed, and local elections have been cancelled. Opposition supporters have been ousted from the civil service and municipal government and their organizations have been shattered."[168]

None of these dynamics bode well for the consolidation of party politics or, for that matter, for the PNA itself. A majority of Palestinians today feel disconnected from political parties, and a steady "de-politicization of the Palestinian discourse" has taken place.[169] In the process, most Palestinians have turned away from organized political parties, many of which have dissolved themselves into NGOs anyway. Today only a handful of political parties have been left standing, including Fatah, Hamas, and the more-radical Islamic Jihad. Some smaller parties have tried to coalesce into the Third Way, but they have not proven to be an effective political force. Most Palestinians, meanwhile, believe that Israel has allowed a weakened PNA to continue to exist in order to exonerate itself from various responsibilities to Palestinians under international law.[170]

There continue to be a number of unresolved issues in Palestinian politics. Most notably, there are persisting ambiguities concerning transformation from a movement to an established polity, ideological inconsistencies, and differences in political practice, none of which are likely to be overcome in the near future. Since the PLC has ceased to function, beginning in 2008, the president has been ruling by decree and therefore further alienating the PNA from its Palestinian constituents. The president himself has been ruling without an electoral mandate since 2009, when his term in office expired. He has been ruling by fiat ever since. PNA cabinet reshuffles, and even the change of PNA prime ministers, are today hardly noticed and discussed by the general public.[171] To maintain that Palestinian state-building has stalled is to simply state the obvious.

Stalled State-Building

Earlier in the chapter, at the risk of splitting hairs, I introduced a distinction between a territorial and an administrative conception of the state. The Palestinians, I argued, see a potential future state in territorial terms, whereas the Israelis are at most willing to concede a highly constrained, administrative version of it. By now it should be clear that neither of these conceptions is likely to become a reality at any time in the future. Despite its declared commitment to ongoing negotiations with Israel, even within the PNA there is growing recognition that a territorial Palestine is now out of reach. In the 2000 Camp David negotiations, Palestinians were offered 65 percent of the West Bank, in discontinuous enclaves with no international boundaries. Among what remains of the Israeli "peace camp" today, there is broad agreement that a future Palestinian state would not be based on the 1967 borders but on approximately 55 percent of the West Bank, that it would include six large settlement blocks, and would be broadly based on borders delineated through the Separation Barrier.[172] The PNA is also keenly aware that without Gaza a Palestinian state would not be viable as a territorial entity; by itself, the West Bank is landlocked and has no access to the high seas, whereas Gaza would provide such an access.[173]

PNA insiders may be hopeful and optimistic, but they are not stupid. They know their predicament. According to confidential documents and transcripts of their negotiations with Israelis, they were quite willing to compromise with their counterparts on what would constitute the fundamentals of a state.[174] At some point they even proposed to take in Israeli settlers as citizens of a Palestinian state and to let them continue to live in their settlements.[175] These negotiations have been ongoing at a time when most Palestinians see them as pointless. In a 2010 poll, two-thirds of Palestinians in both Gaza and the West Bank wanted the PNA to halt negotiations with Israel until the construction of further settlements stopped.[176] No matter how much the Palestinian negotiating team has been willing to compromise, Israel has not halted the rapid pace of settlement building. What the Palestinians have gotten in return is a drop in donor support. Foreign assistance to Palestine went from 28 percent of the GDP in 2008 to 21 percent in 2011, declining from $1.8 billion to $1.1 billion.[177] Helpless and at the mercy of others, the best the Palestinian National Authority can do is to plead for more. The public intellectual and entrepreneur Sam Bahour aptly describes the PNA as "autonomy minus."[178]

With negotiations not going anywhere, the PNA is slowly distancing itself from territorial conceptions of Palestine. According to Khalil Nakhleh, to sell its vision of what a future Palestinian state would look like, the Leadership wants to drop all references to historical Palestine, and it has seen to it that this is the case in Palestinian schoolbooks and in other official documents. The PNA has been downplaying and de-emphasizing historical Palestine, its shape, boundaries, and what it looked like. Instead, it wants to sell a vision of Palestine as a group of small, isolated city-states—Ramallah, Bethlehem, Nablus, and so on—that need neither a president nor a premier but an effective CEO.[179]

Within this context, PNA statehood has come to depend on four mutually reinforcing components. They include public security and the rule of law, building accountable institutions, effective service delivery, and private-sector growth.[180] While implicit in all four components, the notion of territoriality is pushed into the background. The assumption here is that what the PNA lacks in territorial sovereignty it will make up for through what may be broadly labeled as "economic peace." The trade-off proposed by economic peace is that a nonsovereign Palestinian statelike entity may bask in the economic growth of Israel and may even have some economic growth of its own, but in return it will have to postpone or effectively give up its quest for statehood.[181] As such, "the statehood program encourages the idea that citizens may have to acquiesce in occupation but will not be denied the benefits of smoother running traffic, a liberal education curriculum, investor-friendly institutions, efficient public service delivery, and, for the middle class, access to luxury hotel chains and touring theater performances."[182]

As we have seen, however, even administratively the PNA has failed to live up to its promises. The years since the West Bank–Gaza split have seen Hamas become more deeply entrenched in the territory it controls, Fatah in deep disarray, and Palestinian society in despair.[183] The Occupied Palestinian Territories today display all the conditions of state collapse, most notably institutional decay and degraded governance, breakdown of social networks and pervasive violence, widespread resort to the clan and extended family, and sharia-based reconciliation committees for conflict resolution and ensuring security.[184] The PNA itself suffers from deep paralysis, a product of the legacy of Arafat's "debilitating" neopatrimonial management, the marginalization of the PLC, the fragmentation of Fatah, and Israel's policy of border closures.[185] As the veteran Palestinian observer Yezid Sayigh has commented, "the Palestinian state-in-the-making is in the throes of systemic collapse." What we have in

Palestine today, he warns, is "an inherently degenerative status quo" that cannot indefinitely be sustained.[186] Instead of tangible progress toward state-building, there has actually been a regression in law and order and the exertion of central authority in many parts of Gaza and the West Bank. By 2006–2007 central authority had deteriorated to the extent that a number of jihadist groups appeared and started attacking Internet cafes and foreign cultural centers. At around the same time, by early 2007, Gaza appeared headed for "Somalization" and "Iraqization."[187] For now, Hamas appears to have reasserted itself, and, under the rubric of a religious dictatorship of sorts, it has prevented Gaza from slipping into civil chaos. There have also been reports of scattered Salafi-jihadi attacks in the West Bank. If current social, political, and economic conditions in the West Bank and Gaza continue, there is a real possibility that Al Qaeda–type religious radicalism and militancy may spread across the two territories.[188]

For now, Somalization and Iraqization appear mercifully distant possibilities insofar as Palestine is concerned. But what is also a distant possibility is a Palestinian state, whether territorially or administratively. As Nathan Brown has observed, there are "deep problems afflicting Palestinian politics," not the least of which are division, nepotism, occupation, alienation, and far-reaching institutional decay.[189] None of these show signs of dissipating or improving in the near future, making the future of Palestinian politics likely to be more of the same rather than in any way more positive.

Conclusion

At their core, states are made up of three key elements: institutions, individual leaders, and people. The order in which each of these elements becomes consequential varies from case to case and depends largely on the stage of the state's evolution. Initially, at the moment of birth, states are established by leaders who act as founding fathers and who set out to create mechanisms and ground rules for control and power generation. In doing so, they create institutions anew but are also often bound by institutional structures and practices that may have already been in place. Once created and in place, institutions assume a life of their own, shaping and constraining the menu of choices available to political leaders. Leaders, of course, are leaders of a people, a community without whom leadership, institutions, and states would not exist.

In Palestine, all three elements exist. But they exist only separately. And they exist in conditions that do not coalesce into the construction of a viable state.

The PNA is meant to be the institutional framework of the Palestinian state. But despite two decades of autonomy and supposed institution-building, Palestinians are today further rather than closer to forming a state.[190] For most Palestinians the PNA is not much more than a municipal government, one that has no meaningful power, no capacity, and no clearly defined economic policies. The PNA also has no clear development agenda—politically, economically, or otherwise—nor has it fostered any meaningful development in the West Bank and Gaza. It is an administrative apparatus built on favoritism, rentierism, and Israeli manipulation.[191] As one academic and activist commented emphatically, "the PNA is a subcontractor for Israeli occupation, no more, no less—a subcontractor."[192]

The Palestinians' frustrations boiled over in 2011 in a mini Arab Spring of sorts. A wave of protests swept across the West Bank in March 2011, July and September 2012, and November 2012. Triggered by sharp rises in food and fuel prices, protests took place in

Ramallah, Bethlehem, Hebron, Nablus, Jenin, Tulkarem, and Jericho. In an earlier poll, conducted in 2010, two-thirds of Palestinians had felt protests were necessary since people were unable to improve their lives in the future.[193] In response to the 2011 protests, the PNA announced price cuts and salary freezes for top officials, and Israel issued five thousand additional permits to Palestinians to work in Israel. The protests subsided, not because the protestors' demands were met, but because of a sense of resignation that is pervasive across the territories. The PNA almost completely lacks popularity. But there is also an awareness that there is no alternative to it, that it remains the only game in town. Not surprisingly, there is no groundswell of rebellion against the PNA. Ultimately, the PNA remains the only way to chart a future.

Whether or not there are yet leaders who will come to the rescue is a question only history can answer. The Middle East has seen its share of liberators and messiahs in the past and is likely to see them again in the future. Palestine may yet have a Nelson Mandela of its own. In fact, the activist and former Fatah insider Marwan Barghouti is often considered, by Palestinians at least, as the Mandela of Palestine. Despite being imprisoned by Israel since 2002 and out of the public eye for more than a decade, in public-opinion polls Barghouti consistently scores higher than either Mahmoud Abbas or Hamas leader Ismail Haniyeh in a possible presidential race.[194] Earlier, when he first assumed the PNA's presidency, many also saw Abbas as the hope of Palestine's future. Upon assuming the presidency, Abbas sought to introduce "ceasefire, reforms, and negotiations," all of which were initially popular. But, insofar as the United States was concerned, this was not enough of a shift within the PNA. The United States wanted nothing less than a "de-Arafatizing" campaign similar to the de-Baathification of the Iraqi regime after its invasion of Iraq in 2003.[195] Abbas's tenure in office is bound to come to an end. Such an eventually, however, is unlikely to change Palestine's predicament and fate. Ultimately, whatever leader Palestine produces, or whoever the Palestinians uphold as their next savior, will have to contend with the forces and institutions currently in place, not the least of which are the Israeli occupation and the U.S. shadow over the Israeli-Palestinian conflict, as well as, of course, the realities of both the PNA and Hamas.

State-building in Palestine, in sum, is today only a distant dream, a process hijacked by the avarice of political competition and personal ambition, derailed by the cold realities of occupation and territorial loss, stalled by the decay and atrophy of institutions.

6

The Road Ahead

Prolonged intercommunal conflicts often have an ebb and a flow, at times swinging in favor of one side or the other. Since its start, the Palestinian-Israeli conflict has seen a steady withering and erosion of Palestine and all things Palestinian. There has been no swinging of the momentum from one side to the other, no back-and-forth switch in the fortunes of the two sides, with the only ebb and flow present in the degree and intensity of Palestine's dismantling. This conflict, now well more than a century old, has been decidedly unidirectional, going from victory to victory for the Israelis and from defeat to defeat for the Palestinians. The Palestinian catastrophe, the Nakba, did not end in 1948. That is when it started. Israel's policy of "silent transfer" continues, some years more, some years less. Today there is no land for Palestinians. As one Palestinian activist put it, "even if Israel's crimes are forgotten, the question of 'where will I live?' has no answer."[1]

Part of the problem has been the fact that the moral discourses within which the conflict has been embedded have been so foundationally different for each of the sides, with literally no common ground, no matter how slim, where they would intersect. The Israeli narrative has been one of divinely sanctioned redemption, reclamation, the righting of a profound historical wrong compounded over millennia by successive generations of anti-Semites and usurpers.

According to this narrative, the birth, consolidation, and territorial expansion of Israel, which started before 1948 and continues to this day, is the righting of this historical wrong. Justice is finally within grasp.

But for Palestinians, what has befallen them is the precise opposite of justice. It has brought them dispossession, exile, homelessness, confinement, and robbed opportunities. It has dismantled their society, brought their nation to the verge of extinction, placed them at the mercy and avarice of others, and has today confined them to what are at best noncontiguous chunks of land with little water and little potential. This, for Palestinians, is the very meaning of injustice. Daily life, as lived experience because of and through Israel's existence, is fundamentally unjust.

History, it is often said, is written by the victors. So are notions of right and wrong, just and unjust. According to the Israeli academic Ilan Pappe, Israel keeps in place a "strong mechanism of denial" meant to defeat Palestinian claims and "to thwart all significant debate on the essence and moral foundations of Zionism."[2] That may well be. But what is more important is that Israeli political thinking lacks the moral and conceptual tools to accept responsibility for the historic injustice committed against the Palestinians.[3] The very meaning of Israeli citizenship is constructed through the negation of Palestinian citizenship.[4] And Israeli citizenship is forged against a backdrop of a history of persecution and the imperative of making sure that bitter history never again repeats itself.

In a tangible sense, this has given Israel a free hand to do in Palestine as it deems fit. As the maestro of the music, Israel is doing what it wants with complete impunity. It has put meaningful negotiations with the PNA on hold while maintaining the facade of continuing to negotiate; it is continuing to increase the number of settlements and completing work on the Separation Barrier; it is working steadily and methodically on expanding its control over Jerusalem; and it frequently attacks Hamas and others in Gaza—as it did in 2003, 2006, 2008, 2012, and 2014—and maintains its closure of the Strip to make sure of Gaza's continued catastrophization. In the meantime, it continues to deal with an "autonomy-minus" PNA on mundane, administrative matters.[5] As of 2014, no less than sixty-three hundred Palestinians were in Israeli prisons.[6] There is little the PNA, or anyone else for that matter, can do to secure their release. Israel does what it likes, all wrapped in a self-reifying moral framework.

Not surprisingly, today there is a palpable mood of resignation among literally all Palestinians. During the course of my research in the West Bank, not one of the intellectuals, academics, activists, students, and entrepreneurs I met or interviewed held out hope of a better future, never mind of a viable and sovereign Palestine. The activist Sam Bahour's assessment of the Palestinian predicament today may be dark, but not far off the mark. "Today," he told me, "as a Palestinian you are either a refugee or on the verge of becoming one."[7]

For years, Arafat and other PLO stalwarts sought to portray successive Palestinian defeats as victories of one sort or another. Great comfort was sought in small steps often overblown and presented as heroic and victorious. The portrayal of defeat as victory not only enabled the PLO to mask bad decision making and poor leadership, but it also made acceptable to Palestinians a story that involved confronting daunting odds. The PLO-perpetuated narrative enabled Palestinians to make sense of a troubled history.[8] But there is only so much that can be explained away in the contradiction between historical myths and actual facts on the ground. Today, the bitter reality of defeat is hard to deny and harder even to twist into some sort of victory.

Palestinians are angry and frustrated, having to choose between a number of equally unpalatable options. There have been and will continue to be various solutions offered for the conflict. We will explore the more commonly discussed ones in the next section. But these are solutions that are national in aim and international in scope. And, perhaps for that very reason, none so far has done anything to reverse the erosion and deterioration of Palestinian life. None deal with the predicament of the Palestinian man and woman on the street. For now, the options that appear most popular among Palestinians are the so-called BDS movement and the mood of anti-normalization with Israel, whereby meetings and other forms of interaction between Israelis and Palestinians is stopped at all levels.[9]

The BDS movement, advocating "boycott, divestment, and sanctions" against Israel, was initially formed in 2005 but gained momentum beginning in 2008, when it came to be led by the National Committee, which represents "the largest coalition of Palestinian civil society organizations inside historic Palestine."[10] Modeled after the boycotts and divestments that were applied to South Africa in the apartheid era, the BDS movement advocates three goals as "the *minimum* of requirements of a just peace": a return to pre-1967 borders (thus recognizing the right of Israel to exist), ending Israel's "system of racial discrimination against its Palestinians citizens," and giving Palestinian refugees the right to return to their homes and to receive reparations. These are all perceived by Palestinians as components of human rights.[11]

Whether the BDS movement will succeed where armed struggle or prolonged negotiations failed is a question that is seldom asked or answered. But it does appear to signal the embryonic start of a new phase in how the Palestinians are approaching the conflict. Back in 2005, Israel's unilateral disengagement and withdrawal from Gaza was seen by two-thirds of Palestinians as a victory for armed resistance.[12] In reality, the move was meant to deepen and solidify Israel's hold over the West Bank. Israel's withdrawal has brought Gazans little relief from precarious existence on the brink of catastrophe. And neither has armed struggle in general brought the Palestinians much tangible, long-term victory now or in the past. As a grassroots, spontaneous revolution, the intifada succeeded in bringing the Israelis to the negotiating table. That the revolution was hijacked by Fatah and derailed by Likud should not take away from the force of its impact on shaking up the status quo, both Palestinian and Israeli. To what extent the BDS movement will succeed in having similar consequences is something that only history can answer. In the case of the intifada, might—Israeli might—ultimately prevailed. Might may not be right, but it does shape history. For now, history is being written at Palestine's expense.

Solutions and More Solutions

Because the conflict started over territory, its solutions are often also perceived in territorial terms. These solutions generally fall into one of three categories. They include a two-state solution, with Israel being inside its 1948–1967 borders, and Palestine made up of the Gaza Strip and the West Bank; a one-state solution, in which the territory between the Mediterranean and the Jordan River is merged into one country; and a Palestinian-Jordanian confederation comprised of a merging of the West and East Banks of the Jordan River into one country. At different times, each of these solutions have been proposed, and at times pursued, with varying degrees of vigor and enthusiasm. None so far has come to fruition, and none, at least for the foreseeable future, shows any signs of ever doing so.

Of these three possible solutions, none has been as advanced or has come as close to fruition as the two-state solution. The idea gained particular traction in the 1990s and the mid-2000s, shortly after Arafat's death, when Palestinians and to a lesser extent the Israelis were both in a compromising mood. According to public-opinion polls at the time, a majority of Palestinians were willing to accept a two-state solution in which Israel would be "a state for the Jewish People" and Palestine "a state for the Palestinians."[13] As late as the 1990s, both Israelis and Palestinians saw at least open economic borders and trade between Israel and Palestine as inevitable due to "the intermingled nature of both populations."[14]

The rise and speedy fall of the two-state solution was made possible by the convergence of several factors. First, there was a determined effort, mounted by the administration of U.S. President Bill Clinton, to bring the two sides to the negotiating table and to use the good offices of the United States to achieve some sort of tangible progress in the establishment of a Palestinian state alongside Israel. Later analyses have shown that what the United States advocated was far from just and equitable for the Palestinians.[15] But at least the much-needed prodding arm of the United States was present and actively involved.

More importantly, the conditions on the ground were less incongruent with the reality of a two-state solution than they are today. And, though by no means universal, enough people on either side saw the two-state solution as a possibility they could live with. At least insofar as the Palestinians were concerned, it was the best and most feasible alternative they could hope for. Support for the two-state solution lay in the belief that it would end the occupation and offer a way to save the remnants of Palestine and Palestinian identity. It gained traction because of its seeming feasibility and the apparent impossibility of a one-state solution.[16] For some, but by no means all, Israelis, the theoretical embrace of the two-state solution lay in the fear of the reality of the alternative. The Israeli push for a two-state solution, especially by center-left and centrist parties such as Labor and Kadima, was—and continues to be—motivated by a fear of the "demographic threat" posed by Palestinians and the challenges inherent in Israel's continued rule over a hostile and growing Arab population.[17]

Significantly, the two-state solution of the 1990s was also the last hurrah of Labor Zionism. Of the three strands of Zionism currently in existence in Israel—Labor, Revisionist, and Religious Zionism—only the Revisionist and Religious varieties capture the public imagination today and hold popular sway. Whereas Labor Zionism is willing to define the "homeland" in terms of the 1949 armistice boundaries, both Revisionist and Religious Zionism see it in terms of present-day Israel, the West Bank and Gaza, and the Golan Heights.[18] Since the late 1980s, a number of structural and political factors have combined to result in the steady decline of Labor Zionism, not the least of which are the changing nature of the Israeli political economy and the decline of labor as a social and political force, and the steady departure from the scene of the older generation of Israeli leaders who were once stewards of the Labor Zionist movement. In many ways, the Oslo peace process signified the last gasp of Labor Zionism, its final act for a State of Israel it had been so instrumental in creating. But the failure to salvage Oslo in the 1990s and in the aftermath of the frantic efforts of 2000 and 2001 signified the slow death of the storied movement. Although shadows of Labor Zionism still linger today, the movement is not nearly the force it once was.

From the start, the internal contradictions of the two-state solution outweighed its promises. Even when the euphoria of statehood was at its height soon after the signing of the Oslo Accords, veteran observers such as Yezid Sayigh were calling for a sober realization of limitations, such as the fragmentation of a possible Palestinian state into noncontiguous pockets, the administrative and juridical consequences of the intermeshing of Israeli settlers with Palestinians, and the ceding of east Jerusalem and limits on the return of Palestinian refugees. Sayigh warned that even if a state were born out of Oslo, it would be a "weak" state in terms of its administrative, political, economic, and military relations with Palestinian society and with other states.[19] A decade later, a comprehensive study of Palestinian statebuilding by the Rand Corporation concluded that none of the conditions for success can be realized unless Palestinian territory in the West Bank is contiguous. "A Palestine of enclaves," the study team stated emphatically, "is likely to fail."[20]

Ten years hence, Palestine has been even more punctured by Israeli settlements, cut off internally from itself so much so that the "Swiss cheese" state that the Oslo Accords sought to establish has become far too fragmented to make sense.[21] Pretending that the conditions of the 1990s still obtain today is not grounded in reality.[22] According to the Palestinian academic Mazin Qumsiyeh, whoever still believes in the two-state solution suffers from either "ignorance or malice." The two-state solution "is a mirage, an illusion, a myth to facilitate what [the Israelis] want to do for consolidation, a myth to consolidate their hold on land [and] to put a wall around Palestine."[23] The author Saree Makdisi is equally blunt. "The age of the two-state solution," he writes, "has drawn to a close."[24]

There are, of course, still those who hold on to the idea of a two-state solution, perhaps because of its psychological comfort of compartmentalizing nations and their troubles into neat, separate categories, or perhaps still out of fear of the alternative. According to a December 2012 poll conducted in the West Bank and Gaza, for example, 52 percent of Palestinians continue to support a two-state solution, while 48 percent oppose it. This does not automatically translate into widespread support for a one-state solution: 71 percent of Palestinians polled oppose such an alternative, while 27 percent support it.[25] Of Palestinians, 63 percent supported and 33 percent opposed a compromise that would finally lead to a permanent status agreement with Israel.[26] Although 60 percent of Palestinians believe that a two-state solution is no longer viable, only 40 percent support dissolving the PNA, and less than 30 percent support shifting the struggle from a two-state solution to a one-state solution.[27] A majority of Israelis and Palestinians continue to support a two-state solution despite the fact that they live with a one-state reality.[28]

These polls indicate a certain level of popular exhaustion, especially among Palestinians. There is increasing awareness that an independent Palestinian state, comprised of the West Bank, Gaza, and east Jerusalem, is a "geophysical impossibility."[29] As difficult and troubling as this reality may be, its internalization is still easier than coming to terms with the alternative. Most Palestinians are painfully aware that their predicament is at best untenable and at worst deteriorating. But what comes next, or what should come next, is not something over which there is any meaningful consensus.

Nevertheless, there are still alarmist voices on both sides that see a two-state solution as the lesser of the evils, especially if the only other alternative is one state.[30] Such alarmism is particularly strong among Israeli intellectuals and policy makers. According to Asher Susser, a professor at Tel Aviv University, the one-state idea does not fully take into account the depth of mutual animosity and the ferocity of the conflict between Israelis and Palestinians. Such a solution, he argues, is ultimately unworkable. It would be catastrophic for Israelis and Palestinians both, and "infinitely worse than the existing malady."[31] The one-state solution is a prescription for eternal strife between the two peoples, and the idea of Palestinianizing Jordan, which he explores at length, is equally unworkable and only leads to a prolonging of the conflict. The only viable option, he argues, is a two-state solution. Imperfect as it is on multiple counts, it is still the only viable option.[32]

The increasing impossibility of the two-state solution has recently prompted a number of observers to explore the possibility and advantages of a one-state solution. As the Palestinian academic Ghada Karmi has put it, "the barriers to thinking the unthinkable have been breached," and today the idea is discussed widely in academic and intellectual circles.[33] One of the earliest, in-depth analyses of the one-state solution was conducted by Virginia Tilley, who back in 2008 argued that a one-state solution is "already an impending reality." She maintained, "Today, no ideology, no planning, no new 'peace process,' and certainly not the snaking apartheid Wall can make sense of carving this small land into two states."[34] For the likes of Tilley and Karmi, a one-state solution addresses the core issues that perpetuate the conflict—land, resources, the settlements, Jerusalem, and refugees—and restores "a land deformed by half a century of division and colonization to an approximation of the whole country it once was, a rejection of disunity in favor of unity."[35]

Sam Bahour, based in Ramallah, sees the advent of a one-state condition as a natural product of the progression of the conflict. There is a generational shift afoot in Palestine, he maintains. Future generations could conceptualize self-determination in terms of human rights and equal access to state services rather than in terms of national liberation and independence. In the not-too-distant future, Palestinians are likely to recognize that they were defeated in their struggle for a national homeland, and that neither the heroics of armed struggle nor the diplomacy of the Oslo Accords and subsequent attempts at salvaging them worked out. Once the struggle for statehood is dropped, then it becomes a struggle for human rights. "You get to have my land and even Jerusalem. Now, where do I sign up for health insurance?"[36]

According to the Israeli scholars Azoulay and Ophir, the "security fundamentalism" of the occupation regime needs to be replaced by a new imagination, a "new utopian horizon," that realizes that the separatist Jewish national vision cannot be sustained in the face of a binational demographic reality.[37] They advocate searching for means of reducing Israeli-Palestinian differences as much as possible—through the work of both civil society organizations and state-sponsored initiatives—in order to foster a "federative framework" for coexistence.[38] Such a solution, as others have argued, can offer a framework of principles to direct a process of reconciliation between Israelis and Palestinians.[39] As one observer has optimistically noted, within the context of a single, binational state, shared religious roots and modes of reconciliation that are integral to all three Abrahamic religions can provide a basis for reconciliation.[40]

The one-state solution can assume two forms, one a binational model, and another a secular-democratic, one-person–one-vote model. Of these two, according to Karmi, the binational model is the preferred option, as it would allow the two separate communities to retain their own religious and ethnic identities. It would address one of the core concerns of weary Israelis in that it would leave room for a form of Zionism to continue.[41] A binational state may be defined as "an arrangement whereby members of both ethno-national communities would enjoy full political rights and the communities themselves, as well as the individuals within them, would be granted prerogatives typical of a pluralist society and based on non-excludability and joint supply and allocation of goods and resources. . . . Each community is given constitutional or other legal and practical guarantees of the freedom to practise its religion, speak its language and observe its customs and traditions."[42]

One of the more-innovative suggestions, also along the lines of a binational state, has been offered by Sari Nusseibeh, the president of Al-Quds University in Jerusalem and an influential figure within the Palestinian community. His proposal is that "Israel would officially annex the occupied territories, and that Palestinians in the enlarged Israel agree that the state remain Jewish in return for being granted all the civil, though not political, rights of citizenship. Thus the state would be Jewish, but the *country* would be fully binational, all the Arabs within it having their well-being tended to and sustained."[43] Nusseibeh's proposal would effectively relegate Palestinians to second-class citizens within the new national entity.

There is, not surprisingly, strong opposition to and numerous obstacles in the way of a one-state solution. For the most part, it is only Palestinian Israelis who are firmly supportive of the idea of bi-nationality.[44] There are deeply entrenched levels of mistrust, ill-will, and grievance between Israelis and Palestinians for the idea to have much meaningful support. For many Palestinians, Israelis have become accustomed to exploiting Palestinian land and resources and are unlikely to easily relinquish the privileges they have acquired over years of dominance.[45] For their part, many supporters of Israel dismiss the one-state idea as "a Western-sounding solution," one that "leaves no room for Israel as a Jewish state, a self-sufficient refuge from persecution, pogrom, and Holocaust."[46] A binational or unitary state, they argue, whether in Israel or in Jordan, "would most probably set the stage for interminable intercommunal conflict and bloodshed."[47]

Another innovative solution has been the so-called parallel states model, which combines elements of the one- and two-state scenarios. This model would include an Israeli state structure and a Palestinian state structure, both covering the whole area of Mandatory Palestine, "with separate heartlands but with soft and porous borders between them. Israelis and Palestinians could each claim their own state with its own special character and identity, but they would complement each other and not be mutually exclusive."[48] The two states may choose to join a defense, customs, or economic union; have a common currency and labor market; and coordinate external border management. With all citizens free to move about and to settle in the whole area, the two parallel states would share sovereignty and political authority, exercising some functions jointly and others separately.[49]

The ideas of parallel states or a one-state solution challenge the whole notion of Israeli identity and its existence as a Jewish state, something that is not lost on the proponents of these and other alternate solutions to the conflict.[50] For Israelis, the "danger of demography" cannot be overstated, as Israelis of all walks of life remain concerned about the demographic problem.[51] According to a 2006 poll, fully 68 percent of Israeli Jews would like to see the Palestinian citizens of Israel "transferred."[52] The idea of living alongside even more Palestinians as citizens of the same country is simply unfathomable. According to Israeli Prime Minister Benjamin Netanyahu, "if the Arabs form 40 per cent of the population, this is the end of the Jewish state. . . . But 20 per cent is also a problem. If the relationship with this 20 per cent becomes problematic, the state is entitled to employ extreme measures."[53]

It is this fear of losing demographic superiority that has dictated much of Israel's position in its negotiations with the Palestinians over the years. In the 2000 negotiations, Israeli negotiators were not al-lowed to even discuss the Palestinians' right of return, which has long been one of the Palestinians' central demands.[54] Israelis are especially fearful that any agreement on the topic would set a precedent for the further return of Palestinians in the future.[55] So far, Israel has not been able to come up with a workable solution to the demographic problem.[56] The only solution to the issue, therefore, has been to sim-ply keep it off the agenda. Surveys among Palestinian refugees have actually shown that only a small minority are interested in exercising the right of returning to the state of Israel.[57] But for Israelis, even opening the door to such a possibility is a nonstarter. A one-state, binational scenario, in which Israelis would live alongside millions more Palestinians without any borders separating them, is even more frightening.

A third, equally impracticable solution to the conflict that has been offered is the annexation of the West Bank to Jordan, an idea most recently expounded on by the Israeli historian Benny Morris. According to Morris, the prospects for a two-state solution are as bleak as they are for a one-state solution, because "the Palestinian Arabs, in the deepest fiber of their being, oppose such an outcome, demanding, as they did since the dawn of their national movement, all of Palestine as their patrimony. And I would hazard that, in the highly unlikely event that Israel and the PNA were in the coming years to sign a two-state agreement, it would in short order unravel. It would be subverted and overthrown in those forces in the Palestin-ian camp—probably representing Palestinian Arab majority opinion and certainly representing the historic will of the Palestinian national movement—bent on having all of Palestine."[58] Morris maintains that due to economic, political, and demographic reasons, a Palestinian state in Gaza and the West Bank is likely to be inherently expansionist. While a two-state solution is just and would present perhaps the best chance for peace, it is unworkable. Morris sees "the only logical—and possible—way forward" that "would blunt the edge of Palestinian expansionist needs and motivations" as the annexation of the West Bank to Jordan.[59] Whatever state for Palestinians emerges would necessarily be "a cooperative enterprise of the Hashemite regime, based on the core bedouin population of Jordan, and the PNA, based on the Palestinian populations of the West Bank, the Gaza Strip, and Jordan."[60]

Morris, a historian whose detailed examination of Israeli historical archives has helped us rewrite the history of the 1948 ethnic cleansing of Palestinians, is surprisingly loose with details in suggesting a union of the West Bank with Jordan. Perhaps back in 1948, or maybe even in 1967, such a scenario might have worked. But today Israeli settlements line the length of the Jordan River, and any hint of dismantling them is certain to spark a civil war in Israel. By its very actions, Israel has made a potential Palestinian union with Jordan as impossible as a sovereign and viable Palestinian state on its own. Except for a "transfer" of Palestinians of the West Bank to Jordan, whereby some 2.5 million West Bankers are sent to the East Bank of the Jordan River, a confederation or union of Palestine today with Jordan is a territorial—as well as a political and social—impossibility.

What then of the future? As Rashid Khalidi has commented, despite their vigorous sense of collective identity, the Palestinians have not had, and are unlikely to ever have, a truly sovereign state in a clearly demarcated territory of their own.[61] Does this mean the Palestinians are consigned to eternal statelessness? In an intriguing argument, the legal scholar John Quigley maintains that Palestine is actually already a state. Despite its occupation and the various constraints imposed on it, because of its size, citizenship, and control over domestic and foreign policies, Quigley argues that from the perspective of international law, Palestine already meets all the criteria of a state and therefore actually already is a state.[62]

But the core dilemmas of the Palestinian issue still remain unresolved. Even if Palestine has a flag, a seat at the United Nations with full membership privileges, and all the other accoutrements of statehood, does it truly perform for its citizens the full range of functions that a state ought to perform? Also, as Ilan Peleg and Dov Waxman remind us, ending the occupation is only a necessary but insufficient condition for ending the conflict. Addressing the inferior status of Palestinian citizens of Israel is altogether a different matter.[63]

What is it then that the future is likely to hold for Palestine?

Whither Palestine?

Before offering a final thought, a reminder of how Palestine got to where it is today is in order. As I have argued in the preceding chapters, Palestinian society never completely recovered from waves of ethnic cleansing in the late 1940s and in 1967, having to reconstitute itself under the consequences and conditions of exile and occupation. The Palestinian national project entailed the two reinforcing processes of state-building and nation-building. With the Palestinian nation scattered and under siege, the state-building project took precedence, first entrusting itself to bigger brothers in Egypt and elsewhere in the 1960s and the 1970s, but then reasserting itself through the force of arms in the 1970s and the 1980s. The PLO's search for a safe refuge, from Jordan to Lebanon and finally to Tunisia, took it farther and farther away from what remained of Palestine in the West Bank and Gaza, and thus farther away from its intended national constituents. More than a revolution, the intifada was a reassertion of indigenous, homegrown Palestinian nationalism, a reassertion of claims of ownership by Palestinians over their own destiny.

The PLO, and more specifically Fatah, hijacked the intifada and used the ensuing Oslo Accords as an opportunity to once again place themselves at the center of the Palestinian state-building process. And, with promises of a new dawn for Palestine, it set out in earnest to recollect and reassemble a Palestinian nation fractured by decades of dispossession and displacement. In the process, the Palestine National Authority deepened the distance between the West Bank and Gaza, on the one hand, and fostered the growth of an Israeli- and PNA-dependent comprador bourgeoisie, on the other. NGOs also flooded into the Occupied Territories to help in the national reconstruction, inadvertently undermining the very phenomenon they were seeking to deepen. All the while, the Palestinians found their world more constrained and their movements more limited, victim to Israel's insatiable appetite for land, its uncompromising fixation with "security" in all aspects of life, and its determined march toward separation and exclusion. What Israel didn't take away from the Palestinians the PNA and Hamas and their all-too-often-violent rivalry did.

Today, as the Palestinian academic Khalil Shikaki has observed, a one-state reality is emerging, but Palestinians do not seem capable of doing anything about it.[64] This is not the one state that is either binational or secular and democratic. As Shikaki laments, it is "an ugly one-state dynamic [that] has no happy ending," one of continued confinement and conflict.[65] As the Palestinians end up drifting with no clear strategy, the future does not look promising.[66]

Shikaki's arguments closely parallel those of Menachem Klein, who teaches political science at Bar-Ilan University in Israel. According to Klein, "a single state" has become "the current problematic reality rather than a viable solution."[67] "The quantity of Israeli operations created a qualitative change" in the nature of the occupation, Klein maintains, whereby what was once a border conflict has now become an ethnic struggle between a settler and a colonized community.[68] The settlement enterprise has resulted in the formation of large, seemingly permanent, and immovable Israeli communities deep within Palestinian areas. What has emerged as a result is an interethnic conflict with blurred territorial boundaries. "In such a conflict, the Green Line is of little importance; what counts are ethnic affiliation and community origins. The frontier line is not an internationally recognized border but rather an ethnic divide."[69] This morphing of the conflict into an interethnic, communal struggle is an important development to which I will return shortly.

In looking to the future, history offers valuable lessons. The conquest and travails of Palestine ever since 1948 parallel three sets of similar historical examples. Each of these historical parallels had one of three outcomes—death, rebirth, or purgatory. The most extreme and negative of the outcomes, death, is what happened to Tibet. Although precarious as a national entity for much of its life, for a brief interlude—from 1913 to 1951—Tibet was an independent, autonomous state, which has since been subsumed by China. Today, with the exact number of ethnic Tibetans living there hotly disputed between the central government in Beijing and Tibetan activists around the world, only Tibetan identity and symbols remain. In every other way, Tibet as a country has ceased to exist.

At the opposite extreme stands the example of Poland, which ceased to exist as a sovereign state starting in the 1770s but was reborn in 1918. During its period of eclipse as a state, Polish society continued to benefit from industrialization and development, in turn helping to maintain a measure of corporate identity and social cohesion. But what ultimately made the critical difference to the country's fate was the consent of the superpowers of the day, and especially the insistence of U.S. President Woodrow Wilson, that the country regain its independence. Poland's rebirth was as much a product of powerful international patronage as it was an outgrowth of its own national perseverance.

In between these two extremes of death and rebirth lie the examples of native Americans and the aborigines of Australia and New Zealand. Governed by largely informal, underdeveloped power structures, these indigenous civilizations were conquered by industrially more advanced intruders who brought with them superior organization and a zealous drive to succeed. The conquered nations' recoveries from collapse were slow and painstaking, directed—if not impeded—by the conquering powers. What reemerged showed signs and scars of defeat and conquest, limited and underdeveloped in its potential. Today, these indigenous communities live in the shadows of their far more advanced, much more prosperous conquerors. They did not completely die out, nor were they altogether reborn. They live in between life and death, in a purgatory of sorts, their lives and opportunities limited by the vagaries of history and the heavy burdens of defeat and dispossession.

This purgatory is also the predicament of Palestine. And the signposts showing a way out do not look promising. Palestinian identity remains strong and robust. As we saw in chapter 1, despite Israel's best effort and the most hostile of predicaments, the Palestinian nation lives on and is not about to somehow disappear or dissipate. But neither the PNA nor Hamas show any signs of an ability to tap into popular potentials for purposes of mass mobilization, national reconciliation, meaningful state-building, or political development. As the Palestinian Israeli academic As'ad Ghanem correctly points out, a deep "existential crisis . . . currently afflicts the Palestinians and their national movement."[70] The Palestinian national movement is "in a state of shock and internal disintegration, the practical reflection of which is the absence of a political platform accepted by all factions and a broad internal mobilization around defined national goals."[71] According to Ghanem, "in the post-Arafat era the Palestinians and the national movement have sunk into a profound crisis that is manifested in a deep internal schism and an inability to function as a national group with national aspirations and a consensual vision of self-expression."[72]

Even if a new intifada brings to the fore as-yet-unknown dynamics and groups that can tap into the Palestinian people's potentials and create new structures of power, the prevailing physical and territorial realities on the ground are likely to impede the reemergence of forces that can lead to a meaningful reconstitution of Palestine. Even if all the social, political, and economic handicaps that Palestine is grappling with today were somehow magically to disappear, as a viable territorial entity Palestine still could not be patched together. Most importantly, the much-needed international support that was critical in the rebirth of a country like Poland is nowhere to be found in the case of Palestine.

Equally consequential is the transformation of the nature of the conflict from one over territory into an ethnic and communal one. The Palestinian struggle for statehood has been lost. Israel has won. And, at least insofar as Israel's territorial size and the scope of its geographic sovereignty are concerned, they both continue to expand at a steady pace. But Israel's victory has been military and territorial, not national. The project of ethnic cleansing of Palestinians was eventually abandoned in favor of separating them from an ever-expanding Israel. But the territorial expansion of Israeli presence into Palestinian lands has deepened the ethnic dimension of the conflict. Its multiple efforts at separation notwithstanding, Israel has brought into its orbit and into ever-closer proximity a Palestinian population with a strong sense of nationhood and a deeply rooted national identity. So far, Israel has implemented multiple legal, administrative, military, territorial, and physical mechanisms to ensure the separation from it of all things Palestinian. But how long and how effectively these means of separation will hold remains an open question.

In societies riven by divisions and ethnic conflicts, "good governance"—code words for a political system that is transparent and democratic—is often seen as fundamental to ensuring that the "constituency of losers" is never large or powerful enough to threaten social order.[73] One of the more-articulate advocates of this line of argument is David Laitin, who proposes a liberal democratic framework for reducing potential tensions inherent in multiculturalism. Laitin argues that the expected losses in public goods that would follow from a multicultural politics can be mitigated through the identification and consolidation of ethnically distinct communities within larger society.[74] In liberal democratic settings, a strong element of individual identity is involved in the creation of national identities. This is likely to result, admittedly, in cultural enclaves in states that are multicultural. However, "homogenous islands with cosmopolitan centers have the capacity to engender growth that is beyond the group of isolated homogenous communities."[75]

Laitin's elegant formula for the resolution of ethnic conflicts, which even allows for separate identities, could not be further from the realities of Israel and Palestine. At a time when most multinational states keep breaking up into smaller bits—witness, most recently, the secession of South Sudan from Sudan, the de facto breakup of Iraq and Syria, and Scotland's nearly successful push for independence from Britain in 2014—the creation of a new multinational state, one forged out of the blood and tears of generations of Palestinians and Israelis, is unfathomable even in the most optimistic, idealistic scenarios. As we saw earlier in this chapter as well as in chapter 5, the political realities of the Israeli-Palestinian conflict, whether endogenous to the two primary parties themselves or reinforced by external actors, mitigate the possibility of any substantive changes to prevailing political, military, and territorial circumstances.

Even if national policies and international efforts were undertaken to address the underlying causes of ethnic conflict among Israelis and Palestinians, they are unlikely to ever go beyond conflict *management* and result in conflict *settlement* and resolution. Ideally, policies and initiatives aimed at conflict settlement must "successfully tackle structural, political, social, economic, and cultural and perceptual factors and diffuse the security dilemmas arising from them."[76] Settling ethnic conflicts may not even always be possible, and for some conflicts a prolonged period of international conflict management may be needed in order to contain and minimize their worst consequences. Equally important are the individual choices made by leaders who have vision and risk-taking abilities, though the menu of these choices is often dictated by circumstances and structural dynamics beyond the control of individuals.[77] Moreover, both conflict management and conflict settlement often require significant commitment from the international community, in the form of the UN or regional organizations, an essential ingredient that is, again, conspicuously absent from the Israeli-Palestinian conflict.[78]

What all of this ultimately amounts to is an unhappy prognosis for the future of Palestine. Whether viewed from the perspective of the interstate conflict or communal and ethnic struggle, meaningful change in Palestine's predicament—its growing territorial dismemberment, political underdevelopment, institutional atrophy, international neglect, infrastructural decay, and its occasional military devastation—is unlikely to change for the foreseeable future. The Palestinian nation will continue to live on, but only under the most adverse of circumstances.

Sadly, the Palestinian purgatory is likely to continue unabated for some time to come.

Notes

Chapter 1. Introduction

1. This line of argument is often heard not only from the likes of Israeli Prime Minister Benjamin Netanyahu but also from a number of the American diplomats involved in the negotiations. See, for example, Aaron David Miller, "Why Kerry Has Failed," *Los Angeles Times,* May 11, 2014, p. 22.

2. Benny Morris, *The Birth of the Palestinian Refugee Problem, 1947–1949* (Cambridge: Cambridge University Press, 1988). In the book's second edition, entitled *The Birth of the Palestinian Refugee Problem Revisited* and published by Cambridge University Press in 2004, Morris claims (p. 5) that the scale of "expulsions and atrocities by Israeli troops" was much greater than he had tabulated in the first edition, as were "orders and advice to various communities by Arab officials and officers to quit their communities."

3. Ilan Pappe, *The Ethnic Cleansing of Palestine* (Oxford, UK: Oneworld, 2006), p. xvii.

4. Meron Benvenisti, *Sacred Landscape: The Buried History of the Holy Land since 1948,* trans. Maxine Kaufman-Lacusta (Berkeley, CA: University of California Press, 2000).

5. Baruch Kimmerling, *The Invention and Decline of Israeliness: State, Society, and the Military* (Berkeley, CA: University of California Press, 2005).

6. Alain Dieckhoff, *The Invention of a Nation: Zionist Thought and the Making of Modern Israel* (New York: Columbia University Press, 2003), p. 273.

7. Not surprisingly, post-Zionism's emphasis on cultural pluralism, relativism, and minority rights does not always sit well with the tenor of Israeli political culture and body politic, thus keeping the writings of the "new historians" of the late 1980s and the 1990s limited mostly to intellectual, scholarly circles that so far have not succeeded in capturing the public imagination.

8. Central Bureau of Statistics, *Statistical Abstract of Israel 2014* (Jerusalem: Central Bureau of Statistics, 2014), pp. 89, 91.

9. Uzi Rebhun and Gilad Matach, "Demography, Social Prosperity, and the Future of Sovereign Israel," *Israel Affairs* 18, no. 2 (March 2012), p. 180.

10. Palestinian Central Bureau of Statistics, "Population," http://www.pcbs.gov.ps/site/881/default.aspx#Population.

11. Palestinian Central Bureau of Statistics, "Estimated Number of Palestinians in the World by Country of Residence, End Year 2010," http://www.pcbs.gov.ps/Portals/_Rainbow/Documents/PalDis-POPUL-2010E.htm.

12. Pappe, *Ethnic Cleansing of Palestine,* p. 259.

13. Benedict Anderson, *Imagined Communities: Reflections on the Origins and Spread of Nationalism* (London: Verso, 2006), p. 6.

14. Eric Hobsbawm, *Nations and Nationalism since 1780: Programme, Myth, Reality,* 2nd ed. (Cambridge: Cambridge University Press, 1992), p. 8.

15. Azar Gat, *Nations: The Long History and Deep Roots of Political Ethnicity and Nationalism* (Cambridge: Cambridge University Press, 2013), pp. 22–23.

16. David D. Laitin, *Nations, States, and Violence* (Oxford: Oxford University Press, 2007), p. 40. Emphasis added.

17. Ibid., p. 41. Emphasis added.

18. In fairness to Laitin, he does distinguish between nation and state, maintaining that "nations that are commensurate with state boundaries have populations that share common knowledge and points of concern. No wonder the nation-state model has been attractive to political visionaries." Ibid., p. 79.

19. Philip G. Roeder, *Where Nation-States Come From: Institutional Change in the Age of Nationalism* (Princeton, NJ: Princeton University Press, 2007), pp. 11–12.

20. Ibid., p.13. Emphasis added.

21. Ibid., p. 5.

22. Ibid., p. 10.

23. Max Weber, *From Max Weber: Essays in Sociology,* trans. and ed. H. H. Gerth and C. Right Mills (London: Routledge & Kegan Paul, 1964), p. 78. Original emphasis.

24. Laleh Khalili, *Heroes and Martyrs of Palestine: The Politics of National Commemoration* (Cambridge: Cambridge University Press, 2007), pp. 2–3.

25. Ibid., p. 215.

26. Ibid., p. 6.

27. Sidney G. Tarrow, *Power in Movement: Social Movements and Contentious Politics,* 3rd ed. (Cambridge: Cambridge University Press, 2011), p. 11.

28. Khalili, *Heroes and Martyrs of Palestine,* p. 49.

29. Tarrow, *Power in Movement,* pp. 28–29.

30. "Contentious politics," Tarrow argues, "is triggered when changing political opportunities and constraints create incentives to take action for actors who lack resources on their own. People contend through known repertoires of contention and expand them by creating innovation at the margins. When backed by well-structured social networks and galvanized by culturally resonant, action-oriented symbols, contentious politics leads to sustained interaction with opponents—to social movements." Ibid., p. 6.

31. David A. McDonald, *My Voice Is My Weapon: Music, Nationalism, and the Poetics of Palestinian Resistance* (Durham, NC: Duke University Press, 2013), p. 22. McDonald further contends (p. 23) that "Palestinians, through music performance, have fashioned and disseminated markers of a distinct Palestinian identity [that] has been historically articulated through various local, national, and transnational contexts." For an insightful collection of contributions on this topic, see, Mosleh Kanaaneh, Stig-Magnus Thorsen, Heather Bursheh, and David A. McDonald, eds., *Palestinian Music and Song: Expression and Resistance since 1900* (Bloomington, IN: Indiana University Press, 2013).

32. Salam Mir, "Palestinian Literature: Occupation and Exile," *Arab Studies Quarterly* 35, no. 2 (2013), pp. 110–111.

33. For sample works by these and other Palestinian literary figures, see, Salma Khadra Jayyusi, ed., *Anthology of Modern Palestinian Literature* (New York: Columbia University Press, 1992).

34. See Orayb Aref Najjar, "Cartoons as a Site for the Construction of Palestinian Refugee Identity: An Exploratory Study of Cartoonist Naji al-Ali," *Journal of Communication Inquiry* 31, no. 3 (2007), pp. 255–285.

35. Khalili, *Heroes and Martyrs of Palestine,* p. 217.

36. Ibid., p. 3.

37. Ibid., p. 191.

38. Giovanni Capoccia and R. Daniel Keleman, "The Study of Critical Junctures: Theory, Narrative, and Counterfactuals in Historical Institutionalism," *World Politics* 59, no. 3 (April 2007), p. 341.

39. Paul Pierson, *Politics in Time: History, Institutions, and Social Analysis* (Princeton, NJ: Princeton University Press, 2004), p. 135.

40. Capoccia and Keleman, "Study of Critical Junctures," p. 343.

41. See, for example, Muhammad Muslih, *The Origins of Palestinian Nationalism* (New York: Columbia University Press, 1988); Edward Said, *The Question of Palestine* (New York: Vintage, 1992); and Rashid Khalidi, *Palestinian Identity: The Construction of Modern National Consciousness* (New York: Columbia University Press, 1997).

42. Khalili, *Heroes and Martyrs of Palestine,* p. 225.

43. Author interview with Mazin Qumsiyeh, Bethlehem, West Bank, June 11, 2013.

44. Kimmerling, *Invention and Decline of Israeliness,* p. 80.

Chapter 2. The Lessons of History

1. David Day, *Conquest: How Societies Overwhelm Others* (Oxford: Oxford University Press, 2008), pp. 2–4.

2. Baruch Kimmerling, *The Invention and Decline of Israeliness: State, Society, and the Military* (Berkeley, CA: University of California Press, 2005), pp. 44–45.

3. Day, *Conquest,* p. 77.

4. Ibid., pp. 7–8. See also John Collins, *Global Palestine* (New York: Columbia University Press, 2011), pp. 30–36.

5. Morris, "Revisiting the Palestinian Exodus of 1948," in *The War for Palestine,* ed. Eugene L. Rogan and Avi Shlaim (Cambridge: Cambridge University Press, 2001), p. 39. For a discussion of the history of Zionism, see, Michael Brenner, *Zionism: A Brief History,* trans. Shelly L. Frisch (Princeton, NJ: Markus Wiener, 2003).

6. Nur Masalha, *Expulsion of the Palestinians: The Concept of "Transfer" in Zionist Political Thought, 1882–1948* (Washington, DC: Institute for Palestine Studies, 1992), p. 8.

7. Quoted in ibid., p. 14.

8. Meron Benvenisti, *Sacred Landscape: The Buried History of the Holy Land since 1948,* trans. Maxine Kaufman-Lacusta (Berkeley, CA: University of California Press, 2000), p. 6.

9. Ibid., pp. 60–61.

10. Charles D. Smith, *Palestine and the Arab-Israeli Conflict: A History with Documents,* 8th ed. (Boston, MA: Bedford St. Martin's, 2013), p. 113.

11. Nurit Peled-Elhanan, *Palestine in Israeli School Books: Ideology and Propaganda in Education* (London: I. B. Tauris, 2012), p. 2.

12. Mark LeVine, *Overthrowing Geography: Jaffa, Tel Aviv, and the Struggle for Palestine, 1880–1948* (Berkeley, CA: University of California Press, 2005), p. 61.

13. Day, *Conquest*, p. 152.

14. Ibid., p. 153.

15. Zeev Sternhell, *The Founding Myths of Israel*, trans. David Maisel (Princeton, NJ: Princeton University Press, 1998), p. 16.

16. Day, *Conquest*, p. 153.

17. Sternhell, *Founding Myths of Israel*, p. 340.

18. Baylis Thomas, *How Israel Was Won: A Concise History of the Arab-Israeli Conflict* (Lanham, MD: Lexington Books, 1999), pp. 3, 7.

19. Alain Dieckhoff, *The Invention of a Nation: Zionist Thought and the Making of Modern Israel* (New York: Columbia University Press, 2003), p. 269.

20. Sternhell, *Founding Myths of Israel*, pp. 341, 343.

21. Dieckhoff, *Invention of a Nation*, p. 289.

22. Sternhell, *Founding Myths of Israel*, p. 344.

23. Quoted in Masalha, *Expulsion of the Palestinians*, p. 29. For a discussion of Jabotinsky and his arguments, see, Avi Shlaim, *The Iron Wall: Israel and the Arab World* (New York: W. W. Norton, 2001), pp. 11–16.

24. Quoted in Masalha, *Expulsion of the Palestinians*, p. 7.

25. Day, *Conquest*, p. 189.

26. Sternhell, *Founding Myths of Israel*, p. 332.

27. Day, *Conquest*, p. 131.

28. Masalha, *Expulsion of the Palestinians*, p. 2.

29. Ibid., p. 72. For a discussion of the records of the Jewish Agency's meeting on June 7–12, 1938, when the idea was widely discussed, see Morris, "Revisiting the Palestinian Exodus of 1948," p. 44. Morris also cites extensively from Ben-Gurion's diary, in which he writes approvingly and enthusiastically about the idea; see pp. 41–42 and 45–46.

30. Benny Morris, *The Birth of the Palestinian Refugee Problem Revisited* (Cambridge: Cambridge University Press, 2004), pp. 40–43.

31. Morris, "Revisiting the Palestinian Exodus of 1948," p. 43.

32. Morris, *Birth of the Palestinian Refugee Problem Revisited*, pp. 51, 60.

33. Day, *Conquest*, p. 129.

34. Ibid., p. 130.

35. Kimmerling, *Invention and Decline of Israeliness*, p. 65.

36. Day, *Conquest*, p. 152.

37. Kimmerling, *Invention and Decline of Israeliness,* p. 65.

38. Rashid Khalidi, "The Palestinians and 1948: The Underlying Causes of Failure," in Rogan and Shlaim, *War for Palestine,* pp. 12–13.

39. Deborah J. Gerner, *One Land, Two Peoples: The Conflict over Palestine,* 2nd ed. (Boulder, CO: Westview, 1994), pp. 9–10.

40. Glenn E. Robinson, *Building a Palestinian State: The Incomplete Revolution* (Bloomington, IN: Indiana University Press, 1997), pp. 7–9.

41. Benvenisti, *Sacred Landscape,* p. 194.

42. Khalidi, "Palestinians and 1948," pp. 27–28.

43. Morris, *Birth of the Palestinian Refugee Problem Revisited,* p. 23.

44. Khalidi, "Palestinians and 1948," pp. 18, 21.

45. Ibid., p. 31.

46. Ibid., pp. 21–22.

47. Rashid Khalidi, *Palestinian Identity: The Construction of Modern National Consciousness* (New York: Columbia University Press, 1997), p. 149.

48. Ibid., pp. 150–154.

49. Istiqlal had two simple rallying cries: "lethargic" notables have failed Palestine, and British imperialism had made Zionism a real threat. Baruch Kimmerling and Joel S. Migdal, *Palestinians: The Making of a People* (Cambridge, MA: Harvard University Press, 1994), p. 92.

50. Ilan Pappe, *The Ethnic Cleansing of Palestine* (Oxford: Oneworld, 2006), p. 28.

51. Ibid., p. xii.

52. Ibid., p. 88. For full text of Plan D and sections of Plan C, see, Walid Khalidi, "Plan Dalet: Master Plan of the Conquest of Palestine," *Journal of Palestine Studies* 18, no. 1 (Autumn 1988), pp. 4–33.

53. Morris, *Birth of the Palestinian Refugee Problem Revisited,* p. 165. Elsewhere Morris argues that "the Haganah also contributed to the terrorist campaign, though its intended targets were what were believed to be Arab terrorist concentrations rather than civilians." Benny Morris, *Righteous Victims: A History of the Zionist-Arab Conflict, 1881–2001* (New York: Vintage, 2001), p. 198.

54. Pappe, *Ethnic Cleansing of Palestine,* p. xiii.

55. Morris, *Birth of the Palestinian Refugee Problem Revisited,* p. 164.

56. Pappe, *Ethnic Cleansing of Palestine,* p. 146.

57. Morris, *Birth of the Palestinian Refugee Problem Revisited,* pp. 168–169.

58. Quoted in ibid., p. 237.

59. Ibid., p. 238. Ilan Pappe puts the number of the Palestinians massacred at ninety-three, including thirty babies. Pappe, *Ethnic Cleansing of Palestine,* p. 91.

60. Morris, "Revisiting the Palestinian Exodus of 1948," p. 38.

61. Ibid., pp. 55–56.

62. Masalha, *Expulsion of the Palestinians,* p. 198.

63. Ibid., p. 25.

64. Pappe, *Ethnic Cleansing of Palestine,* p. 23.

65. Morris, *Birth of the Palestinian Refugee Problem Revisited,* p. 6.

66. Lila Abu-Lughod and Ahmad H. Sa'di, "Introduction: The Claims of Memory," in *Nakba: Palestine, 1948, and the Claim of Memory,* ed. Ahmad H. Sa'di and Lila Abu-Lughod (New York: Columbia University Press, 2007), p. 3.

67. Morris, *Birth of the Palestinian Refugee Problem Revisited,* p. 264.

68. Ilan Pappe puts the number of Arab villages emptied of their inhabitants at 531, along with 11 urban neighborhoods. Pappe, *Ethnic Cleansing of Palestine,* p. xiii.

69. Khalidi, "Palestinians and 1948," pp. 13–14.

70. Morris, *Birth of the Palestinian Refugee Problem Revisited,* p. 342.

71. Benvenisti, *Sacred Landscape,* p. 7.

72. Ibid., p. 145.

73. Masalha, *Expulsion of the Palestinians,* p. 175.

74. Pappe, *Ethnic Cleansing of Palestine,* p. 224.

75. Benvenisti, *Sacred Landscape,* p. 146.

76. Masalha, *Expulsion of the Palestinians,* p. 175.

77. Abu-Lughod and Sa'di, "Introduction: The Claims of Memory," p. 3.

78. Masalha, *Expulsion of the Palestinians,* p. 199.

79. Ibid.

80. Meron Benvenisti, *City of Stone: The Hidden History of Jerusalem ,* trans. Maxine Kaufman Nunn (Berkeley, CA: University of California Press, 1996), p. 165.

81. Laila Parsons, "The Druze and the Birth of Israel," in Rogan and Shlaim, *War for Palestine,* pp. 62–63, 68.

82. Morris, *Birth of the Palestinian Refugee Problem Revisited,* p. 341.

83. Ibid., p. 506.

84. Quoted in Benvenisti, *Sacred Landscape,* p. 150.

85. Morris, *Birth of the Palestinian Refugee Problem Revisited,* p. 491.

86. Quoted in ibid., p. 484.

87. Joshua Landis, "Syria and the Palestine War: Fighting King 'Abdullah's 'Greater Syria Plan,'" in Rogan and Shlaim, *War for Palestine,* p. 178.

88. Avi Shlaim, "Israel and the Arab Coalition in 1948," in Rogan and Shlaim, *War for Palestine,* p. 81.

89. Charles Tripp, "Iraq and the 1948 War: Mirror of Iraq's Disorder," in Rogan and Shlaim, *War for Palestine,* p. 125.

90. Fawaz A. Gerges, "Egypt and the 1948 War: Internal Conflict and Regional Ambition," in Rogan and Shlaim, *War for Palestine,* pp. 151–153.

91. Landis, "Syria and the Palestine War," p. 180. Qawwatli was eventually overthrown in a military coup in 1949.

92. Ibid., p. 200.

93. Shlaim, "Israel and the Arab Coalition in 1948," p. 80.

94. Benvenisti, *Sacred Landscape,* p. 152.

95. Ibid., p. 153.

96. Pappe, *Ethnic Cleansing of Palestine,* pp. 208–209.

97. Benvenisti, *Sacred Landscape,* p. 212.

98. Pappe, *Ethnic Cleansing of Palestine,* p. 220–221.

99. Ibid., p. 223.

100. Ibid., pp. 192–193, 200–201.

101. Benvenisti, *Sacred Landscape,* p. 202.

102. Abu-Lughod and Sa'di, "Introduction: The Claims of Memory," pp. 4–5.

103. Edward W. Said, "Afterward: The Consequences of 1948," in Rogan and Shlaim, *War for Palestine,* p. 206.

104. Ibid., p. 207.

105. Abu-Lughod and Sa'di, "Introduction: The Claims of Memory," p. 9.

106. Kimmerling and Migdal, *Palestinians,* p. 128.

107. Ibid., pp. 128–129.

108. Said, "Afterward: The Consequences of 1948," p. 208.

109. Ibid., p. 209.

110. David McDowall, *Palestine and Israel: The Uprising and Beyond* (Berkeley, CA: University of California Press, 1989), p. 70.

111. Sternhell, *Founding Myths of Israel,* p. 6.

112. Ibid., p. 7.

113. Ibid., p. 133.

114. Quoted in ibid., pp. 21–22.

115. Kimmerling, *Invention and Decline of Israeliness*, p. 43.

116. Robert Bowker, *Palestinian Refugees: Mythology, Identity, and the Search for Peace* (Boulder, CO: Lynne Rienner, 2003), p. 81. Technically, the 1967 refugees are considered "displaced persons" rather than "refugees" by the United Nations and are thus ineligible for UNRWA benefits.

117. Sternhell, *Founding Myths of Israel*, p. 335.

118. Meron Benvenisti, *Intimate Enemies: Jews and Arabs in a Shared Land* (Berkeley, CA: University of California Press, 1995), p. 65.

119. Quoted in Edward Said, "Afterward: The Consequences of 1948," p. 207.

120. Sternhell, *Founding Myths of Israel*, pp. 332–333. While no longer officially in existence, the Allon Plan continues to guide the fundamental vision of the occupation and Israel's settlement policy to this day. See Saree Makdisi, *Palestine Inside Out: An Everyday Occupation* (New York: Norton, 2010), p. 278.

121. Sternhell, *Founding Myths of Israel*, p. 336.

122. Ibid., p. 327.

123. Dina Matar, *What It Means to Be Palestinian: Stories of Palestinian Peoplehood* (London: I. B. Tauris, 2011), p. 189.

124. Jamil Hilal, "Palestine: The Last Colonial Issue," in *Where Now for Palestine? The Demise of the Two-State Solution*, ed. Jamil Hilal (London: Zed, 2007), p. 4.

125. Sternhell, *Founding Myths of Israel*, pp. 336–337.

126. Benvenisti, *Intimate Enemies*, p. 75.

127. McDowall, *Palestine and Israel*, p. 94.

128. Robinson, *Building a Palestinian State*, p. 14.

129. Avi Shlaim, *Israel and Palestine: Reappraisals, Revisions, Refutations* (London: Verso, 2009), p. 308.

130. Robinson, *Building a Palestinian State*, pp. 11–12.

131. Benvenisti, *Intimate Enemies*, p. 68.

132. Ibid., p. 79.

133. Smith, *Palestine and the Arab-Israeli Conflict*, p. 404.

134. McDowall, *Palestine and Israel*, p. viii.

135. Benvenisti, *Intimate Enemies*, p. 82.

136. Robinson, *Building a Palestinian State*, p. xi.

137. Ibid., pp. ix–x, 14–17.

138. McDowall, *Palestine and Israel*, p. 206.

139. Khalidi, *Palestinian Identity*, p. 200.

140. McDowall, *Palestine and Israel*, p. 110

141. Robinson, *Building a Palestinian State*, p. 64.

142. McDowall, *Palestine and Israel*, p. 119.

143. Robinson, *Building a Palestinian State*, p. 49.

144. McDowall, *Palestine and Israel*, p. 113.

145. Robinson, *Building a Palestinian State*, p. 140.

146. McDowall, *Palestine and Israel*, p. 56.

147. Benvenisti, *Intimate Enemies*, p. 81.

148. Ibid., p. 87.

149. Quoted in Thomas, *How Israel Was Won*, p. 251.

150. Ariella Azoulay and Adi Ophir, *The One-State Condition: Occupation and Democracy in Israel/Palestine*, trans. Tala Haran (Stanford, CA: Stanford University Press, 2013), p. 127.

151. Robinson, *Building a Palestinian State*, p. xi.

152. Thomas, *How Israel Was Won*, p. 268.

153. The precise size of Areas A, B, and C is a matter of debate, with some interpretations of the agreement placing them at 15–17, 23–25, and 60–70 percent respectively. The discrepancy arises from the Accord's deliberate vagueness, specifying only the population centers in each area, with Area A containing the cities of Jenin, Nablus, Tulkarm, Qalqilya, Ramallah, and Bethlehem; Area B made up of approximately 450 smaller towns and rural hamlets (not always adjacent to the larger Palestinian cities); and Area C comprised of everything else. For the text of the agreement, see *The Israel-Arab Reader: A Documentary History of the Middle East Conflict*, ed. Walter Laqueur and Barry Ruben, 6th ed. (New York: Penguin, 2001), pp. 502–521. See also Smith, *Palestine and the Arab-Israeli Conflict*, pp. 450–454.

154. Quoted in Thomas, *How Israel Was Won*, p. 264.

155. Ibid., p. 270.

156. Benvenisti, *Sacred Landscape*, p. 266.

157. Robinson, *Building a Palestinian State*, p. xii.

158. Cheryl A. Rubenberg, *The Palestinians: In Search of a Just Peace* (Boulder, CO: Lynne Rienner, 2003), p. 247.

159. Ibid., p. 88.

160. Thomas, *How Israel Was Won*, p. 271.

161. Rubenberg, *Palestinians: In Search of a Just Peace*, p. 323.

162. Hilal, "Palestine: The Last Colonial Issue," p. 5.

163. Matar, *What It Means to Be Palestinian*, p. 192.

164. Ziad Abu-Amr, "Hamas: From Opposition to Rule," in Hilal, *Where Now for Palestine?*, pp. 169–170. Abu-Amr also lists Hamas's reputation for honesty and integrity as one of the important reasons for the rise of its popularity.

165. Smith, *Palestine and the Arab-Israeli Conflict*, pp. 490–498.

166. Rubenberg, *Palestinians: In Search of a Just Peace*, p. 352.

167. Eyal Raz and Yael Stein, *Operation Defensive Shield: Soldiers' Testimonies, Palestinian Testimonies* (Jerusalem: B'Tselem, 2002), p. 3.

168. Author interview with Khalil Nakhleh, Ramallah, West Bank, June 13, 2013.

169. Quoted in Smith, *Palestine and the Arab-Israeli Conflict*, p. 512.

170. Quoted in ibid., p. 513.

171. Shlaim, *Israel and Palestine*, p. 309.

172. Thomas, *How Israel Was Won*, p. 277.

173. Smith, *Palestine and the Arab-Israeli Conflict*, p. 524.

174. Pappe, *Ethnic Cleansing of Palestine*, p. 239.

175. United Nations Human Rights Council, *Report of the United Nations Fact Finding Mission on the Gaza Conflict*, A/HRC/12/48. 15, September 2009, pp. 10–11.

176. Ibid., pp. 14–16. Since the fact-finding mission was headed by Judge Richard Goldstone from South Africa, the document it produced came to be known as the Goldstone Report.

177. Sara Roy, "Gaza: New Dynamics of Civic Disintegration," *Journal of Political Studies* 22, no. 4 (Summer 1993), pp. 21–23.

178. Sara Roy, "De-development Revisited: Palestinian Economy and Society since Oslo," *Journal of Palestine Studies* 28, no. 3 (Spring 1999), pp. 65–66.

179. Jean-Pierre Filiu, *Gaza: A History*, trans. John King (Oxford: Oxford University Press, 2014), p. 286.

180. Azoulay and Ophir, *One-State Condition*, p. 173.

181. Ibid., p. 172.

182. "The 'Arabs Out' Government," *Haaretz*, June 20, 2013, p. 5.

183. Benvenisti, *Sacred Landscape*, p. 166.

184. Kimmerling, *Invention and Decline of Israeliness,* p. 4.

185. Shlaim, "Israel and the Arab Coalition in 1948," p. 79.

186. Benvenisti, *Sacred Landscape,* p. 334.

187. Shlaim, *Israel and Palestine,* p. 307.

Chapter 3. The Lay of the Land

1. Examples of other noncontiguous countries include Brunei, Denmark, Iceland, Indonesia, Sri Lanka, Malaysia, Malta, New Zealand, Philippines, Papua New Guinea, Singapore, and the United States.

2. Ariella Azoulay and Adi Ophir, *The One-State Condition: Occupation and Democracy in Israel/Palestine,* trans. Tala Haran (Stanford, CA: Stanford University Press, 2013), p. 13.

3. Jamil Hilal, "Class Transformation in the West Bank and Gaza," *Journal of Palestine Studies* 6, no. 2 (Winter 1977), p. 172.

4. Azoulay and Ophir, *One-State Condition,* p. 129.

5. Arie Armon, "Israeli Policy Towards the Occupied Palestinian Territories: The Economic Dimension, 1967–2007," *Middle East Journal* 61, no. 4 (Autumn 2007), pp. 573–574.

6. Ibid., p. 573.

7. Shir Hever, *The Political Economy of Israel's Occupation: Repression Beyond Exploitation* (London: Pluto, 2012), p. 6.

8. Azoulay and Ophir, *One-State Condition,* pp. 19–20.

9. Ibid., p. 8.

10. Ibid., pp. 2–3.

11. Baruch Kimmerling and Joel S. Migdal, *Palestinians: The Making of a People* (Cambridge, MA: Harvard University Press, 1994), p. 161.

12. Amir S. Cheshin, Bill Hutman, and Avi Melamed, *Separate and Unequal: The Inside Story of Israeli Rule in East Jerusalem* (Cambridge, MA: Harvard University Press, 1999), p. 56.

13. Ibid. See also Nir Shalev, *Under the Guise of Legality: Declarations on State Land in the West Bank* , trans. Yael Stein (Jerusalem: B'Tselem, 2012), p. 15.

14. B'Tselem, "Taking Over Palestinian Land in the West Bank by Declaring It 'State Land,'" March 13, 2013, www.btselem.org/area_c/state_lands.

15. Jamil Hilal, "Palestine: The Last Colonial Issue," in *Where Now for Palestine? The Demise of the Two-State Solution,* ed. Jamil Hilal (London: Zed, 2007), p. 17.

16. Azoulay and Ophir, *One-State Condition,* p. 129.

17. As'ad Ghanem, "Israel and the 'Danger of Demography,'" in Hilal, *Where Now for Palestine?,* p. 62.

18. John Collins, *Global Palestine* (New York: Columbia University Press, 2011), p. 88.

19. Azoulay and Ophir, *One-State Condition,* p. 21.

20. Palestinian Central Bureau of Statistics, "Special Statistical Bulletin, On the 65th Anniversary of the Palestinian Nakba," May 14, 2013, http://www.pcbs.gov.ps/site/512/default.aspx?tabID=512&lang=en&ItemID=788&mid=3171&wversion=Staging.

21. Meron Benvenisti, *City of Stone: The Hidden History of Jerusalem,* trans. Maxine Kaufman Nunn (Berkeley, CA: University of California Press, 1996), p. 263.

22. Collins, *Global Palestine,* p. 55.

23. Jad Isaac and Owen Powell, "The Transformation of the Palestinian Environment," in Hilal, *Where Now for Palestine?,* pp. 151, 154.

24. David Day, *Conquest: How Societies Overwhelm Others* (Oxford: Oxford University Press, 2008), pp. 50–52.

25. Quoted in Meron Benvenisti, *Sacred Landscape: The Buried History of the Holy Land since 1948,* trans. Maxine Kaufman-Lacusta (Berkeley, CA: University of California Press, 2000), pp. 12, 14.

26. Ibid., p. 35.

27. Quoted in ibid., p. 17.

28. Ibid., pp. 43–44.

29. For an analysis of competing narratives, see Ilan Pappe, "Critique and Agenda: The Post-Zionist Scholars in Israel," *History and Memory* 7, no. 1 (Spring–Summer 1995), pp. 66–90.

30. Benvenisti, *Sacred Landscape,* p. 78.

31. Ibid., p. 67.

32. Joel Beinin and Lisa Hajjar, "Palestine, Israel and the Arab-Israeli Conflict: A Primer," http://www.thinkingtogether.org/rcream/old/f2003/Primer.pdf, p. 6.

33. Cheshin, Hutman, and Melamed, *Separate and Unequal,* pp. 120–123.

34. Saree Makdisi, *Palestine Inside Out: An Everyday Occupation* (New York: Norton, 2010), p. 110.

35. Kimmerling and Migdal, *Palestinians,* p. 161.

36. World Bank, *The Economic Effects of Restricted Access to Land in the West Bank* (Washington, DC: World Bank, 2012), p. 18.

37. According to the Palestine Monetary Authority, for example, 33 percent of Gaza's labor force is employed in the public sector. Palestine Monetary Authority, *Quarterly Social and Economic Monitor,* vol. 31 (Ramallah: PMA, 2013), p. 7.

38. Ghazi-Walid Falah, "Dynamics and Patterns of the Shrinking of Arab Lands in Palestine," *Political Geography* 22 (2003), p. 179.

39. Azoulay and Ophir, *One-State Condition,* p. 130.

40. Graham Usher, "The Palestinians after Arafat," *Journal of Palestine Studies* 34, no. 3 (Spring 2005), p. 48.

41. World Bank, *Economic Effects of Restricted Access to Land,* p. 6.

42. Makdisi, *Palestine Inside Out,* p. 70.

43. Azoulay and Ophir, *One-State Condition,* p. 88.

44. BADIL, "Seam Zones," *BADIL Occasional Bulletin No. 25* (August 2012), p. 9.

45. Makdisi, *Palestine Inside Out,* pp. 16, 24.

46. BADIL, "Seam Zones," p. 4.

47. Ibid., p. 5.

48. Isaac and Powell, "Transformation of the Palestinian Environment," p. 157.

49. Hever, *Political Economy of Israel's Occupation,* p. 51.

50. Ibid., pp. 52–53.

51. As of January 2014, the Web site www.whoprofits.org, which looks at "the occupation industry," listed more than thirteen hundred private Israeli and international companies involved in settlement-related enterprises.

52. Cheshin, Hutman, and Melamed, *Separate and Unequal,* pp. 44–45.

53. Data collected from www.btselem.org//settlements/statistics.

54. Deborah J. Gerner, *One Land, Two Peoples: The Conflict over Palestine,* 2nd ed. (Boulder, CO: Westview, 1994), pp. 80–81.

55. Baruch Kimmerling, *The Invention and Decline of Israeliness: State, Society, and the Military* (Berkeley, CA: University of California Press, 2005), p. 80.

56. Data collected from Palestinian Central Bureau of Statistics, "Localities in Hebron Governorate by Type of Locality and Population Estimates, 2007–2016," http://www.pcbs.gov.ps/Portals/_Rainbow/Documents/hebrn.htm; and United Nations Office for the Coordination of Humanitarian Affairs, "The Humanitarian

Impact of Israeli Settlements in Hebron City," OCHA Fact Sheet, November 2013, p. 1. For a description of life in Hebron, see Makdisi, *Palestine Inside Out,* pp. 209–221.

57. Isaac and Powell, "Transformation of the Palestinian Environment," p. 152; Meron Benvenisti, *Intimate Enemies: Jews and Arabs in a Shared Land* (Berkeley, CA: University of California Press, 1995), pp. 63–64.

58. Makdisi, *Palestine Inside Out,* p. 33. Original emphasis.

59. Ibid., p. 32.

60. Ibid., p. 19. In March 2012, the United Nation's Human Rights Council established the International Fact-Finding Mission on Israeli Settlements. The useful report that was subsequently produced by the group and presented to the UN in March 2013 is available at www.ohchr.org/Documents/HRBodies/HRCouncil/ RegularSession/Session19/FFM/FFMSettlements.pdf.

61. Gerner, *One Land, Two Peoples,* p. 82.

62. Cheryl A. Rubenberg, *The Palestinians: In Search of Just Peace* (Boulder, CO: Lynne Rienner, 2003), p. 230.

63. Ibid.

64. Leila Stockmarr, "Is It All About Territory? Israel's Settlement Policy in the Occupied Palestinian Territory since 1967," Danish Institute for International Studies, DIIS Report, 2012, pp. 11–12.

65. B'Tselem, "Statistics on Settlements and Settler Population," www.btselem. org/settlements/statistics.

66. Stockmarr, "Is It All About Territory?," p. 23.

67. Makdisi, *Palestine Inside Out,* p. 120.

68. Stockmarr, "Is It All About Territory?," p. 14.

69. Azoulay and Ophir, *One-State Condition,* p. 91.

70. Ibid., p. 94.

71. Ibid., p. 92.

72. Quoted in Stockmarr, "Is it All About Territory?," p. 7.

73. Ibid.

74. Charles D. Smith, *Palestine and the Arab-Israeli Conflict: A History with Documents,* 8th ed. (Boston, MA: Bedford St. Martin's, 2013), p. 438.

75. Ibid., p. 454.

76. United Nations Office for the Coordination of Humanitarian Affairs, "Unprotected: Settler Violence against Palestinian Civilians and Their Property,"

OCHA Special Focus, December 2008, p. 1, http://www.ochaopt.org/documents/ocha_opt_settler_vilonce_special_focus_2008_12_18.pdf.

77. B'Tselem, "Background on Settler Violence," May 6, 2010, www.btselem.org/settler_violence.

78. B'Tselem, "Security Forces Fail to Protect Palestinians from Settler Attacks in Incidents Documented by B'Tselem Over Last Three Months," May 30, 2013, www.btselem.org/settlers_violence/20130529_sf_fail_to_protect_palestinians_from_settlers.

79. Rubenberg, *Palestinians: In Search of a Just Peace,* p. 164.

80. Azoulay and Ophir, *One-State Condition,* p. 7.

81. Ibid., p. 97.

82. Ibid., p. 80. For more on the "hyperregulation" of everyday Palestinian life, see Makdisi, *Palestine Inside Out,* pp. 2–7.

83. BADIL, "Seam Zones," p. 4.

84. Azoulay and Ophir, *One-State Condition,* p. 131.

85. Ibid., p. 142.

86. Ibid., p. 5.

87. Ibid., p. 99.

88. Ibid., p. 144.

89. Makdisi, *Palestine Inside Out,* p. 299.

90. Azoulay and Ophir, *One-State Condition,* pp. 141–142.

91. Hever, *Political Economy of Israel's Occupation,* p. 10.

92. Ibid., p. 8.

93. Ibid., p. 9.

94. Ibid., p. 11.

95. Ibid., pp. 12–13.

96. According to Hever, the business community was well represented in Israel's negotiating team in Oslo. Ibid., p. 12.

97. Armon, "Israeli Policy Towards the Occupied Palestinian Territories," pp. 586–587.

98. Ibid., p. 588.

99. Ibid., p. 595.

100. Hever, *Political Economy of Israel's Occupation,* p. 13.

101. Ibid., p. 45.

102. Azoulay and Ophir, *One-State Condition,* p. 96.

103. World Bank, *Economic Effects of Restricted Access to Land,* p. 1.

104. Palestine Monetary Authority, *Quarterly Social and Economic Monitor,* p. iv.

105. Hever, *Political Economy of Israel's Occupation,* p. 48.

106. Palestine Monetary Authority, *Quarterly Social and Economic Monitor,* p. 14.

107. Hever, *Political Economy of Israel's Occupation,* p. 46.

108. Palestine Monetary Authority, *Quarterly Social and Economic Monitor,* p. 9.

109. Hever, *Political Economy of Israel's Occupation,* p. 46.

110. World Bank, *Economic Effects of Restricted Access to Land,* p. iv.

111. World Bank, *Stagnation or Revival? Palestinian Economic Prospects* (Washington, DC: World Bank, 2012), p. 5.

112. Ibid., p. 4.

113. Julie Trottier, *Hydropolitics in the West Bank and the Gaza Strip* (Jerusalem: PASSIA, 1999), p. 72.

114. World Bank, *West Bank and Gaza: Assessment of Restrictions on Palestinian Water Sector Development* (Washington, DC: World Bank, 2009), p. v.

115. Stockmarr, "Is It All About Territory?," p. 13.

116. World Health Organization, "Health Conditions in the Occupied Palestinian Territory, Including East Jerusalem, and in the Occupied Syrian Golan," A65/27 Rev. 1, May 11, 2012, p. 8.

117. World Bank, *West Bank and Gaza,* p. vi.

118. Isaac and Powell, "Transformation of the Palestinian Environment," p. 149.

119. American Near East Refugee Aid, "Agriculture in the West Bank and Gaza," *ANERA Reports,* 1 (Washington, DC: ANERA, 2010), p. 5. For the IDF's rebuke on the water issue, see The Civil Administration of Judea and Samaria, *Factsheet: Water in the West Bank,* 2012, http://www.cogat.idf.il/Sip_Storage/FILES/4/3274.pdf.

120. American Near East Refugee Aid, "Agriculture in the West Bank and Gaza," p. 5.

121. World Health Organization, "Health Conditions in the Occupied Palestinian Territory, p. 8.

122. American Near East Refugee Aid, "Water in the West Bank and Gaza," *ANERA Reports* 2 (March 2012), p. 7.

123. Cheshin, Hutman, and Melamed, *Separate and Unequal,* p. 41.

124. Benvenisti, *City of Stone,* p. 140.

125. Ibid., p. 68.

126. Benvenisti, *Intimate Enemies,* p. 51.

127. Benvenisti, *City of Stone,* p. 164.

128. Makdisi, *Palestine Inside Out,* p. 64.

129. Nisreen Alyan, Ronit Sela, and Michal Pomerantz, "Policies of Neglect in East Jerusalem," Association for Civil Rights in Israel, May 2012, p. 1.

130. Benvenisti, *City of Stone,* p. 129.

131. Alyan, Sela, and Pomerantz, "Policies of Neglect in East Jerusalem," p. 2.

132. Ibid., p. 6.

133. Cheshin, Hutman, and Melamed, *Separate and Unequal,* p. 124.

134. International Peace and Cooperation Center, *East Jerusalem Housing Review 2013* (Jerusalem: IPCC, 2013), p. 10.

135. Benvenisti, *City of Stone,* p. 224.

136. Ibid., pp. 176–177.

137. Ibid., pp. 227–228.

138. Author interview with Micha Kurtz, Jerusalem, June 7, 2013.

139. Cheshin, Hutman, and Melamed, *Separate and Unequal,* p. 34.

140. Ibid., p. 32.

141. Ibid., pp. 50–51. Melamed and Col. Cheshin both held senior advisory positions within the Jerusalem Municipality, and Hutman was a journalist at *The Jerusalem Post.*

142. Ibid., pp. 55–56.

143. Ibid., p. 211.

144. Rubenberg, *Palestinians: In Search of a Just Peace,* p. 206.

145. Ibid., p. 207.

146. Cheshin, Hutman, and Melamed, *Separate and Unequal,* p. 62.

147. International Peace and Cooperation Center, *East Jerusalem Housing Review 2013,* p. 3.

148. Cheshin, Hutman, and Melamed, *Separate and Unequal,* p. 66. Today, Palestinians make up approximately 37 percent of all of the city of Jerusalem. According to the Palestinian Central Bureau of Statistics, in 2014 more than 416,000 Palestinians lived in the Jerusalem Governorate. Palestinian Central Bureau of Statistics, "Localities in Jerusalem Governorate by Type of Locality and Population Estimates, 2007–2016," http://www.pcbs.gov.ps/Portals/_Rainbow/Documents/jerus.htm.

149. Azoulay and Ophir, *One-State Condition,* pp. 3–4.

150. Scholars have long written on the economic "de-development" of the West Bank and Gaza under Israeli occupation. For two earlier, excellent examples, see Yusif A. Sayigh, "The Palestinian Economy under Occupation: Dependency and Pauperization," *Journal of Palestine Studies* 15, no. 4 (Summer 1986), pp. 46–67; and Sara Roy, *The Gaza Strip: The Political Economy of De-Development* (Washington, DC: Institute for Palestine Studies, 1995).

151. World Health Organization, "Health Conditions in the Occupied Palestinian Territory," p. 8.

152. Ministry of Health, *Palestinian National Health Strategy 2011–2013* (Ramallah: Palestinian National Authority Ministry of Health, 2010), p, 13.

153. World Health Organization, "Health Conditions in the Occupied Palestinian Territory," p. 10.

154. Ibid., p. 2.

155. Hever, *Political Economy of Israel's Occupation,* p. 26.

156. World Health Organization, "West Bank and Gaza," in *Cooperation Strategy at a Glance* (Washington, DC: WHO, April 2006), p. 1.

157. Palestine Monetary Authority, *Quarterly Social and Economic Monitor,* p. 7.

158. Author interview with Mazin Qumsiyeh, Bethlehem, West Bank, June 11, 2013.

159. Jamil Hilal, "Palestine: The Last Colonial Issue," p. 15.

160. Isaac and Powell, "Transformation of the Palestinian environment," p. 164.

161. Azoulay and Ophir, *One-State Condition,* p. 88.

162. Collins, *Global Palestine,* p. 91.

163. Azoulay and Ophir, *One-State Condition,* p. 164.

164. American Near East Refugee Aid, "Agriculture in the West Bank and Gaza," p. 3.

165. Azoulay and Ophir, *One-State Condition,* p.165.

166. Ibid., p. 168.

167. Ibid., p. 174.

168. Ibid., p. 175.

169. Makdisi, *Palestine Inside Out,* p. 170.

170. Ibid., p. 204.

171. World Health Organization, "Health Conditions in the Occupied Palestinian Territory," p. 9.

172. World Health Organization, "West Bank and Gaza," p. 1.

173. World Health Organization, "Health Conditions in the Occupied Palestinian Territory," p. 7.

174. Azoulay and Ophir, *One-State Condition,* pp. 175–176.

175. Palestine Economic Policy Research Institute, *Deceptive Facts: The Myth of Israel's Role in Promoting Growth in the Occupied Palestinian Territory* (Jerusalem: MAS, 2011), p. 12.

176. American Near East Refugee Aid, "Agriculture in the West Bank and Gaza," p. 3.

177. Palestinian Central Bureau of Statistics, "Poverty Rates Among Individuals According to Household, Monthly Consumption in Palestine by Region, 2011," www.pcbs.gov.ps/Portals/_Rainbow/Documents/Poverty_2011_e.htm.

178. Palestine Monetary Authority, *Quarterly Social and Economic Monitor,* p. 12.

179. American Near East Refugee Aid, "Agriculture in the West Bank and Gaza," p. 2.

180. Israeli Security Agency, "Terror Data and Trends," http://www.shabak.gov.il/english/enterrordata/pages/default.aspx.

181. According to the Israeli military, during the summer 2014 war between Israel and Hamas, some 4,000 rockets were launched toward Israel by Hamas, the Islamic Jihad, and other smaller groups, though 875 of them fell inside Gaza (some deliberately, fired at Israeli ground forces inside Gaza). Isabel Kershner, "Israel Says Hamas Is Hurt Significantly," *New York Times,* September 3, 2014, p. 7.

182. B'Tselem, "Fatalities after Operation Cast Lead," www.btselem.org/statistics/fatalities/after-cast-lead/by-date-of-event.

183. All data in this paragraph come from UN Office for the Coordination of Humanitarian Affairs, "Occupied Palestinian Territories: Gaza Emergency," Situation Report, August 28 2014.

184. Quoted in Hever, *Political Economy of Israel's Occupation,* p. 27.

185. Cheshin, Hutman, and Melamed, *Separate and Unequal,* p. 60.

186. Azoulay and Ophir, *One-State Condition,* p. 14.

Chapter 4. One Nation, Divisible

1. The term "comprador bourgeoisie" is generally defined as that section of the middle classes whose economic welfare, activities, and status are closely tied to international capital in the form of business and commercial alliances with foreign

investors, banks, and multinational corporations. For a full definition see Nicos Poulantzas, "On Social Classes," *New Left Review,* no. 78 (March–April 1973), p. 39.

2. Between 1967 and 2011, Israeli occupation authorities shut down more than eighty-eight Palestinian human rights, social, and charitable organizations and forced thirty-three others to move their offices to the West Bank. See Najat Hirbawi and David Helfand, "Palestinian Institutions in Jerusalem," *Palestine-Israel Journal* 17, no. 12 (2011), available at www.pij.org/details.php?id=1306.

3. Ariella Azoulay and Adi Ophir, *The One-State Condition: Occupation and Democracy in Israel/Palestine,* trans. Tala Haran (Stanford, CA: Stanford University Press, 2013), pp. 158–159.

4. Dina Matar, *What It Means to Be Palestinian: Stories of Palestinian Peoplehood* (London: I. B. Tauris, 2011), p. 25.

5. Ibid., p. 130.

6. Ibid., p. 26.

7. Sarah Graham-Brown, "The Changing Society of the West Bank," *Journal of Palestine Studies* 8, no. 4 (Summer 1979), p. 156.

8. Fawaz Turki, "Palestinian Self-Criticism and the Liberation of Palestinian Society," *Journal of Palestine Studies* 25, no. 2 (Winter 1996), p. 73.

9. Jamil Hilal, "Class Transformation in the West Bank and Gaza," *Journal of Palestine Studies* 6, no. 2 (Winter 1977), p. 168.

10. Don Peretz, "Palestinian Social Stratification: The Political Implications," *Journal of Palestine Studies* 7, no. 1 (Autumn 1977), p. 50.

11. Ibid., p. 56.

12. Ibid., p. 48.

13. Matar, *What It Means to Be Palestinian,* p. 58.

14. Peretz, "Palestinian Social Stratification," p. 56.

15. Ibid., p. 68–70.

16. Baruch Kimmerling and Joel S. Migdal, *Palestinians: The Making of a People* (Cambridge, MA: Harvard University Press, 1994), p. 255.

17. As Sam Bahour, a Ramallah-based writer and activist put it when I interviewed him, "On their return after Oslo, the external Palestinians took more than they were due." Interview with Sam Bahour, Ramallah, West Bank, June 14, 2013.

18. Matar, *What It Means to Be Palestinian,* p. xii.

19. Ahmad S. Khalidi, "The Palestinians: Current Dilemmas, Future Challenges," *Journal of Palestine Studies* 24, no. 2 (Winter 1995), p. 11.

20. Kimmerling and Migdal, *Palestinians,* p. 201.

21. BADIL, *One People United: A Deterritorialized Palestinian Identity* (Bethlehem: BADIL, 2012), pp. 29–37.

22. Peretz, "Palestinian Social Stratification," p. 65.

23. Author interview with Amjad Alqasis, Bethlehem, West Bank, June 11, 2013.

24. Fouad Moughrabi, "The Politics of Palestinian Textbooks," *Journal of Palestine Studies* 31, no. 1 (Autumn 2001), p. 6.

25. Ibid., p. 7.

26. Jean-Pierre Filiu, *Gaza: A History,* trans. John King (Oxford: Oxford University Press, 2014), p. xiii.

27. David McDowall, *Palestine and Israel: The Uprising and Beyond* (Berkeley, CA: University of California Press, 1989), p. 105

28. Helga Baumgarten, "The Three Faces/Phases of Palestinian Nationalism, 1948–2005," *Journal of Palestine Studies* 34, no. 4, p. 38.

29. Graham-Brown, "Changing Society of the West Bank," p. 158.

30. BADIL, *One People United,* p. 26.

31. Ibid., p. 27.

32. Sara M. Roy, "Gaza: New Dynamics of Civic Disintegration," *Journal of Palestine Studies* 22, no. 4 (Summer 1993), p. 27.

33. Amal Jamal, *The Arab Public Sphere in Israel: Media Space and Cultural Resistance* (Bloomington, IN: Indiana University Press, 2009), p. 38.

34. Nurit Peled-Elhanan, *Palestine in Israeli School Books: Ideology and Propaganda in Education* (London: I. B. Tauris, 2012), p. 16. Peled-Elhanan's book remains by far one of the most detailed and critical treatments of Palestinians in Israeli school books.

35. Amal Jamal, *Arab Public Sphere in Israel,* p. 29.

36. Kimmerling and Migdal, *Palestinians,* p. 159.

37. Ibid., p. 181.

38. Ibid., p. 180.

39. Ilan Peleg and Dov Waxman, *Israel's Palestinians: The Conflict Within* (Cambridge: Cambridge University Press, 2011), p. 22.

40. Ibid., pp. 23–24.

41. Arthur Nelson, *In Yours Eyes a Storm: Ways of Being Palestinian* (Berkeley, CA: University of California Press, 2011), p. 28.

42. Amal Jamal, *Arab Public Sphere in Israel,* p. 36.

43. Peleg and Waxman, *Israel's Palestinians,* p. 100.

44. BADIL, *One People United,* p. 13.

45. Peleg and Waxman, *Israel's Palestinians,* p. 99.

46. Ariel Ben Solomon, "Arab Israeli Voters 56% Turnout Defies Expectations," *Jerusalem Post,* January 25, 2013.

47. Amal Jamal, *Arab Public Sphere in Israel,* p. 54.

48. BADIL, *One People United,* p. 13.

49. Ibid., p. 2.

50. Peleg and Waxman, *Israel's Palestinians,* pp. 69–70.

51. BADIL, *One People United,* p. 15.

52. Peleg and Waxman, *Israel's Palestinians,* pp. 3–4. For a concise discussion on the potential role of Palestinian Israelis in any future peace, see Dov Waxman, "Israel's Palestinian Minority in the Two-State Solution: The Missing Dimension," *Middle East Policy* 18, no. 4 (Winter 2011), pp. 68–82.

53. See, among others, Daniel Chirot, *How Societies Change,* 2nd ed. (Thousand Oaks, CA: Sage, 2012).

54. According to the Israeli human rights organization B'Tselem, "Curfew is the most sweeping and extreme restriction on freedom of movement imposed on Palestinians in the Occupied Territories because it imprisons an entire population within the confines of their homes." Yehezkel Lein, *Civilians under Siege: Restrictions on Freedom of Movement as Collective Punishment* (Jerusalem: B'Tselem, 2001), pp. 10–12.

55. PASSIA, *The Phenomenon of Collaborators in Palestine* (Jerusalem: PASSIA, 2006), p. 18.

56. Ibid., p. 4.

57. Ibid., pp. 25–26.

58. Ibid., p. 27. According to Article 16.2 of the September 1995 Interim Agreement on the West Bank and the Gaza Strip, also known as Oslo II, "Palestinians who have maintained contact with the Israeli authorities will not be subjected to acts of harassment, violence, retribution or prosecution. Appropriate ongoing measures will be taken, in coordination with Israel, in order to ensure their protection."

59. PASSIA, *Phenomenon of Collaborators in Palestine,* p. 40.

60. In addition to the other sources cited in this chapter, a small representative sample of the literature on the daily of Palestinians in Gaza and the West Bank includes Rene Backmann, *A Wall in Palestine,* trans. A. Kaiser (New York: Picador, 2006); Mourid Barghouti, *I Saw Ramallah,* trans. Ahdaf Soueif (New York: Anchor

Books, 2000); Jonathan Cook, *Disappearing Palestine: Israel's Experiments in Human Despair* (London: Zed, 2010); Amira Hass, *Drinking the Sea at Gaza: Days and Nights in a Land under Siege* (New York: Owl Books, 1999); and Mark LeVine and Gershon Shafer, eds., *Struggle and Survival in Palestine/Israel* (Berkeley, CA: University of California Press, 2012).

61. Hilal, "Class Transformation in the West Bank and Gaza," p. 167.

62. Ibid., p. 175.

63. Graham-Brown, "Changing Society of the West Bank," p. 149.

64. Hilal, "Class Transformation in the West Bank and Gaza," p. 168.

65. Ibid., p. 168.

66. Graham-Brown, "Changing Society of the West Bank," p. 151.

67. Hilal, "Class Transformation in the West Bank and Gaza," p. 169.

68. Graham-Brown, "Changing Society of the West Bank," p. 154.

69. Hilal, "Class Transformation in the West Bank and Gaza," pp. 172–174.

70. Graham-Brown, "Changing Society of the West Bank," p. 157.

71. Peretz, "Palestinian Social Stratification," pp. 58–59.

72. Graham-Brown, "Changing Society of the West Bank," p. 154.

73. Baruch Kimmerling, *The Invention and Decline of Israeliness: State, Society, and the Military* (Berkeley, CA: University of California Press, 2005), pp. 164–165.

74. Ibid., pp. 165–167.

75. Peretz, "Palestinian Social Stratification," pp. 73–74.

76. Glenn E. Robinson, "The Role of the Professional Middle Class in the Mobilization of Palestinian Society: The Medical and Agricultural Committees," *International Journal of Middle East Studies* 25, no. 2 (May 1993), p. 322.

77. Ibid., p. 301.

78. McDowall, *Palestine and Israel,* p. 107.

79. Robinson, "Role of the Professional Middle Class in the Mobilization of Palestinian Society," p. 301.

80. Ibid., p. 302.

81. Ibid., p. 321.

82. Rex Brynen, "The Dynamics of Palestinian Elite Formation," *Journal of Palestine Studies* 24, no. 3 (Spring 1995), p. 38.

83. Ibid., pp. 38–39.

84. This is a rough estimate, conveyed to me in various interviews in Ramallah and Bethlehem. This range can also be corroborated by the data provided by the

Palestinian Central Bureau of Statistics Whereas the population of the West Bank grew by 540,000 people from 1980 to 1990, from 1990 to 2000 it grew by more than double that number, by 1,200,000. During the next ten years, from 2000 to 2010, it grew by 1,001,000. Assuming that growth by 1,000,000 individuals is the new norm, that leaves an extra 200,000, which appears to have been the result of influx of returnees after the accords were signed.

85. Donald Macintyre, "King of the West Bank," *Independent* (London), June 26, 2008, p. 24.

86. Author interview with Sam Bahour, Ramallah, West Bank, June 14, 2013.

87. Author interview with Amjad Alqasis, Bethlehem, West Bank, June 11, 2013. See also Adel Samara, "Globalization, the Palestinian Economy, and the 'Peace Process,'" *Journal of Palestine Studies* 29, no. 2 (Winter 2000), pp. 20–34.

88. Sufyan Alissa, "The Economics of an Independent Palestine," in *Where Now for Palestine? The Demise of the Two-State Solution,* ed. Jamil Hilal (London: Zed, 2007), p. 136.

89. Author interview with Amjad Alqasis, Bethlehem, West Bank, June 11, 2013.

90. Alissa, "Economics of an Independent Palestine," pp. 135–136.

91. McDowall, *Palestine and Israel,* p. 108.

92. Sara M. Roy, "Gaza: New Dynamics," p. 21.

93. Ibid., pp. 22–23.

94. Ibid., p. 23.

95. Nelson, *In Yours Eyes a Storm,* p. 15.

96. Palestine Economic Policy Research Institute, *Deceptive Facts: The Myth of Israel's Role in Promoting Growth in the Occupied Palestinian Territory* (Jerusalem: MAS, 2011), p. 1.

97. Author interview with Samir Abdullah, Ramallah, West Bank, June 13, 2013.

98. Ibid.

99. Ziad Abu-Amr, "Hamas: From Opposition to Rule," in Hilal, *Where Now for Palestine?,* p. 178.

100. McDowall, *Palestine and Israel,* p. 109.

101. Alissa, "Economics of an Independent Palestine," p. 140.

102. Nelson, *In Yours Eyes a Storm,* p. 13.

103. Ibid., p. 14.

104. Ibid., p. 16.

105. Turki, "Palestinian Self-Criticism and the Liberation of Palestinian Society," p. 75.

106. See Palestinian Center for Policy and Survey Research, *Polls Number 50, 51, 52* (Ramallah: PCPSR, 2013, 2014).

107. Palestinian Center for Policy and Survey Research, *Poll Number 50* (Ramallah: PCPSR, 2013), p. 5.

108. Author interview with Sam Bahour, Ramallah, West Bank, June 14, 2013.

109. Amaney A. Jamal, *Barriers to Democracy: The Other Side of Social Capital in Palestine and the Arab World* (Princeton, NJ: Princeton University Press, 2007), p. 13.

110. Ibid., p. 38.

111. Karin A. Gerster and Helga Baumgarten, "Palestinian NGOs," Rosa Luxemburg Foundation in Palestine, December 30, 2011, p. 9.

112. Jamal, *Barriers to Democracy,* pp. 28–29.

113. Ibid., p. 21.

114. Ibid., p. 18.

115. World Bank, *The Role and Performance of Palestinian NGOs in Health, Education, and Agriculture* (Washington, DC: World Bank, 2006), p. 8.

116. Ibid.

117. Ibid., p. 10.

118. Jamal, *Barriers to Democracy,* p. 13.

119. Ibid., pp. 128–129.

120. Islah Jad, "NGOs: Between Buzzwords and Social Movements," *Development in Practice* 17, nos. 4–5 (August 2007), p. 624; Rema Hammami, "Palestinian NGOs since Oslo: From NGO Politics to Social Movements?," *Middle East Report,* no. 214 (Spring 2000), p. 17.

121. Jad, "NGOs: Between Buzzwords and Social Movements," p. 625.

122. Gerster and Baumgarten, "Palestinian NGOs," p. 7. According to the study (p. 3), 48 percent of NGO employees are twenty-six to thirty-seven years old, and 23 percent are in the seventeen-to-twenty-five age bracket.

123. Hammami, "Palestinian NGOs since Oslo," p. 27.

124. Jad, "NGOs: Between Buzzwords and Social Movements," p. 624.

125. Islah Jad, "The NGO-isation of Arab Women's Movements," *IDS Bulletin* 35, no. 4 (October 2004), p. 38.

126. Jad, "NGOs: Between Buzzwords and Social Movements," p. 626.

127. Jad, "NGO-isation of Arab Women's Movements," p. 39.

128. Ibid., p. 40.

129. Shir Hever, *The Political Economy of Israel's Occupation: Repression Beyond Exploitation* (London: Pluto, 2010), p. 41.

130. Jad, "NGO-isation of Arab Women's Movements," p. 40.

131. World Bank, *Role and Performance of Palestinian NGOs in Health, Education, and Agriculture,* p. 11.

132. Gerster and Baumgarten, "Palestinian NGOs," pp. 1–2.

133. McDowall, *Palestine and Israel,* p. 111.

134. Jad, "NGOs: Between Buzzwords and Social Movements," p. 623.

135. Hever, *Political Economy of Israel's Occupation,* p. 40.

136. McDowall, *Palestine and Israel,* p. 111.

137. Jad, "NGOs: Between Buzzwords and Social Movements," p. 628.

138. Ibid., p. 625.

139. Hever, *Political Economy of Israel's Occupation,* p. 41.

140. Author interview with Sam Bahour, Ramallah, West Bank, June 14, 2013.

141. World Bank, *Role and Performance of Palestinian NGOs in Health, Education, and Agriculture,* p. 10.

142. Ibid., p. 9.

143. The study was conducted by Y. Shalabi as part of his MS thesis at Birzeit University, entitled "International and Local Impacts on the Vision and Roles of Palestinian NGOs," and is quoted by Jad, "NGO-isation of Arab Women's Movements," p. 39.

144. Sara Roy, *Hamas and Civil Society in Gaza: Engaging the Islamist Social Sector* (Princeton, NJ: Princeton University Press, 2011), p. 5.

145. Ibid., p. 163.

146. Ibid., p. 5.

147. Ibid., p. 164.

148. Jamal, *Barriers to Democracy,* p. 34.

149. Ibid., pp. 34–35.

150. Roy, *Hamas and Civil Society in Gaza,* p. 163.

151. Gerster and Baumgarten, "Palestinian NGOs," p. 1.

152. World Bank, *Role and Performance of Palestinian NGOs in Health, Education, and Agriculture,* p. 11.

153. Jamal, *Barriers to Democracy,* p. 51.

154. Hammami, "Palestinian NGOs since Oslo," p. 18.

155. Jamal, *Barriers to Democracy,* p. 54.

156. Jad, "NGOs: Between Buzzwords and Social Movements," p. 623.

157. Hever, *Political Economy of Israel's Occupation,* p. 41.

158. Jad, "NGOs: Between Buzzwords and Social Movements," p. 628.

159. Hever, *Political Economy of Israel's Occupation,* p. 23.

160. Jad, "NGOs: Between Buzzwords and Social Movements," p. 622.

161. Jad, "NGO-isation of Arab Women's Movements," p. 34.

162. Jad, "NGOs: Between Buzzwords and Social Movements," p. 623.

163. Author interview with Hillel Cohen, Jerusalem, June 20, 2013.

164. Matar, *What It Means to Be Palestinian,* p. 94.

Chapter 5. The Travails of State-Building

1. Quoted in Clayton E. Swisher, *The Palestine Papers: The End of the Road?* (Chatham: Hesperus, 2011), p. 110.

2. Karmi, "Introduction," in ibid., pp. 10–11.

3. Ibid., p. 27.

4. Ibid., p. 29.

5. U.S. foreign policy in relation to the Palestinian-Israeli conflict has been extensively discussed in a number of excellent books on the topic and is beyond the scope of the subject at hand here. For a small sampling of works on the topic, see Madeleine Albright, *The Mighty and the Almighty: Reflections on America, God, and World Affairs* (New York: Harper Perennial, 2006), pp. 123–144; Bill Clinton, *My Life* (New York: Vintage, 2005); John J. Mearsheimer and Stephen M. Walt, *The Israeli Lobby and U.S. Foreign Policy* (New York: Farrar, Straus and Giroux, 2007); and Donald Neff, *Fallen Pillars: U.S. Policy Towards Palestine and Israel since 1945* (Washington, DC: Institute for Palestine Studies, 1995).

6. Swisher, *Palestine Papers,* p. 33. Although the United States technically considers the settlements to be a violation of the Fourth Geneva Convention of 1949, its criticism of Israeli settlement construction has seldom gone beyond expressions of "concern" and rather muted criticism.

7. Swisher, *Palestine Papers,* p. 35.

8. See President Bush's letter to Prime Minister Sharon dated April 14, 2004, http://georgewbush-whitehouse.archives.gov/news/releases/2004/04/20040414-3.html.

9. Swisher, *Palestine Papers,* p. 60.

10. Ziad Abu-Amr, "The Palestine Legislative Council: A Critical Assessment," *Journal of Palestine Studies* 26, no. 4 (Summer 1997), p. 94.

11. Yezid Sayigh, "Armed Struggle and State Formation," *Journal of Palestine Studies* 26, no. 4 (Summer 1997), p. 21.

12. Sayigh, "Armed Struggle and State Formation," p. 17.

13. Mushtaq Husain Khan, "Introduction: State Formation in Palestine," in *State Formation in Palestine: Viability and Governance During a Social Transformation*, ed. Mushtaq Husain Khan, George Giacaman, and Inge Amundsen (London: Routledge, 2004), p. 2.

14. Barry Rubin, *The Transformation of Palestinian Politics: From Revolution to State-Building* (Cambridge, MA: Harvard University Press, 1999), p. 24.

15. Inge Amundsen and Basem Ezbidi, "PNA Political Institutions and the Future of State formation," in Khan, Giacaman, and Amundsen, *State Formation in Palestine*, p. 154.

16. Author interview with Khalil Nakhleh, Ramallah, West Bank, June 13, 2013.

17. Daron Acemoglu and James A. Robinson, *Why Nations Fail: The Origins of Power, Prosperity, and Poverty* (New York: Crown Business, 2012), p. 101.

18. Giovanni Capoccia and R. Daniel Keleman, "The Study of Critical Junctures: Theory, Narrative, and Counterfactuals in Historical Institutionalism," *World Politics* 59, no. 3 (April 2007), p. 343.

19. Jamil Hilal, "PLO Institutions: The Challenge Ahead," *Journal of Palestine Studies* 23, no. 1 (Autumn 1993), p. 46.

20. Author interview with Khalil Nakhleh, Ramallah, West Bank, June 13, 2013.

21. Author interview with Sam Bahour, Ramallah, West Bank, June 14, 2013.

22. Amundsen and Ezbidi, "PNA Political Institutions and the Future of State Formation," p. 141.

23. Prime Minister Sharon's unstated plan was to split the West Bank 50–50 by annexing most of Area C to Israel. This is similar to what Naftali Bennett, leader of the Jewish Home Party and minister of the economy in Prime Minister Netanyahu's cabinet, proposed in a 2014 *New York Times* op-ed piece: Naftali Bennett, "For Israel, Two-State Is No Solution," *New York Times*, November 7, 2014, p. 31.

24. For a concise summary of the institutional and diplomatic consequences of the 2002 invasion of the West Bank, see Lev Grinberg, "The Arrogance of Occupation," *Middle East Policy* 9, no. 1 (March 2002), pp. 46–52.

25. Graham Usher, "The Democratic Resistance: Hamas, Fatah, and the Palestinian Elections," *Journal of Palestine Studies* 35, no. 3 (Spring 2006), p. 27.

26. Nathan J. Brown, "Constituting Palestine: The Effort to Write a Basic Law for the Palestinian Authority," *Middle East Journal* 54, no. 1 (Winter 2000), p. 32.

27. Author interview with Samir Abdullah, Ramallah, West Bank, June 13, 2013.

28. Rubin, *Transformation of Palestinian Politics,* p. 19.

29. Jamil Hilal and Mushtaq Husain Khan, "Palestinian State Formation under the PNA: Potential Outcomes and Their Viability," in Khan, Giacaman, and Amundsen, *State Formation in Palestine,* p. 86.

30. Brown, "Constituting Palestine," p. 25.

31. Nathan Brown, *Palestinian Politics after the Oslo Accords: Resuming Arab Palestine* (Berkeley, CA: University of California Press, 2003), p. 59.

32. Brown, "Constituting Palestine," p. 35.

33. Ibid., p. 41.

34. Ibid., p. 43.

35. Mahdi Abdul Hadi, "Assessment of Palestinian Elections," in *Dialogues on Palestinian State-Building and Identity,* ed. Mahdi Abdul Hadi (Jerusalem: PASSIA, 1999), p. 12.

36. Amundsen and Ezbidi, "PNA Political Institutions and the Future of State Formation," p. 144.

37. Rex Brynen, "The Dynamics of Palestinian Elite Formation," *Journal of Palestine Studies* 24, no. 3 (Spring 1995), p. 32.

38. Sayigh, "Armed Struggle and State Formation," p. 24.

39. Author interview with Khalil Nakhleh, Ramallah, West Bank, June 13, 2013.

40. Rex Brynen, "The Patrimonial Dimension of Palestinian Politics," *Journal of Palestine Studies* 25, no. 1 (Autumn 1995), p. 23.

41. Ibid., p. 25.

42. Ibid., p. 33.

43. Ibid., p. 24.

44. Ibid., p. 28.

45. Ibid., p. 32.

46. Odd-Helge Fjeldstad and Adel Zagha, "Taxation and State Formation in Palestine 1994–2000," in Khan, Giacaman, and Amundsen, *State Formation in Palestine,* p. 192.

47. Riad Malki, "The Opposition and Its Role in the Peace Process," in Abdul Hadi, *Dialogues on Palestinian State-Building and Identity*, pp. 3–4.

48. Cheryl A. Rubenberg, *The Palestinians: In Search of Just Peace* (Boulder, CO: Lynne Rienner, 2003), pp. 271–272.

49. Nathan Brown, "Fayyad Is Not the Problem, but Fayyadism Is Not the Solution to Palestine's Political Crisis," *Carnegie Commentary*, September 2010, pp. 2–3.

50. Raja Khalidi and Sobhi Samour, "Neoliberalism as Liberation: The Statehood Program and the Remaking of the Palestinian National Movement," *Journal of Palestine Studies* 40, no. 2 (Winter 2011), p. 12.

51. Mushtaq Husain Khan, "Evaluating the Emerging Palestinian State: 'Good Governance' versus 'Transformational Potential,'" in Khan, Giacaman, and Amundsen, *State Formation in Palestine*, p. 49.

52. Ziad Abu-Amr, "Hamas: From Opposition to Rule," in *Where Now for Palestine? The Demise of the Two-State Solution*, ed. Jamil Hilal (London: Zed, 2007), p. 181.

53. Brynen, "Dynamics of Palestinian Elite Formation," p. 32.

54. Rubenberg, *Palestinians: In Search of a Just Peace*, p. 276.

55. Jamil Hilal, "Palestine: The Last Colonial Issue," in Hilal, *Where Now for Palestine?*, p. 15.

56. Ahmad S. Khalidi, "The Palestinians: Current Dilemmas, Future Challenges," *Journal of Palestine Studies* 24, no. 2 (Winter 1995), p. 5.

57. Hilal, "PLO Institutions," p. 58.

58. Nathan Brown, "Are Palestinians Building a State?," *Carnegie Commentary*, June 2010, p. 1.

59. Brown, "Fayyad Is Not the Problem," p. 3.

60. Abu-Amr, "Palestine Legislative Council: A Critical Assessment," p. 90.

61. Ibid., p. 93.

62. Abu-Amr, "Palestine Legislative Council," in Abdul Hadi, *Dialogues*, p. 25.

63. See, for example, "Report by the Palestinian Centre for Human Rights on the Closure Imposed by Israel on the Gaza Strip," April 18, 1996, http://www.pchrgaza.org/files/Reports/English/Closeup7.htm.

64. Abu-Amr, "Palestine Legislative Council," in Abdul Hadi, *Dialogues*, p. 26.

65. Rubin, *Transformation of Palestinian Politics*, p. 29.

66. Brown, *Palestinian Politics after the Oslo Accords*, p. 101.

67. Ibid., p. 106.

68. Abu-Amr, "Palestine Legislative Council," in Abdul Hadi, *Dialogues,* p. 27.

69. Hilal, "Palestine: The Last Colonial Issue," p. 7.

70. PASSIA, *Palestinian Security Sector Governance: Challenges and Prospects* (Jerusalem: PASSIA, 2006), pp. 40–41.

71. According to Brown, although members of the Gaza legal community tended to dominate the top echelons of the PNA's legal structure, West Bankers viewed their own legal structures and personnel as more advanced. Also, Brown argues that while the differences in and confusion over various legal traditions in Gaza and the West Bank were real, they should not be exaggerated. Brown, *Palestinian Politics after the Oslo Accords,* pp. 23–24.

72. Ibid., p. 47.

73. Brown, "Are Palestinians Building a State?," p. 5.

74. PASSIA, *The Phenomenon of Collaborators in Palestine* (Jerusalem: PASSIA, 2006), p. 4.

75. Brown, *Palestinian Politics after the Oslo Accords,* p. 36.

76. Brown, "Are Palestinians Building a State?," p. 4.

77. Beverley Milton-Edwards, "Palestinian State-Building: Police and Citizens as Test of Democracy," *British Journal of Middle Eastern Studies* 25, no. 1 (May 1998), p. 99.

78. Ibid., p. 100.

79. Hilal and Khan, "Palestinian State Formation under the PNA," p. 84.

80. These number are based on U.S. government estimates (Al Jazeera, "The Palestine Papers, 10 October 2009," available at http://transparency.aljazeera.net/files/4865.pdf); and the Security Sector Reform Resource Center, available at http://www.ssrresourcecentre.org/countries/country-profile-palestinian-territories/.

81. Hilal and Khan, "Palestinian State Formation under the PNA," p. 85.

82. Brown, *Palestinian Politics after the Oslo Accords,* pp. 41–43.

83. Khan, "Evaluating the Emerging Palestinian State," p. 13.

84. Milton-Edwards, "Palestinian State-Building," p. 105.

85. PASSIA, *Palestinian Security Sector Governance,* p. 36.

86. Ibid., p. 21.

87. Milton-Edwards, "Palestinian State-Building," p. 100.

88. PASSIA, *Palestinian Security Sector Governance,* p. 35.

89. Khan, "Introduction: State Formation in Palestine," p. 5.

90. Judith Spirig and Hans Heyn, "The Political Economy of the West Bank," Konrad Adenauer Stiftung, December 13, 2010, p. 3.

91. Adel Zagha and Husam Zomlot, "Israel and the Palestinian Economy: Integration or Containment?," in Khan, Giacaman, and Amundsen, *State Formation in Palestine,* p. 136.

92. Ibid., pp. 120–121.

93. Ibid., pp. 122–123.

94. Author interview with Samir Abdullah, Ramallah, West Bank, June 13, 2013.

95. Zagha and Zomlot, "Israel and the Palestinian Economy," p. 124.

96. Ibid., p. 125.

97. Khan, "Evaluating the Emerging Palestinian State," p. 37.

98. Hilal and Khan, "Palestinian State Formation under the PNA," p. 94.

99. Ibid., p. 72.

100. Amundsen and Ezbidi, "PNA Political Institutions and the Future of State Formation," p. 142.

101. Sufyan Alissa, "The Economics of an Independent Palestine," in Hilal, *Where Now for Palestine?,* p. 134.

102. Ahmed Qubaja, *Fiscal Sustainability of the Palestinian National Authority: Experience and Future Prospects* (Jerusalem: MAS, 2012), p. i.

103. Author interview with Samir Abdullah, Ramallah, West Bank, June 13, 2013. Abdullah is director general of the Ramallah-based Palestine Economic Policy Research Institute and former PNA economy minister.

104. Khan, "Evaluating the Emerging Palestinian State," p. 49.

105. Ibid., p. 16.

106. Coalition for Integrity and Accountability, *Corruption Report: Palestine 2012* (Ramallah: AMAN, 2013), p. 26.

107. Hilal and Khan, "Palestinian State Formation under the PNA," p. 75.

108. Qubaja, *Fiscal Sustainability of the Palestinian National Authority,* p. 2.

109. Amundsen and Ezbidi, "PNA Political Institutions and the Future of State Formation," pp. 183–184.

110. Ibid., p. 188.

111. Rubenberg, *Palestinians: In Search of a Just Peace,* p. 258. Rubenberg presents the names of some of the PNA officials directly benefiting from these monopolies at the time.

112. Ibid., p. 259.

113. Khan, "Evaluating the Emerging Palestinian State," p. 60.

114. Ibid., p. 39. On occasion, when it suited their purposes, Israeli authorities would denounce Arafat's slush fund, although they were not only aware of it, they actually funded it.

115. Hilal and Khan, "Palestinian State Formation under the PNA," p. 79.

116. Ibid., pp. 96–97.

117. Fadle Mustafa Al-Naqib, *Towards a Palestinian Developmental Vision* (Jerusalem: Palestine Economic Policy Research Institute, 2003), p. 2.

118. Hilal and Khan, "Palestinian State Formation under the PNA," p. 76.

119. World Bank, *Towards Economic Sustainability of a Future Palestinian State: Promoting Private Sector-Led Growth* (Washington, DC: World Bank, 2012), p. iii.

120. Qubaja, *Fiscal Sustainability of the Palestinian National Authority,* p. i.

121. Sari Hanafi and Linda Tabar, "Donor Assistance, Rent-Seeking and Elite Formation," in Khan, Giacaman, and Amundsen, *State Formation in Palestine,* p. 222.

122. Palestine Economic Policy Research Institute, *Economic and Social Monitor, 2011* (Jerusalem: MAS, 2011), p. 1.

123. World Bank, *Towards Economic Sustainability of a Future Palestinian State,* p. 4.

124. Spirig and Heyn, "Political Economy of the West Bank," p. 6. For a useful and concise summary of the West Bank economy, see David Cobham, *A Macroeconomic Narrative for the Palestinian Economy* (Jerusalem: MAS, 2012), p. 2.

125. Khan, "Introduction: State Formation in Palestine," p. 3.

126. Palestinian Center for Policy and Survey Research, *Palestinian Public Poll Number 46 Press Release* (Ramallah: PCPSR, 2012).

127. Coalition for Integrity and Accountability, *Corruption Report,* p. 15.

128. Palestinian Center for Policy and Survey Research, *Palestinian Public Poll Number 46 Press Release;* Palestinian Center for Policy and Survey Research, *Poll Number 44* (Ramallah: PCPSR, 2012), p. 3.

129. Marie Chene, "Overview of Corruption and Anti-Corruption in Palestine," *Transparency International,* no. 314 (January 19, 2012), p. 1.

130. Ibid., p. 4.

131. Ibid., p. 3.

132. Ibid., p. 9.

133. Coalition for Integrity and Accountability, *Corruption Report,* p. 18.

134. Ibid., p. 34.

135. Malki, "Opposition and Its Role in the Peace Process," p. 7.

136. Ibid.

137. Palestinian Center for Policy and Survey Research, *Palestinian Public Poll Number 46 Press Release.*

138. Michael Bröning, *Political Parties in Palestine: Leadership and Thought* (New York: Palgrave Macmillan, 2013), p. 11.

139. Hilal and Khan, "Palestinian State Formation under the PNA," p. 85.

140. Abu-Amr, "Hamas: A Historical and Political Background," *Journal of Palestine Studies* 22, no. 4 (Summer 1993), p. 8.

141. Sara Roy, *Hamas and Civil Society in Gaza: Engaging the Islamist Social Sector* (Princeton, NJ: Princeton University Press, 2011), p. 6.

142. Hilal, "Palestine: The Last Colonial Issue," p. 6.

143. Helga Baumgarten, "The Three Faces/Phases of Palestinian Nationalism, 1948–2005." *Journal of Palestine Studies* 34, no. 4 (Summer 2005), p. 39.

144. Ibid., pp. 25–26.

145. Roy, *Hamas and Civil Society in Gaza,* p. 165.

146. Rubin, *Transformation of Palestinian Politics,* p. 122.

147. Charles D. Smith, *Palestine and the Arab-Israeli Conflict: A History with Documents,* 8th ed. (Boston, MA: Bedford St. Martin's, 2013), p. 448.

148. Usher, "Democratic Resistance," p. 20.

149. International Crisis Group, "Ruling Palestine I: Gaza under Hamas," *Middle East Report No. 73,* March 19, 2008, pp. 6–8.

150. Khaled Hroub, "Hamas after Shaykh Yasin and Rantisi," *Journal of Palestine Studies* 33, no. 4 (Summer 2004), p. 28.

151. International Crisis Group, "Ruling Palestine I," p. i.

152. Ibid., p. 26.

153. Abu-Amr, "Hamas: From Opposition to Rule," pp. 184–186.

154. Usher, "The Palestinians after Arafat," *Journal of Palestine Studies* 34, no. 3 (Spring 2005), p. 52.

155. Yezid Sayigh, "Inducing a Failed State in Palestine," *Survival* 49, no. 3 (Autumn 2007), p. 29.

156. Lihi Ben Shitrit and Mahmoud Jaraba, "The Threat of Jihadism in the West Bank," *Sada,* February 6, 2014, available at http://carnegieendowment.org/sada/2014/02/06/threat-of-jihadism-in-west-bank/hoae.

157. Roy, *Hamas and Civil Society in Gaza,* p. 15.

158. Author interview with Sam Bahour, Ramallah, West Bank, June 14, 2013.

159. Palestinian Center for Policy and Survey Research, *Palestinian Public Poll Number 37* (Ramallah: PCPSR, 2010). Of those polled, 57 percent opposed the PNA's dissolution.

160. Author interview with Sam Bahour, Ramallah, West Bank, June 14, 2013.

161. Ibid.

162. Palestinian Center for Policy and Survey Research, *Palestinian Public Poll Number 37.*

163. Palestinian Center for Policy and Survey Research, *Poll Number 44* (Ramallah: PCPSR, 2012), p. 2.

164. Anne Le More, "Killing with Kindness: Funding the Demise of a Palestinian State," *International Affair* 81, no. 5 (2005), p. 986.

165. Abu-Amr, "Palestine Legislative Council: A Critical Assessment," p. 96.

166. Khalil Shikaki, "The Peace Process, National Reconstruction, and the Transition to Democracy in Palestine," *Journal of Palestine Studies* 25, no. 2 (Winter 1996), p. 10. Significantly, not all Inside revolutionaries resented Arafat, nor did all wealthy Outsiders necessarily favor him. Rubin, *Transformation of Palestinian Politics,* p. 90.

167. Amaney A. Jamal, *Barriers to Democracy: The Other Side of Social Capital in Palestine and the Arab World* (Princeton, NJ: Princeton University Press, 2007), p. 24.

168. Brown, "Are Palestinians Building a State?," p. 10.

169. Author interview with Amjad Alqasis, Bethlehem, West Bank, June 11, 2013.

170. As'ad Ghanem, "Israel and the 'Danger of Demography,'" in Hilal, *Where Now for Palestine?,* p. 59.

171. Author interview with Amjad Alqasis, Bethlehem, West Bank, June 11, 2013.

172. Jad Isaac and Owen Powell, "The Transformation of the Palestinian Environment," in Hilal, *Where Now for Palestine?,* p. 157.

173. Author interview with Samir Abdullah, Ramallah, West Bank, June 13, 2013.

174. In January 2011 the Al Jazeera television network released confidential transcripts and documents related to Israeli-Palestinian negotiations. Dubbed "The

Palestine Papers," the documents are available at http://www.aljazeera.com/palestinepapers/.

175. Swisher, *Palestine Papers,* p. 113.

176. Palestinian Center for Policy and Survey Research, *Palestinian Public Poll Number 37.*

177. Spirig and Heyn, "Political Economy of the West Bank," p. 4.

178. Author interview with Sam Bahour, Ramallah, West Bank, June 14, 2013.

179. Author interview with Khalil Nakhleh, Ramallah, West Bank, June 13, 2013.

180. Khalidi and Samour, "Neoliberalism as Liberation," pp. 9–10.

181. Ibid., p. 16. For a discussion of liberal peace theory and the evolution of Hamas, see Mandy Turner, "Building Democracy in Palestine: Liberal Peace Theory and the Election of Hamas," *Democratization* 13, no. 5 (December 2006), pp. 739–755.

182. Khalidi and Samour, "Neoliberalism as Liberation," pp. 15–16.

183. Brown, "Fayyad Is Not the Problem," p. 2.

184. Sayigh, "Inducing a Failed State in Palestine," p. 26.

185. Ibid., p. 8.

186. Ibid., p. 21.

187. Ibid., p. 27.

188. Ben Shitrit and Jaraba, "Threat of Jihadism in the West Bank."

189. Brown, "Fayyad Is Not the Problem," p. 1.

190. Brown, "Are Palestinians Building a State?," p. 1.

191. Shir Hever, *The Political Economy of Israel's Occupation: Repression Beyond Exploitation* (London: Pluto, 2012), p. 14.

192. Author interview with Mazin Qumsiyeh, Bethlehem, West Bank, June 11, 2013.

193. Spirig and Heyn, "Political Economy of the West Bank," p. 2.

194. Palestinian Center for Policy and Survey Research, *Poll Number 46,* p. 2.

195. Usher, "Palestinians after Arafat," pp. 46–48.

Chapter 6. The Road Ahead

1. Author interview with Amjad Alqasis, Bethlehem, West Bank, June 11, 2013.

2. Ilan Pappe, *The Ethnic Cleansing of Palestine* (Oxford: Oneworld, 2006), p. 245.

3. Jamil Hilal, "Palestine: The Last Colonial Issue," in *Where Now for Palestine? The Demise of the Two-State Solution,* ed. Jamil Hilal (London: Zed, 2007), p. 11.

4. Ariella Azoulay and Adi Ophir, *The One-State Condition: Occupation and Democracy in Israel/Palestine,* trans. Tala Haran (Stanford, CA: Stanford University Press, 2013), p. 17.

5. Author interview with Sam Bahour, Ramallah, West Bank, June 14, 2013.

6. Figure from the Israeli human rights organization B'Tselem, available at http://www.btselem.org/statistics/detainees_and_prisoners.

7. Author interview with Amjad Alqasis, Bethlehem, West Bank, June 11, 2013.

8. Rashid Khalidi, *Palestinian Identity: The Construction of Modern National Consciousness* (New York: Columbia University Press, 1997), p. 199.

9. Author interview with Sam Bahour, Ramallah, West Bank, June 14, 2013.

10. Omar Barghouti, *BDS: Boycott, Divestment, Sanctions—The Global Struggle for Palestinian Rights* (Chicago: Haymarket Books, 2011), p. 4.

11. Ibid., p. 49. The BDS movement's first declaration, issued on July 9, 2005, appears in ibid., pp. 239–247. More information on the BDS movement is available at www.bdsmovement.net.

12. Khalil Shikaki, "Willing to Compromise: Palestinian Public Opinion and the Peace Process," United States Institute of Peace Special Report, no. 158 (January 2006), p. 9.

13. Ibid., p. 10.

14. Ira Sharansky, "The Problem of a Palestine That Would Be Economically Autonomous: A Commentary," *Policy Studies Journal* 27, no. 4 (1999), p. 667.

15. See, for example, Clayton E. Swisher, *The Truth About Camp David: The Untold Story About the Collapse of the Middle East Peace Process* (New York: Nation Books, 2004).

16. Ghada Karmi, "The One-State Solution: An Alternative Vision for Israeli-Palestinian Peace," *Journal of Palestine Studies* 40, no. 2 (Winter 2011), p. 65.

17. Benny Morris, *One State, Two States* (New Haven, CT: Yale University Press, 2009), p. 163.

18. Nadav G. Shelef, *Evolving Nationalism: Homeland, Identity, and Religion in Israel, 1925–2005* (Ithaca, NY: Cornell University Press, 2010), p. 5.

19. Yezid Sayigh, "Redefining the Basics: Sovereignty and Security of the Palestinian State," *Journal of Palestine Studies* 24, no. 4 (Summer 1995), pp. 6–7.

20. Rand Palestinian State Study Team, *Building a Successful Palestinian State* (Santa Monica, CA: Rand, 2005), p. 8.

21. Roni Krouzman, "21st Century Palestine: Toward a 'Swiss Cheese' State," *Middle East Report*, no. 213 (Winter, 1999), pp. 38–40.

22. Nathan J. Brown, "Fayyad Is Not the Problem, but Fayyadism Is Not the Solution to Palestine's Political Crisis," *Carnegie Commentary*, September 2010, p. 6.

23. Author interview with Mazin Qumsiyeh, Bethlehem, West Bank, June 11, 2013.

24. Saree Makdisi, *Palestine Inside Out: An Everyday Occupation* (New York: Norton, 2010), p. 290.

25. Palestinian Center for Policy and Survey Research, *Poll Number 46* (Ramallah: PCPSR, 2012), p. 8.

26. Palestinian Center for Policy and Survey Research, *Palestinian Public Poll Number 42* (Ramallah: PCPSR, 2011).

27. Khalil Shikaki, "The Future of Israel-Palestine: A One-State Reality in the Making," *NOREF Report*, May 2012, p. 4.

28. Ibid., p. 3.

29. Makdisi, *Palestine Inside Out*, p. 280.

30. For one of these alarmist voices, see, for example, David C. Unger, "The Inevitable Two-State Solution," *World Policy Journal* 25, no. 3 (Fall 2008), pp. 59–67. Unger is a member of the *New York Times* editorial board.

31. Asher Susser, *Israel, Jordan, and Palestine: The Two-State Imperative* (Waltham, MA: Brandeis University Press, 2012), p. 213.

32. Ibid., p. 222. David Unger also points to the "inescapable logic" of the two-state solution and sees it as the only "realistic basis for peace." David C. Unger, "Maps of War, Maps of Peace: Finding a Two-State Solution to the Israeli-Palestinian Question," *World Policy Journal* 19, no. 2 (Summer 2002), pp. 2, 6.

33. Karmi, "One-State Solution," p. 71. For a discussion of some of the debates and issues surrounding the one-state solution, see James Ron, "Palestine, the UN and the One-State Solution," *Middle East Policy* 18, no. 4 (Winter 2011), pp. 59–67. For an even-handed elaboration of the idea, see Jenab Tutunji and Kamal Khaldi, "A Binational State in Palestine: The Rational Choice for Palestinians and the Moral Choice for Israelis," *International Affairs* 73, no. 1 (January 1997), pp. 31–58.

34. Virginia Tilley, *The One-State Solution: A Breakthrough for Peace in the Israeli-Palestinian Deadlock* (Ann Arbor, MI: University of Michigan Press, 2008), pp. 9, 183.

35. Karmi, "One-State Solution," p. 67.

36. Author interview with Sam Bahour, Ramallah, West Bank, June 14, 2013.

37. Azoulay and Ophir, *One-State Condition,* pp. 252–254.

38. Ibid., pp. 263–264.

39. Andrew M. Wender, "Transcending Nationalist Divides: Religious Reconciliation as the Basis for a One-State Solution in Israel/Palestine," *Digest of Middle East Studies* 20, no. 2 (Fall 2011), p. 264.

40. Ibid., p. 261.

41. Karmi, "One-State Solution," p. 67.

42. Tutunji and Khaldi, "Binational State in Palestine," p. 33.

43. Sari Nusseibeh, *What Is a Palestinian State Worth?* (Cambridge, MA: Harvard University Press, 2011), p. 14.

44. As'ad Ghanem, "Israel and the 'Danger of Demography,'" in Hilal, *Where Now for Palestine?,* p. 68.

45. Karmi, "One-State Solution," p. 72.

46. Unger, "Maps of War, Maps of Peace," p. 7.

47. Susser, *Israel, Jordan, and Palestine,* p. 5.

48. Mathias Mossberg, "One Land—Two States? An Introduction to the Parallel States Concept," in *One Land, Two States: Israel and Palestine as Parallel States,* ed. Mark LeVine and Mathias Mossberg (Berkeley, CA: University of California Press, 2014), p. 5.

49. Ibid., p. 15.

50. Eyal Megged, one of the proponents of the parallel-states model and a columnist at *Haaretz,* acknowledges some of these challenges in "Parallel Lives, Parallel States: Imagining a Different Future," in LeVine and Mossberg, *One Land, Two States,* pp. 244–254.

51. Ghanem, "Israel and the 'Danger of Demography,'" p. 49.

52. Pappe, *Ethnic Cleansing of Palestine,* p. 260.

53. Quoted in ibid., p. 250.

54. Ibid., p. 244.

55. Meron Benvenisti, *Sacred Landscape: The Buried History of the Holy Land since 1948,* trans. Maxine Kaufman-Lacusta (Berkeley, CA: University of California Press, 2000), p. 325.

56. Pappe, *Ethnic Cleansing of Palestine,* p. 255.

57. Shikaki, "Willing to Compromise," p. 11.

58. Morris, *One State, Two States,* pp. 193–194.

59. Ibid., pp. 200–201.

60. Ibid., p. 199.

61. Rashid Khalidi, *The Iron Cage: The Story of the Palestinian Struggle for Statehood* (Boston, MA: Beacon, 2006), p. 182.

62. John Quigley, *The Statehood of Palestine: International Law in the Middle East Conflict* (Cambridge: Cambridge University Press, 2010), p. 245.

63. Ilan Peleg and Dov Waxman, *Israel's Palestinians: The Conflict Within* (Cambridge: Cambridge University Press, 2011), p. 6.

64. Shikaki, "Future of Israel-Palestine," pp. 1–10.

65. Ibid., p. 1.

66. Ibid., p. 2.

67. Menachem Klein, *The Shift: Israel-Palestine from Border Struggle to Ethnic Conflict* (New York: Columbia University Press, 2010), p. 5.

68. Ibid., p. 4.

69. Ibid., p. 124.

70. As'ad Ghanem, *Palestinian Politics after Arafat: A Failed National Movement* (Bloomington, IN: Indiana University Press, 2010), p. 182.

71. Ibid., p. 171.

72. Ibid., p. 172.

73. Jeffrey Herbst and Greg Mills, "Introduction: Managing Fault Lines in the Twenty-First Century," in *On the Fault Line: Managing Tensions and Divisions within Societies,* ed. Jeffrey Herbst, Terence McNamee and Greg Mills (London: Profile Books, 2012), p. 15.

74. David D. Laitin, *Nations, States, and Violence* (Oxford: Oxford University Press, 2007), p. 112.

75. Ibid., p. 137.

76. Stefan Wolfe, *Ethnic Conflict: A Global Perspective* (Oxford: Oxford University Press, 2006), p. 139.

77. Ibid., p. 154.

78. Ibid., p. 137.

Bibliography

Abdul Hadi, Mahdi. "Assessment of Palestinian Elections." In *Dialogue on Palestinian State-Building and Identity,* edited by Mahdi Abdul Hadi. Jerusalem: PASSIA, 1999, pp. 11–13.

Abou-El-Haj, Rifaʿat ʿAli. *Formation of the Modern State: The Ottoman Empire, Sixteenth to Eighteenth Centuries.* Syracuse, NY: Syracuse University Press, 2005.

Abu-Amr, Ziad. "Hamas: From Opposition to Rule." In *Where Now for Palestine? The Demise of the Two-State Solution,* edited by Jamil Hilal. London: Zed, 2007, pp. 167–187.

———. "Hamas: A Historical and Political Background." *Journal of Palestine Studies* 22, no. 4 (Summer 1993), pp. 5–19.

———. "The Palestine Legislative Council." In *Dialogues on Palestinian State-Building and Identity,* edited by Mahdi Abdul Hadi. Jerusalem: PASSIA, 1999, pp. 25–29.

———. "The Palestine Legislative Council: A Critical Assessment." *Journal of Palestine Studies* 26, no. 4 (Summer 1997), pp. 90–97.

Abu-Lughod, Lila, and Ahmad H. Saʿdi. "Introduction: The Claims of Memory." In *Nakba: Palestine, 1948, and the Claim of Memory,* edited by Ahmad H. Saʿdi and Lila Abu-Lughod. New York: Columbia University Press, 2007, pp. 1–24.

Acemoglu, Daron, and James A. Robinson. *Why Nations Fail: The Origins of Power, Prosperity, and Poverty.* New York: Crown Business, 2012.

Albright, Madeleine. *The Mighty and the Almighty: Reflections on America, God, and World Affairs.* New York: Harper Perennial, 2006.

Alissa, Sufyan. "The Economics of an Independent Palestine." In *Where Now for Palestine? The Demise of the Two-State Solution,* edited by Jamil Hilal (London: Zed, 2007), pp. 123–143.

Al Jazeera. "The Palestine Papers, 10 October 2009." Available at http://transparency.aljazeera.net/files/4865.pdf.

Al-Naqib, Fadle Mustafa. *Towards a Palestinian Developmental Vision.* Jerusalem: Palestine Economic Policy Research Institute, 2003.

American Near East Refugee Aid. "Water in the West Bank and Gaza." *ANERA Reports* 2 Washington, DC: 2012.

———. "Agriculture in the West Bank and Gaza." *ANERA Reports* 1 Washington, DC: 2010.

Amundsen, Inge, and Basem Ezbidi. "PNA Political Institutions and the Future of State Formation." In *State Formation in Palestine: Viability and Governance During a Social Transformation,* edited by Mushtaq Husain Khan, George Giacaman, and Inge Amundsen. London: Routledge, 2004, pp. 141–167.

Anderson, Benedict. *Imagined Communities: Reflections on the Origins and Spread of Nationalism.* London: Verso, 2006.

Armon, Arie. "Israeli Policy Towards the Occupied Palestinian Territories: The Economic Dimension, 1967–2007." *Middle East Journal* 61, no. 4 (Autumn 2007), pp. 573–595.

Asher, Arian. *Politics in Israel: The Second Republic.* 2nd ed. Washington, DC: CQ Press, 2005.

Azoulay, Ariella, and Adi Ophir. *The One-State Condition: Occupation and Democracy in Israel/Palestine.* Translated by Tala Haran. Stanford, CA: Stanford University Press, 2013.

Backmann, Rene. *A Wall in Palestine.* Translated by A. Kaiser. New York: Picador, 2006.

BADIL. *Israeli Land Grab and Forced Population Transfer of Palestinians.* Bethlehem: BADIL, 2013.

———. *One People United: A Deterrritorialized Palestinian Identity.* Bethlehem: BADIL, 2012.

———. "Seam Zones." *BADIL Occasional Bulletin No. 25* (August 2012).

BADIL and Kairos Palestine. *Palestinian Christians: Ongoing Forcible Displacement Until When?* Bethlehem: BADIL, 2012.

Baker, Abeer, and Anat Matar, eds. *Threat: Palestinian Political Prisoners in Israel.* London: Pluto Press, 2011.

Barghouti, Mourid. *I Saw Ramallah.* Translated by Ahdaf Soueif. New York: Anchor Books, 2000.

Barghouti, Omar. *BDS: Boycott, Divestment, Sanctions—The Global Struggle for Palestinian Rights.* Chicago: Haymarket Books, 2011.

Baumgarten, Helga. "The Three Faces/Phases of Palestinian Nationalism, 1948–2005." *Journal of Palestine Studies* 34, no. 4 (Summer 2005), pp. 25–48.

Beinin, Joel, and Lisa Hajjar. "Palestine, Israel and the Arab-Israeli Conflict: A Primer." http://www.thinkingtogether.org/rcream/old/f2003/Primer.pdf.

Ben Shitrit, Lihi, and Mahmoud Jaraba. "The Threat of Jihadism in the West Bank." *Sada,* February 6, 2014. Available at http://carnegieendowment.org/sada/2014/02/06/threat-of-jihadism-in-west-bank/hoae.

Benvenisti, Meron. *Intimate Enemies: Jews and Arabs in a Shared Land.* Berkeley, CA: University of California Press, 1995.

———. *City of Stone: The Hidden History of Jerusalem.* Translated by Maxine Kaufman Nunn. Berkeley, CA: University of California Press, 1996.

———. *Sacred Landscape: The Buried History of the Holy Land since 1948.* Translated by Maxine Kaufman-Lacusta. Berkeley, CA: University of California Press, 2000.

Bowker, Robert, *Palestinian Refugees: Mythology, Identity, and the Search for Peace.* Boulder, CO: Lynne Rienner, 2003.

Brenner, Michael. *Zionism: A Brief History.* Translated by Shelly L. Frisch. Princeton, NJ: Marcus Weiner, 2003.

Bröning, Michael. *Political Parties in Palestine: Leadership and Thought.* New York: Palgrave Macmillan, 2013.

Brown, Nathan J. "Are Palestinians Building a State?" *Carnegie Commentary,* June 2010, pp. 1–16.

———. "Can Cairo Reassemble Palestine?" Carnegie Endowment for International Peace, Web Commentary, November 2008, pp. 1–8.

———. "Constituting Palestine: The Effort to Write a Basic Law for the Palestinian Authority." *Middle East Journal* 54, no. 1 (Winter 2000), pp. 25–43.

———. "Fayyad Is Not the Problem, but Fayyadism Is Not the Solution to Palestine's Political Crisis." *Carnegie Commentary,* September 2010, pp. 1–9.

———. *Palestinian Politics after the Oslo Accords: Resuming Arab Palestine.* Berkeley, CA: University of California Press, 2003.

Brynen, Rex. "The Dynamics of Palestinian Elite Formation." *Journal of Palestine Studies* 24, no. 3 (Spring 1995), pp. 31–43.

———. "The Patrimonial Dimension of Palestinian Politics." *Journal of Palestine Studies* 25, no. 1 (Autumn 1995), pp. 23–36.

Capoccia, Giovanni, and R. Daniel Keleman. "The Study of Critical Junctures: Theory, Narrative, and Counterfactuals in Historical Institutionalism." *World Politics* 59, no. 3 (April 2007), pp. 341–369.

Carroll, James. *Jerusalem, Jerusalem: How the Ancient City Ignited Our Modern World.* Boston, MA: Houghton Mifflin Harcourt, 2011.

Carter, Jimmy. *Palestine: Peace Not Apartheid.* New York: Simon & Schuster, 2006.

Chatty, Dawn. *Displacement and Dispossession in the Modern Middle East.* Cambridge: Cambridge University Press, 2010.

Chene, Marie. "Overview of Corruption and Anti-Corruption in Palestine." *Transparency International,* no. 314 (January 19, 2012).

Cheshin, Amir S., Bill Hutman, and Avi Melamed. *Separate and Unequal: The Inside Story of Israeli Rule in East Jerusalem.* Cambridge, MA: Harvard University Press, 1999.

Chirot, Daniel. *How Societies Change.* 2nd ed. Thousand Oaks, CA: Sage, 2012.

Civil Administration of Judea and Samaria. *Factsheet: Water in the West Bank,* 2012. www.cogat.idf.il/Sip_Storage/FILES/4/3274.pdf.

Clinton, Bill. *My Life.* New York: Vintage, 2005.

Coalition for Integrity and Accountability. *Corruption Report: Palestine 2012.* Ramallah: AMAN, 2013.

Cobham, David. *A Macroeconomic Narrative for the Palestinian Economy.* Jerusalem: MAS, 2012.

Collins, John. *Global Palestine.* New York: Columbia University Press, 2011.

Cook, Jonathan. *Disappearing Palestine: Israel's Experiment in Human Despair.* London: Zed, 2010.

Daibes, Fadia. *Water in Palestine: Problems, Politics, Prospects.* Jerusalem: PASSIA, 2003.

Day, David. *Conquest: How Societies Overwhelm Others.* Oxford: Oxford University Press, 2008.

Dieckhoff, Alain. *The Invention of a Nation: Zionist Thought and the Making of Modern Israel.* New York: Columbia University Press, 2003.

Divine, Donna Robinson. *Exiled in the Homeland.* Austin, TX: University of Texas Press, 2009.

Dowty, Alan. *Israel/Palestine.* 2nd ed. Cambridge: Polity, 2008.

———. *The Jewish State, A Century Later.* Berkeley, CA: University of California Press, 1998.

Eftekhary, Asghar. *Jame'h Shenasi-ye Siyasi-ye Israel* [Political sociology of Israel]. Tehran: Markaz-e pazhohesh-haye 'Elmi va Motale'at-e Ester-atezhik-e Khavarmiyaneh, 1380/2001.

El-Hasan, Hasan Afid. *Is the Two-State Solution Already Dead?* New York: Algora, 2010.

Falah, Ghazi-Walid. "Dynamics and Patterns of the Shrinking of Arab Lands in Palestine." *Political Geography* 22 (2003), pp. 179–209.

Ferguson, Niall. *Civilization: The West and the Rest.* New York: Penguin, 2011.

Filiu, Jean-Pierre. *Gaza: A History.* Translated by John King. Oxford: Oxford University Press, 2014.

Finkelstein, Norman G. *Beyond Chutzpah: On the Misuse of Anti-Semitism and the Abuse of History.* Berkeley, CA: University of California Press, 2005.

Fjeldstad, Odd-Helge, and Adel Zagha. "Taxation and State Formation in Palestine 1994–2000." In *State Formation in Palestine: Viability and*

Governance During a Social Transformation, edited by Mushtaq Husain Khan, George Giacaman, and Inge Amundsen. London: Routledge, 2004, pp. 192–214.

Freedman, Robert O. ed. *Contemporary Israel: Domestic Politics, Foreign Policy, and Security Challenges.* Boulder, CO: Westview, 2009.

Gelvin, James. *The Israel-Palestine Conflict: One Hundred Years of War.* Cambridge: Cambridge University Press, 2007.

Gat, Azar. *Nations: The Long History and Deep Roots of Political Ethnicity and Nationalism.* Cambridge: Cambridge University Press, 2013.

Gerges, Fawaz A. "Egypt and the 1948 War: Internal Conflict and Regional Ambition." In *The War for Palestine,* edited by Eugene L. Rogan and Avi Shlaim. Cambridge: Cambridge University Press, 2001, pp. 151–177.

Gerner, Deborah J. *One Land, Two Peoples: The Conflict over Palestine.* 2nd ed. Boulder, CO: Westview, 1994.

Gerster, Karin A., and Helga Baumgarten. "Palestinian NGOs." Rosa Luxemburg Foundation in Palestine, December 30, 2011.

Ghanem, As'ad. "Israel and the 'Danger of Demography.'" In *Where Now for Palestine? The Demise of the Two-State Solution,* edited by Jamil Hilal. London: Zed, 2007, pp. 48–74.

———. *Palestinian Politics after Arafat: A Failed National Movement.* Bloomington, IN: Indiana University Press, 2010.

Gilbert, Martin. *The Routledge Atlas of the Arab-Israeli Conflict.* 7th ed. London: Routledge, 2002.

Glick, Caroline B. *The Israeli Solution: A One-State Plan for Peace in the Middle East.* New York: Crown Forum, 2014.

Gordon, Neve. *Israel's Occupation.* Berkeley, CA: University of California Press, 2008.

Gorenberg, Gershon. *The End of Days: Fundamentalism and the Struggle for the Temple Mount.* Oxford: Oxford University Press, 2000.

Graham-Brown, Sarah. "The Changing Society of the West Bank." *Journal of Palestine Studies* 8, no. 4 (Summer 1979), pp. 149–159.

Grinberg, Lev. "The Arrogance of Occupation." *Middle East Policy* 9, no. 1 (March 2002), pp. 46–52.

Guyatt, Nicholas. *The Absence of Peace: Understanding the Israeli-Palestinian Conflict.* London: Zed Books, 1998.

Hammami, Rema. "Palestinian NGOs since Oslo: From NGO Politics to Social Movements?" *Middle East Report,* no. 214 (Spring 2000), pp. 16–19, 27, 48.

Hanafi, Sari, and Linda Tabar. "Donor Assistance, Rent-Seeking and Elite Formation." In *State Formation in Palestine: Viability and Governance During a Social Transformation,* edited by Mushtaq Husain Khan, George Giacaman, and Inge Amundsen. London: Routledge, 2004, pp. 215–238.

Hass, Amira. *Drinking the Sea at Gaza: Days and Nights in a Land under Siege.* New York: Owl Books, 1999.

Herbst, Jeffrey, and Greg Mills. "Introduction: Managing Fault Lines in the Twenty-First Century." In *On the Fault Line: Managing Tensions and Divisions within Societies,* edited by Jeffrey Herbst, Terence McNamee, and Greg Mills. London: Profile Books, 2012, pp. 1–16.

Hever, Shir. *The Political Economy of Israel's Occupation: Repression Beyond Exploitation.* London: Pluto, 2010.

Hilal, Jamil. "Class Transformation in the West Bank and Gaza." *Journal of Palestine Studies* 6, no. 2 (Winter 1977), pp. 167–175.

———. "Palestine: The Last Colonial Issue." In *Where Now for Palestine? The Demise of the Two-State Solution,* edited by Jamil Hilal. London: Zed, 2007, pp. 1–29.

———. "PLO Institutions: The Challenge Ahead." *Journal of Palestine Studies* 23, no. 1 (Autumn 1993), pp. 46–60.

Hilal, Jamil, and Mushtaq Husain Khan. "Palestinian State Formation under the PNA: Potential Outcomes and Their Viability." In *State Formation in Palestine: Viability and Governance During a Social Transformation,* edited by Mushtaq Husain Khan, George Giacaman, and Inge Amundsen. London: Routledge, 2004, pp. 64–119.

Hirbawi, Najat, and David Helfand. "Palestinian Institutions in Jerusalem." *Palestine-Israel Journal* 17, no. 12 (2011). Available at www.pij.org/details. php?id=1306.

Hobsbawm, Eric. *Nations and Nationalism since 1780: Programme, Myth, Reality.* 2nd ed. Cambridge: Cambridge University Press, 1992.

Hoffman, Adina. *My Happiness Bears No Relation to Happiness: A Poet's Life in the Palestinian Century.* New Haven, CT: Yale University Press, 2009.

Hroub, Khaled. "Hamas after Shaykh Yasin and Rantisi." *Journal of Palestine Studies* 33, no. 4 (Summer 2004), pp. 21–38.

International Crisis Group. "Ruling Palestine I: Gaza under Hamas." *Middle East Report No. 73,* March 19, 2008.

International Peace and Cooperation Center. *East Jerusalem Housing Review 2013.* Jerusalem: IPCC, 2013.

Isaac, Jad, and Owen Powell. "The Transformation of the Palestinian Environment. In *Where Now for Palestine? The Demise of the Two-State Solution,* edited by Jamil Hilal. London: Zed, 2007, pp. 144–166.

Jad, Islah. "The NGO-isation of Arab Women's Movements." *IDS Bulletin* 35, no. 4 (October 2004), pp. 34–42.

———. "NGOs: Between Buzzwords and Social Movements." *Development in Practice* 17, nos. 4–5 (August 2007), pp. 622–629.

Jamal, Amal. *The Arab Public Sphere in Israel: Media Space and Cultural Resistance.* Bloomington, IN: Indiana University Press, 2009.

Jamal, Amaney A. *Barriers to Democracy: The Other Side of Social Capital in Palestine and the Arab World.* Princeton, NJ: Princeton University Press, 2007.

Jayyusi, Salma Khadra, ed. *Anthology of Modern Palestinian Literature.* New York: Columbia University Press, 1992.

Jirbawi, Ali. "Palestinian National Identity and the Relation between the Returnees and the People of the Homeland." In *Dialogues on Palestinian State-Building and Identity,* edited by Mahdi Abdul Hadi. Jerusalem: PASSIA, 1999, pp. 56–66.

Kanaaneh, Mosleh, Stig-Magnus Thorsen, Heather Bursheh, and David A. McDonald, eds. *Palestinian Music and Song: Expression and Resistance since 1900.* Bloomington, ID: Indiana University Press, 2013.

Karmi, Ghada. "Introduction." In *The Palestine Papers: The End of the Road?,* by Clayton E. Swisher. Chatham: Hesperus, 2011, pp. 9–16.

————. "The One-State Solution: An Alternative Vision for Israeli-Palestinian Peace." *Journal of Palestine Studies* 40, no. 2 (Winter 2011), pp. 62–76.

Kennedy, Paul. *The Rise and Fall of the Great Powers.* New York: Vintage, 1987.

Khalidi, Ahmad S. "The Palestinians: Current Dilemmas, Future Challenges." *Journal of Palestine Studies* 24, no. 2 (Winter 1995), pp. 5–13.

Khalidi, Raja, and Sobhi Samour. "Neoliberalism as Liberation: The Statehood Program and the Remaking of the Palestinian National Movement." *Journal of Palestine Studies* 40, no. 2 (Winter 2011), pp. 6–25.

Khalidi, Rashid. *Palestinian Identity: The Construction of Modern National Consciousness.* New York: Columbia University Press, 1997.

————. *The Iron Cage: The Story of the Palestinian Struggle for Statehood.* Boston, MA: Beacon, 2006.

————. "The Palestinians and 1948: The Underlying Causes of Failure." In *The War for Palestine,* edited by Eugene L. Rogan and Avi Shlaim. Cambridge: Cambridge University Press, 2001, pp. 12–36.

Khalidi, Walid. "Plan Dalet: Master Plan of the Conquest of Palestine." *Journal of Palestine Studies* 18, no. 1 (Autumn 1988), pp. 4–33.

Khalili, Laleh. *Heroes and Martyrs of Palestine: The Politics of National Commemoration.* Cambridge: Cambridge University Press, 2007.

Khan, Mushtaq Husain. "Evaluating the Emerging Palestinian State: 'Good Governance' versus 'Transformational Potential.'" In *State Formation in Palestine: Viability and Governance During a Social Transformation,* edited by Mushtaq Husain Khan, George Giacaman, and Inge Amundsen. London: Routledge, 2004, pp. 13–63.

————. "Introduction: State Formation in Palestine." In *State Formation in Palestine: Viability and Governance During a Social Transformation,* edited by Mushtaq Husain Khan, George Giacaman, and Inge Amundsen. London: Routledge, 2004, pp. 1–12.

Kimmerling, Baruch. *The Invention and Decline of Israeliness: State, Society, and the Military.* Berkeley, CA: University of California Press, 2005.

Kimmerling, Baruch, and Joel S. Migdal. *Palestinians: The Making of a People*. Cambridge, MA: Harvard University Press, 1994.

Klieman, Ahron. *Compromising Palestine: A Guide to Final Status Negotiations*. New York: Columbia University Press, 2000.

Klein, Menachem. *The Shift: Israel-Palestine from Border Struggle to Ethnic Conflict*. New York: Columbia University Press, 2010.

Krouzman, Roni. "21st Century Palestine: Toward a 'Swiss Cheese' State." *Middle East Report*, no. 213 (Winter 1999), pp. 38–40.

La Guardia, Anton. *War Without End: Israelis, Palestinians, and the Struggle for a Promised Land*. New York: Thomas Dunne, 2003.

Laitin, David D. *Nations, States, and Violence*. Oxford: Oxford University Press, 2007.

Landis, Joshua. "Syria and the Palestine War: Fighting King 'Abdullah's 'Greater Syria Plan.'" In *The War for Palestine*, edited by Eugene L. Rogan and Avi Shlaim. (Cambridge: Cambridge University Press, 2001), pp. 178–205.

Laqueur, Walter, and Barry Rubin, eds. *The Israel-Arab Reader: A Documentary History of the Middle East Conflict*. 6th ed. New York: Penguin, 2001.

Lein, Yehezkel. *Civilians under Siege: Restrictions on Freedom of Movement as Collective Punishment*. Jerusalem: B'Tselem, 2001.

Le More, Anne. "Killing with Kindness: Funding the Demise of a Palestinian state." *International Affair* 81, no. 5 (2005), pp. 981–999.

Lesch, David. *The Arab-Israeli Conflict: A History*. Oxford: Oxford University Press, 2008.

LeVine, Mark. *Overthrowing Geography: Jaffa, Tel Aviv, and the Struggle for Palestine 1880–1948*. Berkeley, CA: University of California Press, 2005.

LeVine, Mark, and Mathias Mossberg, eds. *One Land, Two States: Israel and Palestine as Parallel States*. Berkeley, CA: University of California Press, 2014.

LeVine, Mark, and Gershon Shafir, eds. *Struggle and Survival in Palestine/Israel*. Berkeley, CA: University of California Press, 2012.

Lichbach, Mark Irving. *The Rebel's Dilemma*. Ann Arbor, MI: University of Michigan Press, 1998.

Loewenstein, Anthony, and Ahmed Noor, eds. *After Zionism: One State for Israel and Palestine.* London: Saqi, 2012.

Lustick, Ian S. *For the Land and the Lord: Jewish Fundamentalism in Israel.* New York: Council on Foreign Relations, 1988.

Mahler, Gregory S. *Politics and Government in Israel: The Maturation of the Modern State.* Lanham, MD: Rowman and Littlefield, 2004.

Makdisi, Saree. *Palestine Inside Out: An Everyday Occupation.* New York: Norton, 2010.

Malki, Riad. "The Opposition and Its Role in the Peace Process." In *Dialogues on Palestinian State-Building and Identity,* edited by Mahdi Abdul Hadi (Jerusalem: PASSIA, 1999), pp. 3–10.

Marcus, Amy Dockser. *Jerusalem 1913: The Origins of the Arab-Israeli Conflict.* New York: Penguin, 2008.

Masalha, Nur. *Expulsion of the Palestinians: The Concept of "Transfer" in Zionist Political Thought, 1882–1948.* Washington, DC: Institute for Palestine Studies, 1992.

Matar, Dina. *What It Means to Be Palestinian: Stories of Palestinian Peoplehood.* London: I. B. Tauris, 2011.

Mazza, Roberto. *Jerusalem: From the Ottomans to the British.* London: I. B. Tauris, 2009.

McDonald, David A. *My Voice Is My Weapon: Music, Nationalism, and the Poetics of Palestinian Resistance.* Durham, NC: Duke University Press, 2013.

McDowall, David. *Palestine and Israel: The Uprising and Beyond.* Berkeley, CA: University of California Press, 1989.

Mearsheimer, John J., and Stephen M. Walt. *The Israel Lobby and U.S. Foreign Policy.* New York: Farrar, Straus and Giroux, 2007.

Megged, Eyal. "Parallel Lives, Parallel States: Imagining a Different Future." In *One Land, Two States: Israel and Palestine as Parallel States,* edited by Mark LeVine and Mathias Mossberg. Berkeley, CA: University of California Press, 2014, pp. 244–254.

Milton-Edwards, Beverley. "Palestinian State-Building: Police and Citizens as Test of Democracy." *British Journal of Middle Eastern Studies* 25, no. 1 (May 1998), pp. 95–119.

Milton-Edwards, Beverley, and Peter Hinchcliffe. *Conflicts in the Middle East since 1945.* 2nd ed. London: Routledge, 2004.

Ministry of Health. *Palestinian National Health Strategy 2011–2013.* Ramallah: Palestinian National Authority Ministry of Health, 2010.

Mir, Salam. "Palestinian Literature: Occupation and Exile." *Arab Studies Quarterly* 35, no. 2 (2013), pp. 110–129.

Mossberg, Mathias. "One Land—Two States? An Introduction to the Parallel States Concept." In *One Land, Two States: Israel and Palestine as Parallel States,* edited by Mark LeVine and Mathias Mossberg. Berkeley, CA: University of California Press, 2014, pp. 1–28.

Morris, Benny. *The Birth of the Palestinian Refugee Problem Revisited.* Cambridge: Cambridge University Press, 2004.

———. *One State, Two States.* New Haven, CT: Yale University Press, 2009.

———. "Revisiting the Palestinian Exodus of 1948," in *The War for Palestine,* edited by Eugene L. Rogan and Avi Shlaim (Cambridge: Cambridge University Press, 2001), pp. 37–59.

———. *Righteous Victims: A History of the Zionist-Arab Conflict, 1881–2001.* New York: Vintage, 2001.

Moughrabi, Fouad. "The Politics of Palestinian Textbooks." *Journal of Palestine Studies* 31, no. 1 (Autumn 2001), pp. 5–19.

Najjar, Orayb Aref. "Cartoons as a Site for the Construction of Palestinian Refugee Identity: An Exploratory Study of Cartoonist Naji al-Ali." *Journal of Communication Inquiry* 31 no. 3 (2007), pp. 255–285.

Nakhleh, Khalil. *Globalized Palestine: The National Sell-Out of a Homeland.* Trenton, NJ: Red Sea Press, 2012.

Neff, Donald. *Fallen Pillars: US Policy Towards Palestine and Israel since 1945.* Washington, DC: Institute for Palestine Studies, 1995.

Nelson, Arthur. *In Your Eyes a Sandstorm: Ways of Being Palestinian.* Berkeley, CA: University of California Press, 2011.

Nusseibeh, Sari. *What Is a Palestinian State Worth?* Cambridge, MA: Harvard University Press, 2011.

Palestine Economic Policy Research Institute. *Deceptive Facts: The Myth of Israel's Role in Promoting Growth in the Occupied Palestinian Territory.* Jerusalem: MAS, 2011.

———. *Economic and Social Monitor, 2011.* Jerusalem: MAS, 2011.

Palestine Monetary Authority. *Quarterly Social and Economic Monitor.* Vol. 31. Ramallah: PMA, 2013.

Palestinian Center for Policy and Survey Research. *Palestinian Public Poll Number 37.* Ramallah: PCPSR, 2010.

———. *Palestinian Public Poll Number 42.* Ramallah: PCPSR, 2011.

———. *Palestinian Public Poll Number 46 Press Release.* Ramallah: PCPSR, 2012.

———. *Poll Number 44.* Ramallah: PCPSR, 2012.

———. *Poll Number 46.* Ramallah: PCPSR, 2012.

———. *Poll Number 50.* Ramallah: PCPSR, 2013.

———. *Poll Number 51.* Ramallah: PCPSR, 2014.

———. *Poll Number 52.* Ramallah: PCPSR, 2014.

Palestinian Central Bureau of Statistics. "Special Statistical Bulletin, On the 65th Anniversary of the Palestinian Nakba." May 14, 2013. http://www.pcbs.gov.ps/site/512/default.aspx?tabID=512&lang=en&ItemID=788&mid=3171&wversion=Staging.

Pappe, Ilan. "Critique and Agenda: The Post-Zionist Scholars in Israel." *History and Memory* 7, no. 1 (Spring–Summer 1995), pp. 66–90.

———. *The Ethnic Cleansing of Palestine.* Oxford: Oneworld, 2006.

———. *A History of Modern Palestine: One Land, Two Peoples.* Cambridge: Cambridge University Press, 2004.

———. *The Idea of Israel: A History of Power and Knowledge.* London: Verso, 2014.

———, ed. *The Israel/Palestine Question: Rewriting Histories.* London: Routledge, 1999.

Parsons, Laila. "The Druze and the Birth of Israel." In *The War for Palestine,* edited by Eugene L. Rogan and Avi Shlaim. (Cambridge: Cambridge University Press, 2001), pp. 60–78.

PASSIA. *Palestinian Security Sector Governance: Challenges and Prospects.* Jerusalem: PASSIA, 2006.

———. *The Phenomenon of Collaborators in Palestine.* Jerusalem: PASSIA, 2006.

Pedahzur, Ami. *The Triumph of Israel's Radical Right.* Oxford: Oxford University Press, 2012.

Peled-Elhanan, Nurit. *Palestine in Israeli School Books: Ideology and Propaganda in Education.* London: I. B. Tauris, 2012.

Peleg, Ilan, and Dov Waxman. *Israel's Palestinians: The Conflict Within.* Cambridge: Cambridge University Press, 2011.

Peres, Shimon. *The New Middle East.* New York: Henry Holt, 1993.

Peres, Shimon, and Robert Little. *For the Future of Israel.* Baltimore, MD: Johns Hopkins University Press, 1998.

Peretz, Don. "Palestinian Social Stratification: The Political Implications." *Journal of Palestine Studies* 7, no. 1 (Autumn 1977), pp. 48–74.

Pierson, Paul. *Politics in Time: History, Institutions, and Social Analysis.* Princeton, NJ: Princeton University Press, 2004.

Poulantzas, Nicos. "On Social Classes." *New Left Review,* no. 78 (March–April 1973), pp. 27–54.

Qubaja, Ahmed. *Fiscal Sustainability of the Palestinian National Authority: Experience and Future Prospects.* Jerusalem: MAS, 2012.

Quigley, John. *The Case for Palestine: An International Law Perspective.* Durham, NC: Duke University Press, 2005.

———. *The Statehood of Palestine: International Law in the Middle East Conflict.* Cambridge: Cambridge University Press, 2010.

Rand Palestinian State Study Team. *Building a Successful Palestinian State.* Santa Monica, CA: Rand, 2005.

Raviv, Dan, and Yossi Melman. *Spies against Armageddon: Inside Israel's Secret Wars.* Sea Cliff, NY: Levant Books, 2012.

Rebhun, Uzi, and Gilad Matach. "Demography, Social Prosperity, and the Future of Sovereign Israel." *Israel Affairs* 18, no. 2 (March 2012), pp. 177–200.

Robinson, Glenn E. *Building a Palestinian State: The Incomplete Revolution.* Bloomington, IN: Indiana University Press, 1997.

————. "The Role of the Professional Middle Class in the Mobilization of Palestinian Society: The Medical and Agricultural Committees." *International Journal of Middle East Studies* 25, no. 2 (May 1993), pp. 301–326.

Roeder, Philip G. *Where Nation-States Come From: Institutional Change in the Age of Nationalism.* Princeton, NJ: Princeton University Press, 2007.

Rogan, Eugene L., and Avi Shlaim, eds. *The War for Palestine: Rewriting the History of 1948.* Cambridge: Cambridge University Press, 2001.

Ron, James. "Palestine, the UN and the One-State Solution." *Middle East Policy* 18, no. 4 (Winter 2011), pp. 59–67.

Roy, Sara M. "Gaza: New Dynamics of Civic Disintegration." *Journal of Palestine Studies* 22, no. 4 (Summer 1993), pp. 20–31.

————. *The Gaza Strip: The Political Economy of De-Development.* Washington, DC: Institute for Palestine Studies, 1995.

————. "De-development Revisited: Palestinian Economy and Society since Oslo." *Journal of Palestine Studies* 28, no. 3 (Spring 1999), pp. 64–82.

————. *Hamas and Civil Society in Gaza: Engaging the Islamist Social Sector.* Princeton, NJ: Princeton University Press, 2011.

Rubenberg, Cheryl A. *The Palestinians: In Search of a Just Peace.* Boulder, CO: Lynne Rienner, 2003.

Rubin, Barry. *The Transformation of Palestinian Politics: From Revolution to State-Building.* Cambridge, MA: Harvard University Press, 1999.

Said, Edward W. "Afterward: The Consequences of 1948." In *The War for Palestine,* edited by Eugene L. Rogan and Avi Shlaim. Cambridge: Cambridge University Press, 2001, pp. 206–219.

————. *Peace and Its Discontents: Essays on Palestine in the Middle East Peace Process.* New York: Vintage, 1996.

————. *The Question of Palestine.* New York: Vintage, 1992.

Saidi, Ahmad, and Lila Abu-Lughod, eds. *Nakba: Palestine, 1948, and the Claims of Memory.* New York: Columbia University Press, 2007.

Samara, Adel. "Globalization, the Palestinian Economy, and the 'Peace Process.'" *Journal of Palestine Studies* 29, no. 2 (Winter 2000), pp. 20–34.

Savir, Uri. *The Process: 1,100 Days that Changed the Middle East.* New York: Vintage, 1998.

Sayigh, Yezid. "Armed Struggle and State Formation." *Journal of Palestine Studies* 26, no. 4 (Summer 1997), pp. 17–32.

———. "Inducing a Failed State in Palestine." *Survival* 49, no. 3 (Autumn 2007), pp. 7–40.

———. "Redefining the Basics: Sovereignty and Security of the Palestinian State." *Journal of Palestine Studies* 24, no. 4 (Summer 1995), pp. 5–19.

Sayigh, Yusif A. "The Palestinian Economy under Occupation: Dependency and Pauperization." *Journal of Palestine Studies* 15, no. 4 (Summer 1986), pp. 46–67.

Scott, James C. *Weapons of the Weak: Everyday Forms of Peasant Resistance.* New Haven, CT: Yale University Press, 1985.

Selbin, Eric. *Revolution, Rebellion, Resistance: The Power of Story.* London: Zed, 2010.

Shalev, Nir. *Under the Guise of Legality: Declarations on State Land in the West Bank.* Translated by Yael Stein. Jerusalem: B'Tselem, 2012.

Sharansky, Ira. "The Problem of a Palestine that Would Be Economically Autonomous: A Commentary." *Policy Studies Journal* 27, no. 4 (1999), pp. 665–667.

Shelef, Nadav G. *Evolving Nationalism: Homeland, Identity, and Religion in Israel, 1925–2005.* Ithaca, NY: Cornell University Press, 2010.

Shikaki, Khalil. "The Future of Israel-Palestine: A One-State Reality in the Making." *NOREF Report,* May 2012, pp. 1–10.

———. "The Peace Process, National Reconstruction, and the Transition to Democracy in Palestine." *Journal of Palestine Studies* 25, no. 2 (Winter 1996), pp. 5–20.

———. "Willing to Compromise: Palestinian Public Opinion and the Peace Process." United States Institute of Peace Special Report, no. 158 (January 2006), pp. 1–16.

Shindler, Colin. *A History of Modern Israel.* Cambridge: Cambridge University Press, 2008.

Shipler, David. *Arabs and Jews: Wounded Spirits in a Promised Land.* New York: Penguin, 1987.

Shlaim, Avi. *The Iron Wall: Israel and the Arab World.* New York: Norton, 2001.

———. "Israel and the Arab Coalition in 1948." In *The War for Palestine,* edited by Eugene L. Rogan and Avi Shlaim. Cambridge: Cambridge University Press, 2001), pp. 79–103.

———. *Israel and Palestine: Reappraisals, Revisions, Refutations.* London: Verso, 2009.

Smith, Charles D. *Palestine and the Arab-Israeli Conflict: A History with Documents.* 8th ed. Boston: Bedford St. Martin's, 2013.

Spirig, Judith, and Hans Heyn. "The Political Economy of the West Bank." Konrad Adenauer Stiftung, December 13, 2010.

Sternhell, Zeev. *The Founding Myths of Israel.* Translated by David Maisel. Princeton, NJ: Princeton University Press, 1998.

Stockmarr, Leila. "Is It All About Territory? Israel's Settlement Policy in the Occupied Palestinian Territory since 1967." Danish Institute for International Studies, DIIS Report, 2012.

Swisher, Clayton E. *The Palestine Papers: The End of the Road?* Chatham: Hesperus, 2011.

———. *The Truth About Camp David: The Untold Story About the Collapse of the Middle East Peace Process.* New York: Nation Books, 2004.

Susser, Asher. *Israel, Jordan, and Palestine: The Two-State Imperative.* Waltham, MA: Brandeis University Press, 2012.

Taraki, Lisa. "Enclave Micropolis: The Paradoxical Case of Ramallah/al-Bireh." *Journal of Palestine Studies* 37, no. 4 (Summer 2008), pp. 6–20.

Tarrow, Sidney G. *Power in Movement: Social Movements and Contentious Politics.* 3rd ed. Cambridge: Cambridge University Press, 2011.

———. *Strangers at the Gates: Movements and States in Contentious Politics.* Cambridge: Cambridge University Press, 2012.

Tessler, Mark. *A History of the Israeli-Palestinian Conflict.* Bloomington, IN: Indiana University Press, 1994.

Thomas, Baylis. *The Dark Side of Zionism: Israel's Quest for Security through Dominance.* Lanham, MD: Lexington Books, 2009.

———. *How Israel was Won: A Concise History of the Arab-Israeli Conflict.* Lanham, MD: Lexington, 1999.

Tilley, Virginia. *The One-State Solution: A Breakthrough for Peace in the Israeli-Palestinian Deadlock.* Ann Arbor, MI: University of Michigan Press, 2008.

Tilly, Charles, and Lesley J. Wood. *Social Movements, 1768–2012.* 3rd ed. Boulder, CO: Paradigm, 2013.

Tripp, Charles. "Iraq and the 1948 War: Mirror of Iraq's disorder." In *The War for Palestine,* edited by Eugene L. Rogan and Avi Shlaim. Cambridge: Cambridge University Press, 2001, pp. 125–150.

Trottier, Julie. *Hydropolitics in the West Bank and the Gaza Strip.* Jerusalem: PASSIA, 1999.

Turki, Fawaz. "Palestinian Self-Criticism and the Liberation of Palestinian Society." *Journal of Palestine Studies* 25, no. 2 (Winter 1996), pp. 71–76.

Turner, Mandy. "Building Democracy in Palestine: Liberal Peace Theory and the Election of Hamas." *Democratization* 13, no. 5 (December 2006), pp. 739–755.

Tutunji, Jenab, and Kamal Khaldi. "A Binational State in Palestine: The Rational Choice for Palestinians and the Moral Choice for Israelis." *International Affairs* 73, no. 1 (January 1997), pp. 31–58.

Unger, David C. "The Inevitable Two-State Solution." *World Policy Journal* 25, no. 3 (Fall 2008), pp. 59–67.

———. "Maps of War, Maps of Peace: Finding a Two-State Solution to the Israeli-Palestinian Question." *World Policy Journal* 19, no. 2 (Summer 2002), pp. 1–12.

United Nations Human Rights Council. Report of the International Fact-Finding Mission on Israeli Settlements. March 18, 2013. www.ohchr.org/Documents/HRBodies/HRCouncil/RegularSession/Session19/FFM/FFMSettlements.pdf.

United Nations Office for the Coordination of Humanitarian Affairs. "Unprotected: Settler Violence against Palestinian Civilians and Their

Property." *OCHA Special Focus,* December 2008. www.ochaopt.org/documents/ocha_opt_settler_vilonce_special_focus_2008_12_18.pdf.

Usher, Graham. "The Democratic Resistance: Hamas, Fatah, and the Palestinian Elections." *Journal of Palestine Studies* 35, no. 3 (Spring 2006), pp. 20–36.

———. "The Palestinians after Arafat." *Journal of Palestine Studies* 34, no. 3 (Spring 2005), pp. 42–56.

Viorst, Milton. *UNRWA and Peace in the Middle East.* Washington, DC: Middle East Institute, 1984.

Waxman, Dov. "Israel's Palestinian Minority in the Two-State Solution: The Missing Dimension." *Middle East Policy* 18, no. 4 (Winter 2011), pp. 68–82.

Weber, Max. *From Max Weber: Essays in Sociology.* Translated and edited by H. H. Gerth and C. Right Mills. London: Routledge & Kegan Paul, 1964.

Wender, Andrew M. "Transcending Nationalist Divides: Religious Reconciliation as the Basis for a One-State Solution in Israel/Palestine." *Digest of Middle East Studies* 20, no. 2 (Fall 2011), pp. 261–276.

Wolfe, Stefan. *Ethnic Conflict: A Global Perspective.* Oxford: Oxford University Press, 2006.

World Bank. *The Economic Effects of Restricted Access to Land in the West Bank.* Washington, DC: World Bank, 2012.

———. *The Role and Performance of Palestinian NGOs in Health, Education, and Agriculture.* Washington, DC: World Bank, 2006.

———. *Stagnation or Revival? Palestinian Economic Prospects.* Washington, DC: World Bank, 2012.

———. *Towards Economic Sustainability of a Future Palestinian State: Promoting Private Sector-Led Growth.* Washington, DC: World Bank, 2012.

———. *West Bank and Gaza: Assessment of Restrictions on Palestinian Water Sector Development.* Washington, DC: World Bank, 2009.

World Health Organization. "West Bank and Gaza." In *Cooperation Strategy at a Glance.* Washington, DC: WHO, April 2006.

———. "Health Conditions in the Occupied Palestinian Territory, Including East Jerusalem, and in the Occupied Syrian Golan." A65/27 Rev. 1, 11 May 2012.

Wright, Robin. *Dreams and Shadows: The Future of the Middle East.* New York: Penguin, 2008.

Zagha, Adel, and Husam Zomlot. "Israel and the Palestinian Economy: Integration or containment?" In *State Formation in Palestine: Viability and Governance During a Social Transformation,* edited by Mushtaq Husain Khan, George Giacaman, and Inge Amundsen. London: Routledge, 2004, pp. 120–140.

Zuhur, Sherifa. "Gaza, Israel, Hamas, and the Lost Claim of Operation Cast Lead." *Middle East Policy* 16, no. 1 (Spring 2009), pp. 40–52.

Index

Abbas, Mahmoud, 66–67, 162, 174; election of, 62, 66, 174; presidency of, 66, 186, 189, 199, 200

absolutism, 57

Abu-Amr, Ziad, 192

Al-Ali, Naji, 16

Al-Aqsa Intifada, 13, 58–59, 83, 168, 174; causes of, 58; economic effects of, 94, 156, 183; and state formation, 167, 173; violence of, 126–127, 178. *See also* second intifada

Algeria, 25

aliyah, 27

Allon, Yigal, 47, 49

Allon Plan, 85; provisions of, 87–88

Al Qaeda, 197

Al-Qassam Brigade, 189

al-qiyadah, 171. *See also* Leadership

Al-Quds Hospital, 64

Al-Quds University, 101, 212

al-rais, 164, 167

Anderson, Benedict, 9

anti-normalization, 204

anti-Semitism, 201

apartheid: in South Africa, 25, 204; spatial, 80, 210

Arab-Israeli war of *1948:* destruction in, 14; and ethnic cleansing, 215;

as moral basis, 49; and Palestinian society, 6–7, 32, 35–44, 67–68, 118; and refugees, 46, 123. *See also* War of Independence

Arab-Israeli war of *1967:* and east Jerusalem, 98–99; expulsion of Palestinians, 19, 46, 216; and Palestinian identity, 115, 118–119, 125; refugees from, 105; and seam zone, 81–82; and territorial occupation, 48–49, 71–73, 111, 115

Arab-Israeli war of *1973,* 19, 131

Arab League, diplomacy by, 48

Arab Revolt (1936–1939), 27; consequences of, 32–34

Arabian Peninsula, 96

Arabism, as identity, 34

Arafat, Yasser, 18, 89, 162–163, 203, 220; de-Arafatization, 199; death of, 62, 66, 168, 174, 206; and PLC elections, 175; as PLO leader, 48, 54; as president, 57–59, 163–171, 177–179, 184, 196

archaeology, 28–29

Area A, 2, 56, 66, 90; population in, 111; size of, 56

Area B, 111; size of, 56